VOLUME FOUR

The
Great
Democracies

A HISTORY OF THE
ENGLISH-SPEAKING PEOPLES

The Great
Democracies

Winston S. Churchill

DODD, MEAD & COMPANY · NEW YORK
1958

MANUFACTURED IN THE UNITED STATES OF AMERICA
LIBRARY OF CONGRESS CATALOG CARD NO. 56–6868

ACKNOWLEDGMENTS

I desire to record my thanks again to Mr F. W. Deakin and Mr G. M. Young for their assistance before the Second World War in the preparation of this work; to Professor Asa Briggs of Leeds University, to Mr Maldwyn A. Jones of Manchester University, and to Mr Maurice Shock of University College, Oxford, who have since helped in its completion; and to Mr Alan Hodge, Mr Denis Kelly, Mr Anthony Montague Browne and Mr C. C. Wood. I have also to thank many others who have kindly read these pages and commented upon them.

For permission to include a quotation from *The Oxford History of the United States* acknowledgment is due to the Oxford University Press.

Preface

THE downfall of Napoleon in 1815 left Britain in unchallenged dominion over a large portion of the globe. France and indeed the whole continent of Europe was exhausted. A United Germany had not yet arisen and Italy still lay in fragments. Russia was withdrawing from Western Europe. The Spanish and Portuguese peoples were busy in their peninsula and in their tropical possessions overseas. In the following decades revolution and civil commotion smote many of the Powers of Europe, and new nations were born. Britain alone escaped almost unscathed from these years of unrest. There was an unparalleled expansion of the English-speaking peoples both by birth and emigration.

The break between Britain and America made by the American Revolution was neither complete nor final. Intercourse continued and grew across the Atlantic. While America devoted her energies to the settlement of half of the North American continent, Britain began to occupy and develop many vacant portions of the globe. The Royal Navy maintained an impartial rule over the oceans which shielded both communities from the rivalry and interference of the Old World.

The colonisation of Australia and New Zealand, and the acquisition of South Africa in the decline of Holland, created the new and wider British Empire still based upon sea-power and comprising a fifth of the human race, over which Queen Victoria, in the longest reign of British history, presided. In this period moral issues arising from Christian ethics became prominent. The slave trade, from which Britain had so shamelessly profited in the past, was suppressed by the Royal Navy. By a terrible internal struggle, at the cost of nearly a million lives, slavery was extirpated from the United States; above all, the Union was preserved.

The nineteenth century was a period of purposeful, progressive, enlightened, tolerant civilisation. The stir in the world arising from the French Revolution, added to the Industrial Revolution unleashed by the steam-engine and many key-inventions, led inexorably to the democratic age. The franchise was extended steadily in all the Western States of Europe, as it had been in America, until it became practically universal. The aristocracy, who had guided for centuries the advance of Britain, was merged in the rising mass of the nation. In the United States the Party system and the Money Power, which knew no class distinctions, preserved the structure of society during the economic development of the American continent.

At the same time the new British Empire or Commonwealth of Nations was based upon Government by consent, and the voluntary association of autonomous states under the Crown. At the death of Queen Victoria it might well have been believed that the problems of past centuries were far on the highroad to gradual solution. But meanwhile in Europe the mighty strength of the Teutonic race, hitherto baffled by division or cramped in lingering medieval systems, began to assert itself with volcanic energy. In the struggle that ensued Great Britain and the United States were to fight for the first time side by side in a common cause.

W.S.C.

Chartwell
Westerham
Kent
February 10, 1957

Contents

BOOK X

RECOVERY AND REFORM

BOOK XI

THE GREAT REPUBLIC

· ix ·

CONTENTS

BOOK XII

THE VICTORIAN AGE

MAPS

BOOK TEN

RECOVERY AND REFORM

The Victory Peace

AFTER a generation of warfare peace had come to Europe in the summer of 1815. It was to be a long peace, disturbed by civil commotions and local campaigns, but flaring into no major blaze until the era of German expansion succeeded the age of French predominance. In the Revolutionary and Napoleonic struggles Britain had played an heroic part. The task that had united and preoccupied her people was now at last accomplished. Henceforth they could bend their energies to developing the great resources of industrial and commercial skill which had accumulated in the Island during the past half-century and been tested and sharpened by twenty-two years of war. But the busy world of trade and manufacture and the needs and aspirations of the mass of men, women, and children who toiled in its service were beyond the grasp of the country's leading statesmen on the morrow of Waterloo. The English political scene succumbed to stagnation. The Tories, as we may call them, though not all would have acknowledged the name, were firmly in power. They had won the struggle against Napoleon with the support of a War Cabinet drawn largely from their own party. They embodied the tradition of resistance to the principles of Revolutionary France and the aggressive might of the Napoleonic empire. Throughout the country they had innumerable allies among men of substance and independent mind, who would have scorned to wear a party label but nevertheless shared the prevailing Tory outlook. They regarded themselves as the defenders not only of the Island, but of the almost bloodless aristocratic settlement achieved by the Revoultion of 1688. Under the shock of the French Terror the English governing classes had closed their minds and their ranks to change. Prolonged exertions had worn out the nation. Convalescence lasted until 1830.

The principal figures in the Government were Lord Liverpool, Lord Castlereagh, and, after 1818, the Duke of Wellington. Castlereagh and Wellington towered above their colleagues. Much of the credit for the broad peace which Europe enjoyed after the fall of Napoleon was due to the robust common sense and shrewd judgment of Wellington and to the aloof disinterestedness of Castlereagh. In spite of many setbacks and some military blunders these men had led the country to victory. Liverpool was the son of Charles Jenkinson, organiser of Government patronage under George III and close colleague of the younger Pitt. He was a man of conciliatory temper, a mild chief, and an easy colleague. He had held a variety of public offices almost continuously since the start of the war with France. In 1812 he became Prime Minister, and for fifteen years presided over the affairs of the realm with tact, patience, and laxity.

Castlereagh had served his political apprenticeship as Chief Secretary for Ireland. In the difficult days of the negotiation for Union with Ireland, when the powers of patronage were extensively used, he had seen eighteenth-century jobbery at its worst. He had joined the war-time Cabinet as Secretary for War, but was obliged to resign after a celebrated quarrel with his colleague Canning, which led to a duel between them on Putney Heath. In 1812 Castlereagh had returned to the Government and had been appointed to the Foreign Office. He was the architect of the coalition which gained the final victory and one of the principal authors of the treaties of peace. For home affairs he cared little, and he was unable to expound his far-sighted foreign policy with the eloquence that it deserved. Castlereagh was no orator. His cool, collected temperament was stiffened with disdain; he thought it beneath him to inform the public frankly of the Government's plans and measures. Nevertheless he was Leader of the House of Commons. Seldom has that office been filled by a man with fewer natural qualifications for it.

In Wellington all men acknowledged the illustrious General who had met and beaten Napoleon. His conception of politics was simple. He wished to unite all parties, and imbue them with the duty of preserving the existing order. The rest of the Cabinet were Tories of the deepest dye, such as the Lord Chancellor, Eldon; Addington, now Viscount Sidmouth, once Prime Minister and now at the Home Office; and Earl Bathurst, Colonial Secretary, whom Lord Rosebery has described as "one of those strange children of our political system who fill the most dazzling offices with the most complete obscurity." These men had begun their political life under the threat of world revolution. Their sole aim in politics was an unyielding defence of the system they had always known. Their minds were rigid, and scarcely capable of grasping the changes pending in English society. They were the upholders of the landed interest in government, of the Protestant ascendancy in Ireland, and of Anglicanism at home. Castlereagh was a specialist in foreign and Wellington in military affairs. The others were plain Tory politicians resolved to do as little as possible as well as they could.

They had many advantages. The sea-power, the financial strength, and the tenacity of Britain had defeated Napoleon. In the summer of 1815 Britain and Castlereagh stood at the head of Europe, and upon the terms of the European settlement now to be concluded the peace of generations depended. The sundered or twisted relations between the leading states must be replaced by an ordered system; France must be rendered harmless for the future. An international structure must be raised high above the battlefields of nations, of theories, and of class. The treaties which created the new Europe involved Britain in obligations she had never assumed before. She was a party to the settlement of the new frontiers of France, which deprived the restored Bourbons of what is now the Saarland and of parts of Savoy. France was reduced to the frontiers of 1789, and Prussia established as the chief Power upon the river Rhine. The Allied army of occupation in North-Eastern France, which included thirty thousand British troops out of a hundred and fifty thousand men, was commanded by the Duke of Wellington. Although Tory opinion even in the day of triumph was fearful of Continental commitments, Castlereagh resolved that Britain should not abandon the position of authority she had won during the war. Immune from popular passions, race hatreds, or any desire to trample on a fallen enemy, he foresaw the day when France would be as necessary to the balance of Europe and to the interests of Britain as Prussia, Austria, and Russia. With Wellington he stood between France and her vindictive foes. Unrestrained, Prussia, Austria, and Russia would have divided between them the states of Germany, imposed a harsh peace upon France, and fought each other over the partition of Poland. The moderating influence of Britain was the foundation of the peace of Europe.

In the eighteenth century the European Powers had no regular organisation for consulting each other, and little conception of their common interests. The Revolution in France had united them against the common danger, and they were now determined to remain together to prevent a further outbreak. An alliance of the four Great Powers already existed, sworn to confer as occasion demanded upon the problems of

Europe. This was now supplemented by a Holy Alliance between the three autocratic rulers on the Continent, the Emperors of Russia and Austria and the King of Prussia. Its main purpose was to intervene in any part of Europe where revolution appeared and in the name of legitimacy instantly to suppress it.

This made small appeal to Castlereagh. He was opposed to any interference in the affairs of sovereign states, however small and whatever liberal complexions their Governments might assume. Although caricatured as a reactionary at home he was no friend to Continental despotism. To him the Quadruple Alliance and the Congress at Vienna were merely pieces of diplomatic machinery for discussing European problems. On the other hand, the Austrian Chancellor Metternich and his colleagues regarded them as instruments for preserving the existing order. This divergence between the Great Powers was in part due to the fact that Britain had a Parliamentary Government which represented, however imperfectly, a nation. Castlereagh's European colleagues were the servants of absolute monarchs. Britain was a world-Power whose strength lay in her ranging commerce and in her command of the seas. Her trade flourished and multiplied independently of the reigning ideas in Europe. Moreover, her governing classes, long accustomed to public debate, did not share the absolutist dreams that inspired, and deluded, the Courts of the autocrats.

In spite of these differences the Congress of Vienna stands as a monument to the success of classical diplomacy. The intricacies of its negotiations were immense. No fewer than twenty-seven separate agreements were concluded during the first six months of 1815, in addition to the formidable Final Act of the Congress itself, and some twenty other treaties signed elsewhere in the same period. Talleyrand, with his background of double-dealing and treachery to his Emperor, nevertheless displayed an unswerving and ingenious determination to restore his country's position in Europe. But to modern eyes Castlereagh was pre-eminent as the genius of the conference. He reconciled opposing views, and his modest expectation that peace might be ensured for seven years was fulfilled more than fivefold. He represented, with its faults and virtues, the equable detached and balanced approach to Continental affairs that was to characterise the best of British foreign policy for nearly a century. After the Congress was concluded split became inevitable, but Castlereagh achieved at least one triumph before the eventual collapse. Within three years of the signing of the peace treaty British troops had evacuated French territory, the war indemnity had been paid, and France was received as a respectable nation into the European Congress. Wellington, released from military duties in France, thereupon entered the Cabinet in the not inappropriate office of Master-General of the Ordnance.

* * * * *

At home the Government were faced with the delicate and perplexing task of economic reconstruction. For this their members were supremely unfitted. The dislocation caused by the end of the war and the novel problems posed by the advance of industry were beyond the power of these men to remedy or solve. Earlier than her neighbours Britain enjoyed the fruits and endured the rigours of the Industrial Revolution. She gained a new domain of power and prosperity. At the same time the growing masses in her ill-built towns were often plunged into squalor and misery, the source of numerous and well-grounded discontents. Her technical lead was due to the ingenuity and success of British inventors and men of business in the eighteenth century and to the fortunate proximity of her main coal and iron deposits to each other and to the coast. Supremacy at sea, the resources of the colonial empire, and the use of capital accumulated from its trade nourished the industrial movement. Steam engines were gradually harnessed to the whole field of contemporary industry. In engineering accurate tools were perfected which brought a vast increase in output. The spinning of cotton was mechanised, and the factory system grew by degrees. The skilled man, self-employed, who had hitherto worked in his home, was steadily displaced. Machinery, the rise of population, and extensive changes in employment all presented a formidable social problem. The Government were by their background and upbringing largely unaware of the causes of the ills which they had to cure. They concentrated upon the one issue they understood, the defence of property. In a society which was rapidly becoming industrial most of them represented the abiding landed interest. They were incapable of carrying out even moderate reforms because of their obsessive fears of bloody revolution.

Napoleon had closed the Continent to British commerce, and the answering British blockade had made things worse for industry at home. There was much unemployment in the industrial North and the Midlands. Smashing of machinery during the Luddite riots of 1812 and 1813 had exposed the complete absence of means of preserving public order. There was no co-ordination between the Home Office in London and the Justices of the Peace in the country. Disorder was in the end suppressed only by the tactful and efficient behaviour of the officers commanding the troops sent to put down the rioters. Often before in the eighteenth century low wages and lack of employment had caused widespread unrest, which had been fanned into riot whenever a succession of bad harvests drove prices high and made food dearer. Bad harvests now added to the prevailing distress. But eighteenth-century riots were generally soon over. They were snuffed out by a few hangings and sentences of transportation to the colonies. The sore-pates who remained at home were more inclined to blame nature for their woes than either the economic or political system. After Waterloo the public temper was very different. Extremist Radical leaders came out of hiding and kept up a perpetual and growing agitation. Their organisations, which had been suppressed during the French Revolution, now reappeared, and began to take the shape of a political movement, though as yet scarcely represented in the House of Commons.

In the Radical view it was the Government alone, and not chance or Act of God, that was to blame for the misfortunes of the people. The Tory Cabinet in the face of such charges knew not what to do. It was no part of Tory philosophy to leave everything to be settled by the chaffer of the market-place, to trust to good luck and ignore the bad. The Tories of the time recognised and sometimes gloried in the responsibility of the governing classes for the welfare of the whole nation. The tasks of government were well understood to be as Burke had defined them—"the public peace, the public safety, the public order, the public prosperity." It was the last of these that was now foremost. The trouble was that the Government, in the unprecedented conditions that confronted them, had no idea how to secure the public prosperity. And even if they had hit upon a plan they possessed no experienced body of civil servants to put it into effect. As a result the only remedy for misery was private charity or the Poor Law.

It was a misfortune for Britain in these years that the Parliamentary Opposition was at its weakest. A generation in the wilderness had demoralised the Whig Party, which had not been effectively in office since 1783. Among themselves the Whigs were deeply divided, and none of them had any better or broader plans for post-war reconstruction than the Tories. Indeed, their interests were essentially the same. Like their rivals, they represented the landed class, and also the City of London. The only issues upon which they seriously quarrelled with the Government were Catholic Emancipation and the enfranchisement of the middle classes in the rising industrial towns. In the 1790's the Whigs had favoured the cause of Parliamentary Reform. It had been a useful stick with which to beat the administration of the younger Pitt. But they had been badly scared by the headlong course of events in France. Their leaders only gradually and reluctantly regained their reforming zeal. In the meantime, as Hazlitt put it, the two parties were like competing stage-coaches which splashed each other with mud but went by the same road to the same place. The Radicals who found their way into Parliament were too few to form an effective Opposition. One of their veteran leaders, John Cartwright, had for forty years in a litter of pamphlets been advocating annual Parliaments and universal suffrage. He was a landed gentleman, liked by many Members, but he never sat in the House of Commons. Under the unreformed franchise no constituency would adopt him. The violence of language used by the Radicals frightened Tories and Whigs alike. It stiffened the resistance of the upper middle classes, both industrial and landed, to all proposals for change.

*   *   *   *   *

English political tradition centred in Parliament, and men still looked to Parliament to cure the evils of the day. If Parliament did nothing, then the structure of Parliament must be changed. Agitation therefore turned from airing social discontents to demanding Parliamentary Reform. Huge meetings were held, and protests vociferously made. But the tactics of the Radicals were much too like those of the French Revolutionaries to gain support from the middle classes. Though still denied much weight in Parliament, the middle classes were bound by their fear of revolution to side in the last resort with the landed interest. The Cabinet was thoroughly perturbed. Habeas corpus was suspended, and legislation passed against the holding of seditious meetings. Throughout the country a fresh wave of demonstrations followed. A large body of men set out to march from Manchester to London to present a petition against the Government's measures, each carrying a blanket for his night's shelter. This march of the "Blanketeers" disturbed the authorities profoundly. The leaders were arrested and the rank and file quickly dispersed. Another rising in Derbyshire was easily suppressed.

These alarums and excursions revealed the gravity of conditions. Not only was there grinding poverty among the working population, but also a deep-rooted conflict between the manufacturing and agricultural classes. The economy of the country was dangerously out of balance. The war debt had reached alarming proportions. The fund-holders were worried at the instability of the national finances. The country had gone off the gold standard in 1797, and the paper currency had seriously depreciated. In 1812 a Parliamentary committee advised returning to gold, but the Bank of England was strongly adverse and nothing was done. The income tax, introduced by Pitt to finance the war, was highly unpopular, especially among the industrial middle class. It took 10 per cent of all incomes over £150 a year, and there were lower rates for smaller incomes. The yield in 1815 was fifteen million pounds, which was a large proportion of the Budget. Agriculture as well as industry quaked at the end of the war. Much capital had been sunk in land for the sake of high profits. Peace brought a slump in the prices fetched by crops,

and landowners clamoured for protection against the impor-
tation of cheap foreign corn. This had been granted by the
Corn Law of 1815, which excluded foreign wheat unless the
domestic price per quarter rose above eighty shillings. The
cost of bread went up, and the manufacturing classes had to
raise wages to save their workers from hunger. The manufacturers in their turn got the income tax abolished, which
helped them but imperilled the Budget. The Chancellor of
the Exchequer, Nicholas Vansittart, struggled vainly with the
chaos of a mounting deficit, and an unstable currency, while
behind these technical problems distress grew and gaped.

In 1819 an incident took place which increased the un-
popularity and quickened the fears of the Government. A
meeting of protest was held at St Peter's Fields, outside Manchester, attended by over fifty thousand people, including
women and children. The local magistrates lost their heads,
and, after reading the Riot Act, ordered the yeomanry to
charge. Eleven people were killed, two of them women, and
four hundred were injured. This "massacre of Peterloo," as it
was called in ironic reference to the Battle of Waterloo,
aroused widespread indignation, which was swelled still further when the Government took drastic steps to prevent the
recurrence of disorder. Six Acts were passed regulating public
meetings, empowering the magistrates to seize seditious lit-
erature, forbidding unauthorised drilling in military formations, imposing a heavy tax upon the Press to restrict the
circulation of Radical newspapers, regulating the issue of
warrants and the bringing of cases to trial. Soon afterwards
a conspiracy was discovered against the whole Cabinet. A
small gang of plotters was arrested in Cato Street, a turning
off the Edgware Road, where they had met to plan to murder
all the Ministers at a dinner party and seize the Bank of England.

The attack by the Government upon the traditional principles of English liberty aroused the conscience of the Whigs. They considered that "Peterloo" was no excuse for invading the rights of the subject. They demanded an inquiry. Liberty was at stake, and this was a struggle they well understood. When they were outvoted however they took their defeat with some equanimity; for they were as frightened as the Tories by the social unrest that was gripping all Europe. Compared with most Continental countries, Britain came lightly out of these years of disturbance. But the spectacle of convulsions abroad darkened counsel at home. By the end of 1819 trade and harvests had improved. A commission under the chairmanship of Robert Peel, a young Tory politician who had been Chief Secretary for Ireland at the age of twenty-four, recommended a return to the gold standard. Peel brought in and carried a Bill embodying the principles of their report. Stabilisation of the currency was at last achieved, and by a Private Member of Parliament. Though the landed interests suffered some hardship, not without raising their voices in complaint, it seemed that a corner had been turned.

* * * * *

Once again in English history the personal affairs of the royal family now exploded into public view. Victory over Napoleon had been a triumph for the Divine Right of Kings and the cause of monarchy. But the republican influence of the French Revolution had left its mark on public opinion in most European countries, and the vices or incapacity of many monarchs made them easy targets for criticism and abuse. In England King George III had long been intermittently mad, and English politicians had had to reckon with the virtual demise of the Crown for considerable intervals. In 1788 the first madness of the King had confronted Pitt with a grave political crisis. An acrimonious dispute with Fox and the

Whigs over the powers that should be exercised by the Prince of Wales as Regent was brought to a conclusion only by George III's sudden recovery. In 1810 the old King finally sank into incurable imbecility. He lived for another ten years, roaming the corridors of Windsor Castle with long white beard and purple dressing-gown. The Prince became Regent, with unrestricted royal prerogatives. To the consternation of his old Whig friends, he had kept his Tory advisers in power and prosecuted the war with vigour. Whatever the faults of George IV, his determination as Regent to support Wellington and Castlereagh and to stand up to Napoleon should earn him an honourable place in his country's history.

The royal family of the house of Hanover had by now implanted itself firmly on English soil. "Farmer George," as George III was called in his happier middle years, had become a popular figure. He had been the only person who had not lost his nerve at the time of the Gordon Riots, when a crazy Protestant mob, led by an unbalanced member of the aristocracy, reduced London to panic. He had endured the disasters of the American War of Independence. But though he commanded his people's affection he scarcely inspired their leaders' respect. He married a German princess, Queen Charlotte, who bore him a brood of sons, seven of whom grew to manhood. None of them added dignity or lustre to the royal house.

The atmosphere of the Court was like that of a minor German principality. All was stiff, narrow, fusty. The spirited lad who was to be George IV soon rebelled against his decorous mother and parsimonious father. A gift for facile friendship, often with dubious personages, alienated him still further from the home circle. He was early deprived of the companionship of his brothers, who were dispatched to Germany, there to receive a thorough Teutonic grounding. George, as heir to the throne, had to have an English background; and in the circle of his more intimate friends, Charles James Fox, Richard Sheridan, and Beau Brummel, he soon acquired the attributes of the eighteenth-century English gentleman—the arts of acquiring debts, of wearing fine clothes, and making good conversation. His natural intelligence and good taste went undisciplined and his talent for self-expression was frequently squandered in melodramatic emotion. Self-indulgence warped his judgment and frivolity marred his bearing. When pleasure clashed with royal duty it was usually pleasure that won. The loneliness of his position, both as Regent and King, cast a harsh emphasis upon his not unamiable weaknesses.

In 1784 the Prince had fallen in love. His choice was unfortunate. Maria Fitzherbert was not only a commoner of obscure family, but also a Roman Catholic. Her morals were impeccable and she would be content with nothing less than marriage. The Prince's Whig friends were alarmed when the heir to the most Protestant throne in Europe insisted on marrying a Roman Catholic widow who had already survived two husbands. Under the Royal Marriages Act the union was illegal, and George's behaviour was neither creditable to himself nor to his position. The clandestine beginnings of this relationship and the volatile temperament of George did their work. Mrs Fitzherbert, prim and quiet, was not the woman to hold him for long. The relationship slid back into the secrecy from which it had unwillingly emerged. It was finally broken off, but not until some years after George had contracted a second, legal, and dynastic marriage.

At the bidding of his parents in 1796 he was wedded to Caroline of Brunswick, a noisy, flighty, and unattractive German princess. George was so appalled at the sight of his bride that he was drunk for the first twenty-four hours of his married life. A few days after his wedding he wrote his wife a letter absolving her from any further conjugal duties. For some years thereafter he consoled himself with Lady Jersey. He acquired a growing hatred for Caroline. A high-spirited, warm-hearted girl was born of their brief union, Princess Charlotte, who found her mother quite as unsatisfactory as her father. In 1814 George banned his wife from Court, and after an unseemly squabble she left England for a European tour, vowing to return to plague her husband when he should accede to the throne.

The Government were perturbed about the problem of the succession. Princess Charlotte married Prince Leopold of Saxe-Coburg, later King of the Belgians, but in 1817 she died in childbirth. Her infant was stillborn. George's brothers, who were all in different ways eccentric, were thoroughly unpopular; as Wellington said, "the damnedest millstone about the necks of any Government, . . . who had personally insulted two-thirds of the gentlemen of England." They lacked not only charm, but lawful issue. But they were well aware of the importance of their position. They had a cash value to the Government on the royal marriage market. Most of them were already illegally involved in long-standing relationships with women. In 1818 however the obliging Dukes of Clarence and Kent did their royal duty—for a sum. Kent made a German marriage, and retired to Gibraltar to exercise his martial talents upon the Rock. The offspring of this alliance was the future Queen Victoria.

The Prince of Wales had long played with the idea of divorcing his itinerant wife. But Liverpool's Government were apprehensive. The Prince's extravagance, his lavish architectural experiments at Brighton and Windsor, were already causing them anxiety and giving rise to hostile speeches in Parliament. The Lord Chancellor, bluest of Tories, was vehemently opposed to any idea of divorce. The bench of bishops adopted a similar and suitable attitude. But George was persistent. He got a commission appointed to inquire into the Princess's conduct. It posted to Italy to collect evidence from the unsavoury entourage of Caroline. In July 1819 the Government received a report producing considerable circumstantial evidence against her. George was delighted, Liverpool and the Cabinet dismayed. Ever since 1714 the quarrels of the royal family had provided ammunition for party political warfare. The Opposition would certainly take up the cause of the injured wife.

The Princess's chief legal adviser was Henry Brougham, the ablest of the younger Whigs. This witty, ambitious, and unscrupulous attorney saw the value of the case to his party, though he was unconvinced of his client's innocence. He entered into confidential relations with the Government, hoping for a compromise which would bring advancement to himself. But in January 1820 the mad old King died and the position of the new sovereign's consort had to be determined. George IV fell seriously ill, but his hatred of Caroline sustained and promoted his recovery. He insisted upon her name being struck from the Church liturgy. The Cabinet presented him with a nervous note pointing out the difficulties of action. But now he was King. He warned them he would dismiss the lot, and threatened to retire to Hanover. The Whigs were as much alarmed as the Tories by the King's determination. They too feared the effect on public opinion outside Parliamentary and political circles. Whatever happened there would be a scandal which would bring the monarchy into dangerous disrepute.

Caroline now showed her hand. In April 1820 an open letter appeared in the London Press, signed by her, and recounting her woes. The Radical sympathy of the City of London was easily aroused in her favour. Alderman Wood entered into active correspondence with her and promised her a warm reception. The Radicals saw their chance of discrediting the traditional political parties. The Government made a last effort. Brougham was sent to intercept the Queen on her journey to England. A hurried meeting took place at St Omer. But nothing would stop the infuriated woman, whose obstinacy was inflamed by Radical advice. In June she landed, and she drove amid stormy scenes of enthusiasm from Dover to London. Her carriage was hauled most of the way by exuberant supporters. Her arrival produced a tumult of agitation.

The Government reluctantly decided that they must go through with the business. A Secret Committee of the Lords was set up, and their report persuaded Liverpool to agree to introduce a Bill of Pains and Penalties if the Queen were proved guilty of adultery. Popular feeling against the conditions of England was now diverted into a national inquiry into the condition of the monarchy. The characters of the royal personages concerned came under merciless scrutiny. A well-organised campaign was launched on behalf of Queen Caroline, led by the City Radicals, and, now that there was no turning back, by Brougham. Cheering crowds gathered every day outside her house in London. Her appearance in public places was loudly acclaimed. Politicians known to oppose her case were stoned in their carriages. In July the hearing of the charges was opened in Westminster Hall. In lengthy sessions the Attorney-General put the case for the Government, producing unreliable Italian witnesses from Caroline's vagabond Court. Her Master of Ceremonies, Bergami, had installed his numerous relations with bogus titles around her person, and this motley company had for some years been touring the Mediterranean countries, earning derision and insults from several Governments. The conflicting and sordid evidence of lackeys and chambermaids was displayed before the audience in Westminster Hall. Stories of keyholes, of indecorous costumes and gestures, regaled the public ear. The London Press openly attacked the credibility of the witnesses with their broken Italianate English and their uninspiring appearance. Leigh Hunt wrote a pungent verse:

> You swear—you swear—"O Signore, si,"
> That through a double door, eh,
> You've seen her *think* adulterously?
> "Ver' true, Sir—Si, Signore!"

"For fifteen days," wrote a contemporary historian, "the whole people was obscene." Brougham led the defence. With great effect he produced George's letter of 1796 absolving his wife from all marital obligations. It was not difficult to show that the conflicting evidence produced hardly justified the divorce clause in the Bill of Pains and Penalties. He boldly attacked the veiled personage behind the case, the King himself, malevolently referring to George's obesity in a wounding quotation from *Paradise Lost:*

> The other shape—
> If shape it could be called—that shape had none
> Distinguishable in member, joint or limb;
> Or substance might be called that shadow seemed,
> For each seemed either. . . .
> What seemed its head
> The likeness of a kingly crown had on.

The peers thought the Queen guilty, but doubted the wisdom of divorce, and the Bill passed through their House by only nine votes. The Whigs, when compromise had become impossible, voted against the Government. Their leader, Earl

Grey, had declared his belief in the innocence of Caroline. The Cabinet now decided that there was small chance of forcing the Bill through the Commons. They withdrew it and the affair was dropped. The London mob rioted in joy; the whole city was illuminated. The windows of the Ministers' houses were broken. Lord Sidmouth, who had prudently kept the newspapers from his daughters, was the first to suffer. But the bubbling effervescence of the masses quickly subsided. Caroline was granted an annuity of £50,000, which she was not too proud to accept. One political result of the crisis was the resignation of George Canning, who had been on friendly terms with the Queen. This gifted pupil of Pitt had rejoined the administration in 1816 as President of the Board of Control, which supervised the Government of India. He had made his influence felt in other spheres as well, and his departure was a serious loss to the Cabinet.

Two more awkward scenes closed this regrettable story. In July 1821 George IV was crowned in pomp at Westminster Abbey. Caroline attempted to force her way into the Abbey, but was turned away because she had no ticket. A month later she died. An attempt by the authorities to smuggle her coffin out of the country was frustrated and a triumphant and tumultuous funeral procession struggled through the City of London. This was the last victory that the Radicals gained from the affair.

The agitation over the Queen had been essentially the expression of discontent. It marked the highest point of the Radical movement in these post-war years. Towards the end of 1820 however industry and trade revived and popular disturbances subsided. The mass of the country was instinctively Royalist and the personal defects of the sovereign had little effect upon this deep-rooted tradition. The monarchy was inseparable from the settlement of 1688. Canning himself had

underrated the nation's deep conservatism. The Duke of Bedford had at one moment so far lost his nerve in the crisis as
to declare, "The monarchy is finished." Eldon showed better
judgment. "The lower orders here are all Queen's folks; few
of the middling or higher orders are, except the profligate, or
those who are endeavouring to acquire power through mis-
chief. . . . There is certainly an inclination to disquiet
among the lower orders; but it is so well watched that there
is no great cause for uneasiness on that account."

The political effects of the episode did not end at Canning's resignation. The Tory administration, which consisted
largely of ageing reactionaries, had been gravely weakened.
It was isolated from general opinion and badly in need of
new recruits. The Whigs too had been forced to recognise
their lack of popular backing, and the younger Members
saw that the "old and natural alliance between the Whigs
and the people" was now in danger. They began henceforth
to renew their interest in Parliamentary Reform, which soon
became the question of the hour.

Canning and the Duke

D URING the ten years' reign of King George IV the old party groupings in politics were fast dissolving. For more than a century Whig and Tory on different contentious issues had faced and fought one another in the House of Commons. Whig also fought Whig. Modern scholars, delving deeply into family connections and commercial interests, have sought to show that there was no such thing as a two-party system in eighteenth-century Britain. If caution must be the hall-mark of history, all that may be said is that the men in power were vigorously opposed by the men who were out, while in between stood large numbers of neutral-minded gentlemen placidly prepared to support whichever group held office. It is not much of a conclusion to come to about a great age of Parliamentary debate. The ins and outs might as well have names, and why not employ the names of Whig and Tory which their supporters cast at one another? At any rate, in the 1820's a Government of Tory complexion had been in power almost without interruption for thirty years.

This Government had successfully piloted the country through the longest and most dangerous war in which Britain had yet been engaged. It had also survived, though with tarnishing reputation, five years of peace-time unrest. But the Industrial Revolution posed a set of technical administrative problems which no aristocratic and agricultural party, Whig or Tory, was capable of handling. The nineteenth century called for a fresh interpretation of the duties of government. New principles and doctrines were arising which were to break up the old political parties and in the Victorian age reshape and recreate them. These developments took time, but already the party built up by the younger Pitt was feeling their stir and stress. Pitt had enlisted the growing mercantile and commercial interests of his day on the Tory side, and his policy of free trade and efficient administration had won over leaders of industry such as the fathers of Robert Peel and William Gladstone. But Pitt's tradition had faded during the years of war. Faithful disciples among the younger men strove to carry on his ideas, but his successors in office lacked his prestige and broad vision. Without skilful management an alliance between the landed gentry and the new merchant class was bound to collapse. The growers of corn and the employers of industrial labour had little in common, and they began to quarrel while Pitt was still alive. Disruption was postponed to the days of Peel, but the conflict had been sharpening since the end of the war amid falling agricultural prices and weary bickering over the Corn Laws. Caroline's divorce had discredited and weakened the Government. Parties were not yet expected to work out and lay before the country ambitious programmes of action. But even to its friends Lord Liverpool's administration seemed to have no aim or purpose beyond preserving existing institutions.

The younger Tories, headed by George Canning and supported by William Huskisson, spokesman of the merchants, advocated a return to Pitt's policy of free trade and intelligent commercial legislation. But even they were disunited. The issue of Catholic Emancipation was soon to confuse and split the Tory Party, and on this they were opposed by one of their own generation. Robert Peel during his six years in Ireland had successfully upheld the English ascendancy against heavy discontent and smouldering rebellion. He believed that "an honest despotic Government would be by far the fittest for Ireland." By a mixture of coercion and adroit patronage he had imposed comparative quiet and orderliness. In the nature of things neither his methods nor their results endeared him to the Irish. He had come home convinced that Catholic Emancipation would imperil not only Protestantism in Ireland but the entire political system at Westminster. Long before the nineteenth century was over events proved him right. Meanwhile Peel became Canning's rival for the future leadership of the Tories. Personalities added their complications. Canning had played a leading part in the conception and launching of the Peninsular War. His chief interest lay in foreign affairs. But this field seemed barred to him by his quarrel with Castlereagh. The older Members distrusted him. Brilliant, witty, effervescent, he had a gift for sarcasm which made him many enemies. A legend of unreliability grew up, his seniors thought him an intriguer, and when he resigned over the royal divorce in 1820 a Tory lord declared with relish, "Now we have got rid of those confounded men of genius." In August 1822 Canning was offered the post of Governor-General of India. He reconciled himself to this honourable exile; his political life seemed at an end. But then Fate took a hand. As the ship came up the Thames to take him to the East, Castlereagh, his mind unhinged by overwork, cut his throat in the dressing-room of his home. Canning's presence in the Government was now essential: he was appointed Foreign Secretary, and in this office he dominated English politics until his death five years later.

The Ministry was reconstructed to include Peel at the Home Office and Huskisson at the Board of Trade. The Government now had as many as three leading members in the

Commons. In 1815 three-quarters of the Cabinet had been in the Lords. The following years saw a more enlightened period of Tory rule. Canning, Peel, and Huskisson pursued bold policies which in many respects were in advance of those propounded by the Whigs. The penal code was reformed by Peel, and the London police force is his creation. Huskisson overhauled the tariff system, and continued Pitt's work in abolishing uneconomic taxes and revising the customs duties. Canning urged a scaling down of the duty on corn as the price rose at home. This was bound to bring conflict in the Tory ranks. He realised the distress and the political danger it would cause in the country, and declared on one occasion, "We are on the brink of a great struggle between property and population. . . . Such a struggle is only to be averted by the mildest and most liberal legislation." This soothing task he set before himself, but it was Peel who had to face the crisis when it came.

Annual motions for a Bill of Catholic Emancipation were brought in, to the disquiet of the reactionary supporters of the Government. But on one issue Canning was firm. He was a stubborn defender of the existing franchise. He believed that by far-sighted commercial measures and a popular foreign policy the problems of Parliamentary Reform could be evaded. Length of years was not given him in which to perceive himself mistaken.

* * * * *

A crisis in Spain confronted Canning with his first task as Foreign Secretary. The popular elements which had led the struggle against Napoleon now revolted against the autocratic Bourbon Government, formed a revolutionary Junta, and proclaimed a constitution on the model of that set up in France in 1815. Canning had backed the Spanish national rising in 1808, and was naturally sympathetic, but Metternich and the Holy Alliance saw the revolt, which soon spread to the Bourbon Kingdom of Naples, as a threat to the principle of monarchy and to the entire European system. A Congress at Verona in the autumn of 1822 discussed intervention in Spain on behalf of the Bourbons. Wellington had gone out as British representative with instructions from Castlereagh that Britain was to play no part in such a move. Canning vehemently agreed with this view and gave it wide publicity in England, and indeed the whole tradition of British foreign politics was against intervention in the domestic affairs of other states. But Austria and Russia were determined to act. An instrument lay ready to their hand. The ex-enemy, France, coveted respectability. Her restored Bourbon Government feared the revolutionaries and offered to send a military expedition to Spain to recover for King Ferdinand his absolutist powers. This was accepted at Verona. Canning would have nothing to do with it. There was great excitement in London. English volunteers went to Spain to serve in the defence forces of the Spanish "Liberals," a name which entered English politics from this Spanish revolt, while "Conservative" came to us from France. But Canning was equally against official intervention on the side of "Spanish Liberalism," and it was upon this that the Whigs attacked him. These heart-searchings in Britain made little difference to the outcome in Spain. The French expedition met with no serious resistance, and the Spanish Liberals retired to Cadiz and gave in.

A much larger issue now loomed beyond the European scene. Britain had little direct interest in the constitution of Spain, but for two centuries she had competed for the trade of Spain's colonies in South America. Their liberties were important to her. During the wars with Napoleon these colonies had enjoyed the taste of autonomy. They had no relish, when the Bourbons were restored in Madrid, for the revival of royal Spanish rule. Up and down the whole length of the Andes campaigns were fought for South American liberation. By Canning's time at the Foreign Office most of the republics that now figure on the map had come into separate if unstable existence. In the meanwhile British commerce with these regions had trebled in value since 1814. If France or the Holy Alliance intervened in the New World, if European troops were sent across the Atlantic to subdue the rebels, all this was lost, and much besides. These dangers gave Canning great anxiety. The business elements in England, whose support he was keen to command, were acutely sensitive to the peril. He acted with decision. He urged the United States to join Britain in opposing European interference in the countries across the Atlantic. While the Americans meditated on this proposal Canning also made an approach to the French. France had no desire to start an overseas quarrel with Britain. She disclaimed the use of force in South America and forswore colonial ambitions there. Thus was the Holy Alliance checked. As Canning later declared in a triumphant phrase, he had "called the New World into existence to redress the balance of the Old."

The New World meanwhile had something of its own to say. The United States had no wish to see European quarrels transferred across the ocean. They had already recognised the independence of the principal Latin-American republics. They did not want aspiring princes of the royal houses of Europe to be ferried over and set up as monarchs on the democratic continent. Still less would they contemplate European reconquest and colonisation. Canning's suggestion for a joint Anglo-American declaration began to grow attractive. Two honoured ex-Presidents, Jefferson and Madison, agreed with President Monroe that it would be a welcome and momentous step. They all had in mind Russian designs in the Pacific Ocean, as well as menaces from Europe; for the Russians occupied Alaska, and the territorial claims of the Czar stretched down the Western coast of America to California, where his agents were active. Monroe however had in John Qunicy Adams a Secretary of State who was cautious and stubborn by temperament and suspicious of Britain. Adams distrusted Canning, whom he earnestly thought to possess "a little too much wit for a Minister of State." He believed that the United States should act on their own initiative. If at some future time Cuba, or even Canada, desired to enlist in the Great Republic, might not a joint statement with Britain about the inviolability of the continent prejudice such possibilities? It was wiser for America to keep her hands free. As Adams noted in his diary, "It would be more candid, as well as more dignified, to avow our principles explicitly to Russia and France, than to come as a cock-boat in the wake of the British man-of-war." Hence there was propounded on December 2, 1823, in the President's annual message to Congress a purely American doctrine, the Monroe Doctrine, which has often since been voiced in transatlantic affairs. "The American continents," Monroe said, "by the free and independent condition they have assumed and maintain, are henceforth not to be considered as subjects for future colonisation by any Europen Powers. . . . We should consider any attempt on their part to extend their [political] system to any portion of this hemisphere as dangerous to our peace and safety." These were resounding claims. Their acceptance by the rest of the world depended on the friendly vigilance of the "British man-of-war," but this was a fact seldom openly acknowledged. For the best part of a century the Royal Navy remained the stoutest guarantee of freedom in the Americas. Thus shielded by the British bulwark, the American continent was able to work out its own unhindered destiny.

Monroe's famous message conveyed a warning to Britain as well as to the authoritarian Powers. Canning understood the risks of competition and dispute with the United States upon the continent in which the Americans now claimed predominance. He was determined to avert all conflicts which might embarrass Britain and harm her own proper interests. There was no purpose however in arguing about dangers which still lay largely in the future. His private comment was short and to the point. "The avowed pretension of the United States," he wrote, "to put themselves at the head of the confederacy of all the Americas and to sway that confederacy against Europe (Great Britain included) is not a pretension identified with our interests, or one that we can countenance or tolerate. It is, however, a pretension which there is no use in contesting in the abstract, but we must not say anything that seems to admit the principle."

Soon afterwards Britain officially recognised the independence of the South American states. King George IV, who bore no love for republics, and many of Canning's colleagues in the Government, had strenuously opposed this step. Even now the King refused to read the Royal Speech containing the announcement. It was read for him by a reluctant Lord Chancellor. So Canning's view prevailed. His stroke over South America may probably be judged his greatest triumph in foreign policy. But this was not the only field in which decisive action was required of him.

*   *   *   *   *

During the worst years of the Napoleonic wars Britain's greatest military effort had been launched in defence of Portugal. Now our oldest ally again called for assistance. Once more South America was involved. The Portuguese colony of Brazil had proclaimed its independence, and surprisingly accepted as its ruler a resident prince of the royal house. Canning recognised the new Empire of Brazil, and persuaded the Portuguese to do so. But affairs took a fresh turn. The King of Portugal died and his throne lay in dispute. His rightful heiress was the daughter of the Brazilian Emperor, eight years old, around whom the Liberal and constitutional forces rallied. But another claimant appeared in her absolutist uncle, who enjoyed the smiles of the Holy Alliance and the active support of Spain. It was, and always has been, British policy that Lisbon must not fall into the possession of unfriendly hands, and it now seemed that the whole of Portugal might succumb to authoritarian intervention. Under the terms of the ancient alliance British troops were dispatched to the Tagus in December 1826. Canning declared his views to the House of Commons. The movement of troops was not intended, he said, "to prescribe constitutions, but to defend and preserve the independence of an ally." Our ambassador in Lisbon described the wild scenes when the ships of the Royal Navy were sighted in the Tagus. "No one is afraid to be a constitutionalist now. . . . England has spoken, and some of her troops have already arrived. The lion's awakening [*ce revéil du lion*] has been majestic." Nevertheless the Portuguese problem was only temporarily settled. It remained to perplex Canning's successors in office for some years to come.

Another crisis had meanwhile erupted in the Eastern Mediterranean. After four centuries of subjection to the Turks the spirit of liberty was stirring among the Greeks. They broke into revolt, and in 1822 declared their independence. In England there was widespread enthusiasm for their cause. It appealed to the educated classes who had been brought up on the glories of Thermopylæ and Salamis. Enlightened circles in London were eager for intervention. Subscriptions were raised, and Byron and other British volunteers went to the aid of the Greeks. Before he met his death at Missolonghi Byron was deeply disillusioned. Not for the first or last time in the history of Greece a noble cause was nearly ruined by faction. But for the pressure of the Powers of Europe, the Greeks would have succumbed. With the aid of an army supplied by Mahomet Ali, the formidable Pasha of Egypt, the Sultan of Turkey was almost everywhere victorious. Unfortunately for the Greeks, the Powers were themselves divided. The Greek revolt had split the Holy Alliance, Austria and Russia taking opposite sides. Canning, like Castlereagh before him, was all for mediation. On the other hand, he feared that Russia would intervene, set up a client state in Greece, and exact her own price from the Turks. If Russia grew at Turkey's expense British interests in the Middle East and in India would be put in jeopardy. Here lay the origins of the "Eastern Question," as it was called, which increasingly preoccupied and baffled the Powers of Europe down to the First World War. After complicated negotiations Britain, France, and Russia agreed in 1827 on terms to be put to the Turks. British and French squadrons were sent to Greek waters to enforce them. This was the last achievement of Canning's diplomacy. The next act in the Greek drama was played after his death.

Canning's colleagues had become increasingly critical of the activities of their Foreign Secretary. Wellington was particularly disturbed by what he regarded as Canning's headlong courses. The two wings of the administration were only held together by the conciliatory character of the Prime Minister, and in February 1827 Liverpool had a stroke. A major political crisis followed. Canning abroad and Huskisson at home had alienated the old Tories in the party. Who was now to lead the Government? The whole future of the Tories was at stake. Were they to go upon the road of Wellington or of Canning? The choice of Prime Minister still lay with the Crown, and Georve IV hesitated for a month before making his decision. The Whigs could offer no alternative administration. They were divided among themselves and without hope of gaining a majority from the existing electorate. So it had to be one or other of the Tory wings. Many members of Liverpool's Cabinet, including Wellington and Eldon, declined to serve under Canning. On the other hand, Canning could command the support of a number of the leading Whigs. Should a Whig-Tory coalition be formed? That would break up the old party loyalties on which the Governments of the realm had for so long been based. Or should pure Tory rule be tried? That would be unpopular in the House of Commons and unacceptable to the country outside. Or could some neutral personage be found who might preside benignly and ineffectively over the factious scene? Exciting weeks and long conversations followed round the dinner-tables of Windsor Castle. It soon became plain that no Government could be constructed which did not include Canning and his friends, and that Canning would accept all or nothing. His final argument convinced the King. "Sire," he said, "your father broke the domination of the Whigs. I hope your Majesty will not endure that of the Tories." "No," George IV replied, "I'll be damned if I do." In April 1827 Canning became Prime Minister, and for a brief hundred days held supreme political power.

Canning's Ministry signalled the coming dissolution of the eighteenth-century political system. He held office by courtesy of a section of the Whigs. The only able Tory leader in the House of Commons whom he had lost was Robert Peel. Peel resigned partly for personal reasons and partly because he knew that Canning was in favour of Catholic Emancipation. But the Opposition Tories and the die-hard Whigs harassed the new Government. Had Canning been granted a longer spell of life the group he led might have founded a new political allegiance. But on August 8, after a short illness, Canning died. He was killed, like Castlereagh, by overwork.

Canning had played a decisive part in the shaping of the new century. In war and in peace he had proved himself a man of large views and active determination. His quick mind and hasty temper made him an uneasy party colleague. As his friend Sir Walter Scott said of him, he wanted prudence. Through Canning however the better side of the Pitt tradition was handed on to the future. In many ways he was in sympathy with the new movements stirring in English life. He was also in close touch with the Press and knew how to use publicity in the conduct of government. As with Chatham, his political power was largely based on public opinion and on a popular foreign policy. Belief in Catholic Emancipation marked him as more advanced in view than most of his Tory colleagues. His opposition to Parliamentary Reform was part of the curse which lay upon all English politicians who had had contact with the French Revolution. On this perhaps he might have changed his mind. At any rate, after his death his followers amid the ruins of the Tory Party were converted to the cause. Disraeli bore witness to this striking man. "I never saw Canning but once. I remember as if it were but yesterday the tumult of that ethereal brow. Still lingers in my ear the melody of that voice."

*   *   *   *   *

Canning's death at a critical moment at home and abroad dislocated the political scene. A makeshift administration composed of his followers, his Whig allies, and a group of Tories struggled ineptly with the situation. It leader was the lachrymose Lord Goderich, formerly Chancellor of the Exchequer. More than half the Tory Party, under Peel and Wellington, was in opposition. Quarrels among Whig and Tory members of the Government ruptured its unity. There had been a hitch in carrying out Canning's policy of nonintervention in Greece—which did mean something, in spite of Talleyrand's malicious definition, "un mot métaphysique et politique qui signifie à peu près la même chose qu'intervention." Admiral Codrington, one of Nelson's captains, who had fought at Trafalgar and was now in command of the Allied squadron in Greek waters, had on his own initiative destroyed the entire Turkish fleet in the Bay of Navarino. There was alarm in England in case the Russians should take undue advantage of this victory. The battle, which meant much to the Greeks, was disapprovingly described in the King's Speech as an "untoward incident," and the victor narrowly escaped court-martial. The Government, rent by Whig intrigues, abruptly disappeared. There was no question of a purely Whig Government. That party was weak and indifferently led. Wellington and Peel were instructed to form an administration. This they did. Wellington became Prime Minister, with Peel as Home Secretary and Leader of the House of Commons. The old Tories were to fight one more action. It was a stubborn rearguard.

The political views of the new Government were simple—defence of existing institutions, conviction that they alone stood between order and chaos, determination to retreat only if pressed by overwhelming forces. Peel was one of the ablest Ministers that Britain has seen. But his was an administrative mind. General ideas moved him only when they had seized the attention of the country and become inescapable political facts. The Government's first retreat was the carrying of an Opposition measure repealing the Test and Corporation Acts which excluded the Nonconformists from office. After a long struggle they at last achieved political rights and equality. Not so the Catholics. Their emancipation was not merely a matter of principle, a step in the direction of complete religious equality, but it was also an Imperial concern. The greatest failure of British Government was in Ireland. Irish discontent had seriously weakened Britain's strategic position during the Napoleonic wars. The social and political monopoly of a Protestant minority, which had oppressed Irish life since the days of Cromwell, would not be tolerated indefinitely. British Governments were perpetually threatened with revolution in Ireland. A main dividing line in politics after 1815 was upon this issue of Catholic Emancipation. It had sundered Canning and his followers, together with the Whigs, from Wellington and Peel. A decision had been postponed from year to year by "gentlemen's agreements" among the English politicians. But the patience of the Irish was coming to its end. They were organising under Daniel O'Connell for vehement agitation against England. O'Connell was a landlord and a lawyer. He believed in what later came to be called Home Rule for Ireland under the British Crown. Though not himself a revolutionary, he was a powerful and excitable orator, and his speeches nourished thoughts of violence.

A minor political incident in England fired the train. The leader of the Canningites, William Huskisson, had been forced out of the Government along with his followers, and an Irish Protestant landowner, Vesey Fitzgerald, was promoted to one of the vacant Ministerial posts. Appointment to office in those days involved submitting to the electorate at a by-election, and so a poll was due in County Clare. O'Connell stood as candidate, backed by the whole force of his organisation, the Catholic Association. He was of course debarred by existing legislation from taking a seat in Parliament, but in spite of the efforts of the local Protestant gentry he was triumphantly elected. Here was a test case. If the English Government refused to enfranchise the Catholics there would be revolution in Ireland, and political disaster at home.

Peel, whose political career had been built up in Ireland, had long been the symbol of opposition to any concessions to the Catholics. It was upon that view that his political reputation was based. He was a Member for that most Anglican of constituencies, Oxford University. His attitude in the growing crisis was unavoidably delicate. Wellington's position was happier. He was less committed and more able to take without qualm the line of expediency. The position in Ireland was simple. An independent association of the Irish people had sabotaged the official administration. The choice was either Catholic Emancipation or the systematic reconquest of Ireland. In August 1828 Wellington put the matter to the King. "The influence and powers of government in that country are no longer in the hands of the officers of the Government, but have been usurped by the demagogues of the Roman Catholic Association, who, acting through the influence of the Roman Catholic clergy, direct the country as they think proper. . . . We have a rebellion impending over us in Ireland, . . . and we in England a Parliament which we cannot dissolve, the majority of which is of opinion . . . that the remedy is to be found in Roman Catholic Emancipation, and they would unwillingly enter into the contest without making such an endeavour to pacify the country."

The Protestants in Ireland were thoroughly alarmed. They had nothing to gain from an Irish revolt. Political equality for the Catholics was a bitter draught for them to swallow, but if emancipation was not conceded the whole land settlement would be in danger. Either the Catholics got the vote or the Protestants stood to lose their estates. In December the Chief Secretary for Ireland made the dangers clear to Peel. "I have little doubt that the peasantry of the South at present look forward to the period of O'Connell's expulsion from the House of Commons as the time of rising. But any occurrence in the interval which might appear to be adverse to the Roman Catholic body might precipitate this result." And one of the English Opposition in a letter described the view of the Irish Protestants: "I know from the most unquestionable authority that very many of the Orange Protestants in Ireland are now so entirely alarmed at their own position that they express in the most unqualified terms their earnest desire for any settlement of the question at issue on any terms."

As a general Wellington knew the hopelessness of attempting to repress a national rising. He had seen civil war at close quarters in Spain. He himself came from an Irish family and was familiar with the turbulent island. He used plain language to the House of Lords. "I am one of those who have probably passed a longer period of my life engaged in war than most men, and principally in civil war; and I must say this, that if I could avoid by any sacrifice whatever even one month of civil war in the country to which I was attached I would sacrifice my life in order to do it."

The only opponents of Emancipation were the English bishops, the old-fashioned Tories, and the King. The bishops and the Tories could be outvoted; but the King was a more serious obstacle. Wellington and Peel had had a most unsatisfactory interview with him at Windsor, and they had not yet consulted their Cabinet as a whole. Peel was growing more and more uncomfortable, but the attitude of the King would dictate his own. He felt justified in remaining in an administration which was about to introduce a measure he had opposed all his political life only if his presence were vital to its success. The fact that the Opposition could force Parliament to carry Catholic Emancipation did not weigh with him. They lacked the confidence of the Crown, and this was still indispensable. Wellington could not carry the measure without Peel, and the Whigs could not carry it without the King. This determined Peel. He resigned his High Tory seat at Oxford and bought himself in for Westbury. His offer to stand by Wellington finally persuaded George IV, who dreaded a Whig administration. Peel himself introduced the Bill for Catholic Emancipation into the House of Commons, and it was carried through Parliament in 1829 with comfortable majorities. Revolution in Ireland was averted. But the unity of the English Tories had received another blow. The "Old Guard," still powerful under the unreformed franchise, never forgave Peel and Wellington for deserting the principle of the Anglican monopoly of power in Great Britain. Toryism meant many different and even conflicting things to its followers, but the supremacy of Protestantism had long been one of its binding political beliefs.

Wellington's military view of politics had led him to overawe his critics by a characteristic challenge to a duel. Lord Winchilsea had overstepped the bounds of decorum in an attack upon the Prime Minister in the House of Lords, accusing Wellington of dishonesty. A full-dress challenge followed. The meeting took place in Battersea Park. The Field-Marshal, now aged sixty, was most nonchalant, slow and deliberate in his movements. This was much more his line than smoothing the susceptibilities of politicians, or, as he once put it in a moment of complaint, "assuaging what gentlemen call their feelings." Turning to his second, who was also his Secretary at War, he said, "Now then, Hardinge, look sharp and step out the ground. I have no time to waste. Damn it! don't stick him up so near the ditch. If I hit him he'll tumble in." Neither party was wounded and Winchilsea signed a paper withdrawing his insinuations. Later in the day Wellington called upon the King. "I have another subject to mention to your Majesty, personal to myself. I have been fighting a duel this morning." George graciously replied that he was glad of it; he had always been in favour of upholding the gentleman's code of honour. Politics, alas, are not always so easily managed.

The Duke's administration showed little sign of continuing its Liberal course. After the resignation of the Canningites two Cabinet posts had been given to ex-members of Wellington's staff. This military and aide-de-campish Government was increasingly out of touch with political opinion, and the forces of Opposition were gathering. But upon the surface the atmosphere was calm. In June 1830 King George IV died, with a miniature of Mrs Fitzherbert round his neck. "The first gentleman of Europe" was not long mourned by his people. During his last illness his mistress, Lady Conyngham, was busy collecting her perquisites. This once handsome man had grown so gross and corpulent that he was ashamed to show himself in public. His extravagance had become a mania, and his natural abilities were clouded by years of self-indulgence. No tyrant by nature, he yet enjoyed fancying himself as an autocrat. But with thrones tottering on the Continent he realised that the less he said on this subject the better. His memory was bespattered by the Victorians. He was not in his conduct much worse or better than most contemporary men of fashion.

* * * * *

George IV was succeeded on the throne by his brother, the Duke of Clarence, the most eccentric and least obnoxious of the sons of George III. He had been brought up in the Navy, and had passed a life of total obscurity, except for a brief and ludicrous interval when Canning had made him Lord High Admiral in 1827. For many years he had lived with an actress at Bushey Park. But in the end he too had had to do his duty and marry a German princess, Adelaide of Saxe-Meiningen. She proved to be a generous-hearted and acceptable Queen. Good-nature and simplicity of mind were William IV's in equal measure. The gravest embarrassments he caused his Ministers sprang from his garrulity. It was difficult to restrain his tactlessness at public functions. At an official dinner given to Cabinet Ministers and foreign diplomats he rose, and, with nautical bluntness, proposed a coarse toast, adding, "Honi soit qui mal y pense," to the embarrassment of the company. When he at last sat down one of the guests turned to the French Ambassador, Talleyrand, saying, "Eh bien, que pensez-vous de cela?" "C'est bien remarquable," replied the Frenchman, not a muscle of his face moving.

But the royal pair were popular, although the diarist, Charles Greville, Clerk to the Privy Council and a close observer, was not certain if the kingly wits would last until the calling of Parliament. The Queen was not a beauty, but her quiet homeliness was a welcome change after the domestic life of George IV. The bluffness of the monarch was attractive to the lower orders, though once, when he spat out of the window of the State coach, a reproving voice from the crowd said, "George the Fourth would never have done that!" In any case, the life and manners of London society did not depend upon the example of the Court.

It had been expected that the new King might prefer a Whig administration. As Duke of Clarence he had been dismissed from the Admiralty by the Duke of Wellington. But on his accession William IV welcomed and retained the Duke. His reputation for fairness proved to be of political value. Wellington bore witness to it. "It is impossible for one man to have treated another man better or more kindly than the King did me from that day [his accession] to the day of his death. And yet it was also impossible for one man to have run another as hard as I did him as Lord High Admiral. But he showed no resentment of it." "Sailor William" needed every ounce of fairness. There were heavy seas ahead. Revolution had again broken out in France, and the Bourbon monarchy was at an end. As the news swept across the Channel there were mutterings of a coming storm in England.

Reform and Free Trade

I N 1830 the Liberal forces in Europe stirred again. The July Revolution in France set up a constitutional monarchy under the house of Orleans. The new King, Louis Philippe, was the son of the Revolutionary Philippe Égalité, who had voted for the death of his cousin, Louis XVI, and himself been guillotined later. Louis Philippe was a wiser and more honourable man than his father. He was to keep his uneasy throne for eighteen years, and he also kept his head. Encouraged by events in Paris, the Belgians rebelled against the Kingdom of the Netherlands, in which they had been incorporated by the peace treaties of 1815. Britain had played a big part in this arrangement. It had long been British policy, and still is, to support the independence of the Low Countries and prevent any of their provinces from passing under the control of a menacing Power. The twentieth century needs no reminding of the great wars that have been fought with this as a leading cause. In 1815 an enlarged united Netherlands had seemed a promising experiment. After all, it at last realised the dreams of the first William of Orange in the days of Queen Elizabeth. But the Dutch and Belgians were divided by language, religion, and commercial interests, and these barriers could not easily be overcome. The Belgians demanded autonomy, and then independence. Much diplomatic activity ensued before a peaceful solution was eventually found. Meanwhile a wave of revolts spread across Germany into Poland. The Europe of Metternich and the Holy Alliance was severely shaken, though not yet overturned.

These agitations on the European continent, largely orderly in character and democratic in purpose, were much acclaimed in England; and their progress was closely and excitedly studied. The Tory Government and the Duke of Wellington alone seemed suspicious and hostile. With some reason the Government feared that France might annex Belgium or establish a French prince in Brussels upon a new throne. Wellington was even suspected of intending to restore the Kingdom of the Netherlands by armed force. This was not true. The preservation of peace was his chief care. But Opposition speakers were pleased to attribute to him an aim he did not profess, and the rumour was enough to inflame the hot tempers of the times. Poverty in the villages and on the farms had already led to rioting in South-East England. In the growing towns and cities industrial discontent was driving men of business and their workers into political action. Turmoil, upheaval, even revolution, seemed imminent. Instead there was a General Election.

At the polls the Whigs made gains, but the result was indecisive. The Whig leader was Earl Grey, a friend and disciple of Fox. It is given to few men to carry out late in life a great measure of reform which they have advocated without success for forty years. Such was to be Grey's achievement. He had held office briefly under Fox in the Ministry of 1806. For the rest, since the early years of the younger Pitt he had been not only continuously out of office, but almost without expectation or desire of ever winning it. Now his hour was at hand. Grey was a landowner who regarded politics as a social duty, and much preferred his country estates to the lobbies of Westminster. He had however made careful study of the insurrections on the Continent, and realised that they were not as sinister as Wellington thought. His judgment on home affairs was also well directed. He and his colleagues perceived that the agitation which had shaken England since Waterloo issued from two quite separate sources—the middle classes, unrepresented, prosperous, respectable, influenced by the democratic ideas of the French Revolution, but deeply law-abiding in their hunger for political power; and on the other side a bitter and more revolutionary section of working men, smitten by the economic dislocation of war and its aftermath, prepared to talk of violence and perhaps even to use it. An alliance with the middle classes and a moderate extension of the franchise would suffice, at any rate for a time, and for this Grey prepared his plans. He had the support of Lord John Russell, son of the Duke of Bedford, who was a man of impulsive mind, with a high devotion to the cause of liberty in the abstract, whatever the practical consequences might be. With them stood Henry Brougham, expectant of office, an advanced politician who had made his name as the defender of Queen Caroline. Brougham was fertile with modern ideas, and a friend of leading Radicals and newspaper editors.

Parliament met in November. There were some who hoped that the Tories would do again what they had done over Catholic Emancipation and, after a rearguard action, reform the franchise themselves. One group of Tories was convinced that a wider electorate would be more staunchly Protestant. Others were in touch with the popular associations which were campaigning for reform. But Wellington was adverse. To the House of Lords he said, "I never read or heard of any measure . . . which in any degree satisfies my mind that the state of representation can be improved. . . . I am fully convinced that the country possesses at the present moment a legislature which answers all the good purposes of legislation, and this to a greater degree than any legislature ever has answered in any country whatever. . . . The representation of the people at present contains a large body of the property of the country, and in which the landed interest has a preponderating influence. Under these circumstances I am not prepared to bring forward any measure of the description alluded to." When he sat down he turned to his Foreign Secretary, the Earl of Aberdeen. "I have not said too much, have I?" He received no direct answer, but in reporting the incident later the Foreign Secretary described Wellington's speech briefly. "He said that we are going out."

Wellington hoped that the Whigs were too disorganised to form a Government, but his own party was even more disunited. Those who had followed Canning would have nothing more to do with the Tory "Old Guard," and now made common cause with the Whigs. A fortnight later the Tories were defeated and King William IV asked Grey to form a Government. With one brief interval the Whigs had been out of office for nearly fifty years. Now at a bound they were at the summit of power and influence.

They were confronted with an ugly scene. French threats to intervene in Belgium made it imperative but unpopular to increase the military estimates. The Chancellor of the Exchequer failed to provide an effective Budget. Law and order were breaking down in the south-eastern counties, and Lord Melbourne, the new Home Secretary, acted decidedly. Over four hundred farm workers were sentenced to transportation. The Radicals were indignant and disillusioned. Only Parliamentary Reform could save the Government, and to this they now addressed themselves.

A secret Cabinet committee was appointed to draft the scheme, and in March 1831 Lord John Russell rose in the House of Commons to move the first Reform Bill. Amid shouting and scornful laughter he read out to their holders a list of over a hundred "rotten" and "pocket" boroughs which it was proposed to abolish and replace with new constituencies for the unrepresented areas of the Metropolis, the industrial North, and the Midlands. To the Tories this was a violation of all they stood for, an affront to their deepest political convictions, a gross attack on the rights of property. A seat was a thing to be bought or sold like a house or an estate, and a more uniform franchise savoured of an arithmetical conception of politics dangerously akin to French democracy. Many Whigs, too, who had expected a milder measure were at first dumbfounded by the breadth of Russell's proposals. They soon rallied to the Government when they saw the enthusiasm of the country, for the Whigs believed that Reform would forestall revolution. The Tories, on the other hand, feared that it was the first step on the road to cataclysm. To them, and indeed to many Whigs, English government meant the rule, and the duty to rule, of the landed classes in the interests of the community. A wider franchise would mean the beginning of the end of the old system of administration by influence and patronage. Could the King's Government be carried on in the absence of these twin pillars of authority? It was not altogether a vain question. After 1832 Britain was to see many unstable Ministries before the pattern was changed by the rise of disciplined parties with central organisations and busy Whips.

Radical leaders were disappointed by what they conceived to be the moderation of the Bill, but in their various ways they supported it. There was not much in common between them. Jeremy Bentham and James Mill were philosophical advocates of democracy and middle-class education; William Cobbett was a vigorous, independent-minded journalist; Francis Place, the tailor of Charing Cross, and Thomas

Attwood, the banker of Birmingham, were active political organisers. But they were all determined that the Bill should not be whittled away by amendment and compromise. Agitation spread through the country. There was no economic crisis to distract public attention from the one burning issue or to shake the popular belief that an extension of the right to vote and a redistribution of seats to accord with the Industrial Revolution would cure all national ills. A cataract of journals and newspapers appeared in support of the cause. To avoid the tax upon the Press, a relic of the repressive legislation of 1819, weekly news-letters were sent through the post.

In the House of Commons the Tories fought every inch of the way. The Government was by no means sure of its majority, and although a small block of Irish votes controlled by O'Connell, leader of the emancipated Catholics, was cast for Grey the Bill was defeated. A roar of hatred and disappointment swept the country. Grey asked the King for a dissolution, and William IV had the sense to realise that a refusal might mean revolution. The news caused uproar in the Lords, where a motion was introduced asking the King to reconsider his decision, but as the shouting rose from the benches and peers shook their fists across the floor of the House the thunder of cannon was heard as the King left St James's to come in person to pronounce the dissolution. The Tories stormed. One of them, jumping to his feet, shouted to the jubilant Whigs, "The next time that cannons are heard they will not be firing blanks and it will be your heads that they will carry off." "Those who were present," wrote Greville in his memoirs, "tell me it resembled nothing but what we read of the *Serment du Jeu de Paume,* and the whole scene was as much like the preparatory days of revolution as well can be imagined."

Excited elections were held on the single issue of Reform.

It was the first time a mandate of this kind had been asked of the British people. They returned an unmistakable answer. The Tories were annihilated in the county constituencies and the Whigs and their allies gained a majority of 136 in the House of Commons. When Parliament reassembled the battle was shifted to the House of Lords. Wellington rose again and again to put the case against Reform. "A democracy," he declared, "has never been established in any part of the world that it has not immediately declared war against property, against the payment of the public debt, and against all the principles of conservation, which are secured by, and are in fact the principal objects of the British Constitution as it now exists. Property and its possessors will become the common enemy." Most of his political experience had been gathered in Spain, and he was oppressed with memories of revolutionary Juntas. Reform would break "the strength which is necessary to enable his Majesty to protect and keep in order his foreign dominions and to ensure the obedience of their inhabitants. We shall lose these colonies and foreign possessions, and with them our authority and influence abroad." On the night of October 7, 1831, the critical division took place. The peers were sharply divided, and it was the twenty-one bishops in the Upper House who decided the issue; they were against Reform. Thus the Tories triumphed. The Bill was defeated and a new constitutional issue was raised—the Peers against the People.

Next morning the newspapers, bordered in black, proclaimed the news. Rioting broke out in the Midlands; houses and property were burned; there was wild disorder in Bristol. The associations of Reformers in the country, called Political Unions, strove to harness enthusiasm for the Bill and to steady the public temper. Meanwhile the Government persevered. In December Russell introduced the Bill for the third time, and the Commons carried it by a majority of two to one. In the following May it came again before the Lords. It was rejected by forty-four votes. There was now no question of another dissolution and Grey realised that only extreme remedies would serve. He accordingly drove to Windsor and asked the King to create enough new peers to carry the Bill. The King refused and the Cabinet resigned. William IV asked Wellington and Peel to form an administration to carry Reform as they had carried Catholic Emancipation, and thus avoid swamping the Lords. But Peel would not comply; he was not prepared to assume Ministerial responsibility for a measure of which he disapproved. Feeling in the country became menacing. Plans were made for strikes and a general refusal of taxes. Banners and placards appeared in the London streets with the caption "To Stop the Duke Go for Gold," and there was a run on the Bank of England. Radical leaders declared they would paralyse any Tory Government which came to power, and after a week the Duke admitted defeat. On the afternoon of May 18 Grey and Brougham called at St James's Palace. The King authorised them to draw up a list of persons who would be made peers and could be counted on to vote for the Whigs. At the same time he sent his private secretary to tell the leading Tories of his decision and suggest that they could avoid such extremities by abstaining. When the Bill was again introduced the Opposition benches were practically empty. It was carried by an overwhelming majority, and became law on June 7, 1832.

*　*　*　*　*

The new electors and the Radicals were not content to stop at extending the franchise, and during the next five years the younger politicians forced through an equally extensive reform of public administration. The Whigs became more and more uncomfortable, and Grey, feeling he had done enough, retired in 1834. The new leaders were Lord Melbourne and Lord John Russell. Russell was a Whig of the old school, sensitive to any invasion of political liberty and rights. He saw the need for further reforms in the sphere of government, but the broadening paths of democracy did not beckon him. Melbourne in his youth had held advanced opinions, but his lack of any guiding aim and motive, his want of conviction, his cautious scepticism, denied him and his party any theme or inspiration. Personal friendships and agreeable conversation mattered more to him than political issues. He accepted the office of Prime Minister with reluctance, genuinely wondering whether the honour was worth while. Once in power his bland qualities helped to keep his divided team together. But his administration wore an eighteenth-century air in the midst of nineteenth-century stress.

One of Melbourne's ablest colleagues was Lord Palmerston, who held the Foreign Office for nearly eleven years. Under the wise guidance of Lord Grey, Palmerston had secured a settlement of the Belgian problem which still endures. The Dutch and French were both persuaded to withdraw, Belgian claims to Dutch territory were abated, and Prince Leopold of Saxe-Coburg was installed at Brussels as an independent sovereign. The neutrality of the country was guaranteed by international treaty. Thus was a pledge given which was to be redeemed with blood in 1914. Under Melbourne Palmerston did much as he pleased in foreign affairs. His leading beliefs were two: that British interests must everywhere be stoutly upheld, if necessary by a show of force, and that Liberal movements in the countries of Europe should be encouraged whenever it was within Britain's power to extend them sympathy or even aid. There was a jaunty forthright self-assurance about everything Palmerston did which often gave offence in the staider chancelleries of Europe and alarmed his more nervous colleagues. But his imperturbable spirit gradually won the admiration of the mass of his fellow countrymen. He was in these years building up the popularity which later made him appear the embodiment of mid-Victorian confidence.

The Whig rank and file were perplexed and uncertain. Champions of political reform, they wavered and boggled at the sterner and more fateful issue of social reorganisation. In the past they had quarrelled with the Tories over constitutional issues—the limits of the royal prerogative, the position of the Established Church, religious toleration—but all this was now dead and settled, and the problems and perils of the Industrial Revolution glowered across obsolete party alignments. With the passing of the Reform Bill the Whig Party had done its work. Its leaders neither liked nor understood the middle classes. They looked on Radicalism as a fashionable creed to be held in undergraduate days and dropped on reaching maturity, and they perceived, uneasily and dimly, that they were being pushed from behind by mass agitation and organisation into strange and perilous paths.

Moreover, their hold on the country was by no means certain. Some quarter of a million voters had been added by the Reform Bill to the electorate, which now numbered nearly 700,000 persons. This meant that about one adult male in six had the vote. However, they by no means gave their undivided support to the Whigs. The strange habit of English electors of voting against Governments which give them the franchise now made itself felt, and it was with great difficulty that the Whig administrations preserved a majority with the help of O'Connell's Irish votes. Their only hope was to unite with the Radicals, who, though few in Parliament, had the backing of the middle class and the Press, and whose strength was not truly reflected in the number of seats they held. But the Whigs hesitated. One of the few who favoured such an alliance was "Radical Jack"—John Lambton, Earl of Durham, Grey's son-in-law. But his hot temper made him a prickly colleague. He soon left the Government, and later became absorbed in the problems of colonial government, greatly to the advantage of Canada and the whole Imperial connection. His early death removed all hope of domestic fusion between Radicals and Whigs.

Nevertheless the legislation and the commissions of these years were by no means unfruitful. The slaves in the West Indies were finally emancipated in 1833. For the first time in English history the Government made educational grants to religious societies. The Poor Law was reformed on lines that were considered highly advanced in administrative and intellectual circles, though they did not prove popular among those they were supposed to benefit. The first effective Factory Act was passed, though the long hours of work it permitted would horrify the twentieth century and did not satisfy the humanitarians of the time. The whole system of local government was reconstructed and the old local oligarchies abolished. Politics meanwhile centred on the position of the Established Church and the maintenance of order in Ireland, and it was their failure to deal with these issues and to balance their Budgets that in due course ruined the Whigs. Moreover, great forces were at work outside the House of Commons. A large mass of the country still remained unenfranchised. The relations of capital and labour had scarcely been touched by the hand of Parliament, and the activities of the early trade unions frightened the Government into oppressive measures. The most celebrated case was that of the Tolpuddle "Martyrs" of 1834, when six labourers from that Dorsetshire village of curious name were sentenced to transportation for the technical offence of "administering unlawful oaths" to members of their union. Public agitation eventually secured their pardon, but not until they had served two years in New South Wales. While unrest for many reasons spread, the position of the monarchy itself showed signs of weakness. The Whigs were not the men to bridge the gulf which seemed to yawn between official political circles and the nation.

Sir Robert Peel, on the other hand, was not slow to adjust the Tories to the new times and a speedy reorganisation of their machinery was set on foot. "I presume," he declared in 1833, "the chief object of that party which is called Conservative will be to resist Radicalism, to prevent those further encroachments of democratic influence which will be attempted as the natural consequence of the triumph already achieved." He made it clear that the Tories would support administrative changes which increased efficiency, but oppose any weakening of the traditional institutions of the State. A disciplined, purposeful, but not factious Opposition gradually took shape under his leadership. In the following year the party was heartened by a rousing election address which Peel had issued to his constituency. They took their stand upon an enlightened conservation of the best elements in the existing institutions in the country, and Peel showed considerable cleverness in revealing his desire to modify the whole position of the Established Church. The Nonconformist voters did not forget this in the coming years, for religion still counted in politics. As the great Acts of reform succeeded each other so further interests were antagonised and the Conservative sentiment in the country gradually rallied to Peel. In the elections of 1834 the Tories won a hundred seats, and for some months he presided over a minority Government. Then the Whigs returned, as divided among themselves as ever. They seemed to be playing with fire. They were arousing hopes that no Government could fulfil. The dangers of spasmodic and uncoordinated reform were borne in upon the middle classes by their fumbling leadership. The Whig coach was clattering down a twisting, unknown road, and many supporters alighted in the course of the journey.

* * * * *

In 1837 King William IV died. Humorous, tactless, pleasant, and unrespected, he had played his part in lowering esteem for the monarchy, and indeed the vices and eccentricities of the sons of George III had by this time almost destroyed its hold upon the hearts of the people. An assault on the institution which had played so great a part in the history of England appeared imminent, and there seemed few to defend it. The new sovereign was a maiden of eighteen. She had been brought up by a dutiful mother, who was shocked at the language and habits of the royal uncles, and had secluded her in Kensington Palace from both the Court and the nation. Her education was supervised by a German governess, with occasional examinations by Church dignitaries, and a correspondence course on her future duties with her maternal uncle, King Leopold of Belgium. The country knew nothing of either her character or her virtues. "Few people," wrote Palmerston, "have had opportunities of forming a correct judgment of the Princess; but I incline to think that she will turn out to be a remarkable person, and gifted with a great deal of strength of character." He was right. On the eve of her accession the new Queen wrote in her diary: "Since it has pleased Providence to place me in this station, I shall do my utmost to fulfil my duty towards my country; I am very young, and perhaps in many, though not in all things, inexperienced, but I am sure that very few have more real good will and more real desire to do what is fit and right than I have." It was a promise she was spaciously to fulfil.

By the time Queen Victoria came to the throne the Whigs

had shot their bolt. The Court and the governing circles were isolated and unpopular; the middle classes were fearful of unrest and beginning to vote for the Tories. Meanwhile Lord Melbourne, who had little faith in law-making, with grace and pleasantness was doing nothing. On top of all this there appeared towards the end of the year the first signs of a great economic depression. Conditions in the industrial North soon became as bad as after Waterloo, and in May 1838 a group of working-class leaders published a "People's Charter." Chartism, as it was called, in which some historians discern the beginnings of socialism, was the last despairing cry of poverty against the Machine Age. The Chartists, believing, like the agitators for Reform before 1832, that an extension of the franchise would cure all their miseries, demanded annual Parliaments, universal male suffrage, equal electoral districts, the removal of the property qualification for Membership of Parliament, the secret ballot, and the payment of Members. Their only hope of success was to secure, as the Radicals had done, the backing of a Parliamentary party and of the progressive middle classes. But they deliberately refused to bid for middle-class support. Their leaders quarrelled among themselves and affronted respectable people by threatening and irresponsible speeches. They had no funds, and no organisation such as the Catholic Association had found in the parishes of the Irish clergy, or the Labour Party was to find later in the trade unions. For a time England was flooded with petitions and pamphlets, but the ferment varied in warmth from one part of the country to another. Whenever conditions improved the popular temper cooled, and no united national movement emerged as a permanent force. The few unions which then existed soon deserted the cause and the more prosperous artisans were lukewarm. Agitation revived from time to time in the years that followed, culminating in the revolutionary year of 1848. But in the end the whole muddled, well-intentioned business came to nothing.

Peel drew the right conclusions. He discerned, much more clearly than the Whigs, the causes of the unrest, and, though steadfast against Radicalism, he believed that the remedy lay in efficient administration and an enlightened commercial policy. The younger Tories supported him, and like him were oppressed by the division of the country into "two nations," the rich and the poor, as portrayed in the novels of a young Jewish Member of Parliament called Benjamin Disraeli. A small group of Conservatives were already seeking an alliance with the working men against the middle classes.

In 1839 Melbourne offered to resign, but for another two years Victoria kept him in office. His charm had captured her affections. He imparted to her much of his wisdom on men and affairs, without burdening her with his scepticism, and she refused to be separated from her beloved Prime Minister. In February of the following year a new figure entered upon the British scene. The Queen married her cousin, Prince Albert of Saxe-Coburg. The Prince was an upright, conscientious man with far-ranging interests and high ideals. He and the Queen enjoyed for twenty-one years, until his early death, a happy family life, which held up an example much in accord with the desires of her subjects. After the excesses of George IV and his brothers the dignity and repute of the monarchy stood in need of restoration, and this was Victoria and Albert's achievement. At first the Prince found his presence in England resented by the political magnates of the time. They would not let him take a seat in the House of Lords, they cut down his annual allowance, and he was not granted even the title of Prince Consort until 1857. Nevertheless the patronage which he earnestly extended to science, industry, and the arts, and to good causes of many kinds, gradually won him a wide measure of public respect. As permanent adviser to the Queen, on all issues laid before her, he played a scrupulous, disinterested part. Wise counsels from his uncle, King Leopold, and his former tutor, Baron Stockmar, taught him the rôle and duties of a constitutional sovereign. Eventually the party leaders in England learnt to value his advice, especially on foreign affairs, though they did not always pay heed to it. The Queen was a woman of strong mind, who had begun her reign as a vehement partisan of the Whigs. Under Albert's influence she came to perceive that in public at least she must be impartial and place her trust in whichever Minister could command a majority in the House of Commons. This did not prevent her from entertaining vivid likes and dislikes for her chief servants, to which she gave vigorous expression in private letters. Together the Queen and the Prince set a new standard for the conduct of monarchy which has ever since been honourably observed.

Peel, unlike Melbourne, had given the Queen an impression of awkwardness and coldness of manner; but at last in 1841 a General Election brought him to power. Before long he had won her confidence. His abilities now came into full play. He had absolute control of his Cabinet, himself introduced his Government's more important Budgets, and supervised the work of all departments, including that of William Gladstone at the Board of Trade. Tariffs were once again reformed, customs duties greatly reduced, and income tax was reimposed. These measures soon bore fruit. In 1843 trade began to revive, prosperity returned, and the demand for political reform was stilled. Once again the sky seemed clear at Westminster. But a storm was gathering in Ireland.

*   *   *   *   *

The immediate issue was the price of bread. To promote foreign commerce Peel had reduced import duties on everything except corn. Dear bread however meant either high wages or misery for the masses, and Peel gradually realised that cheap imported food could alone sustain the continued prosperity of the nation. Free Trade in corn seemed imperative, but the political obstacles were formidable. The Tory Party leaned heavily on the votes of the landowners, who had invested much capital in their properties during the Napoleonic wars. Peace had brought cheaper corn from abroad, and the cry for protection had led in 1815 to a prohibition of the import of foreign grain except when the price in the home market was abnormally high. The repeal or modification of this and later Corn Laws now overclouded all other issues. The landowners were accused of using their power in Parliament to safeguard their interests at the expense of the rest of the community. The enmity of the manufacturers and industrialists sharpened the conflict, for the Corn Laws not only caused great distress to the working classes, but angered many employers. Protection in their view prevented them from building up new markets overseas and from competing on fair terms in old ones.

Hostility to the Corn Laws had grown during the depression of 1838–42. An Anti-Corn Law League was formed at Manchester to press for their abolition. It soon exerted a powerful influence on public opinion, and produced two remarkable leaders and organisers who became the Free Trade prophets of nineteenth-century England, Richard Cobden, a calico printer, and John Bright, a Quaker mill-owner. The movement was strongly supported. There were large subscriptions to its funds. The new penny postage, introduced by Sir Rowland Hill in 1840, carried circulars and pamphlets cheaply all over the country. Meetings were held throughout the land. The propaganda was effective and novel: a few simple ideas hammered into the minds of audiences by picked lecturers and speakers. Never had there been such a shrewdly conducted agitation. Monster petitions were sent to Parliament. Cobden persuaded prosperous townspeople to buy forty-shilling free-holds in the county constituencies and thus secure a double vote. This so increased the number of Anti-Corn Law electors that instead of only petitioning Parliament from outside, the League started influencing it from within.

Cobden and Bright's thundering speeches against the landed classes reverberated through the nation. "Let them go on, and in a short time they will find themselves like the French nobility previous to the Revolution an isolated, help-less, powerless class—a class that, in their own inherent qualities, in their intellectual and moral powers, are inferior to any other classes of society. They not only cling to feudal abuses, but they actually try to put a restraint upon the supply of food for the people. They are warring against the progres-sion of the age. They fancy that their feudal system is neces-sary to the existence of the community. Why, their feudal system has gone in France; it has gone in Germany; in Amer-ica it has never existed."

Peel, like Cobden and Bright, came from the middle class, and such arguments bit deeply into his mind. England's trade and prosperity demanded the abolition of the Corn Laws, but at least half his supporters were landowners, and such a step would wreck the Conservative Party. By 1843 however Peel was determined to act. His position was very difficult, for some of his followers felt he had betrayed them once already over Catholic Emancipation. But he was sure of himself. Perhaps he believed that his personal ascendancy would carry the majority with him; but he needed time to convince his party, and time was denied him.

In August 1845 the potato crop failed in Ireland. Famine was imminent and Peel could wait no longer, but when he put his proposals to the Cabinet several of his colleagues revolted and in December he had to resign. The Whig leader Russell refused to form an administration, and Peel returned to office to face and conquer the onslaught of the Tory Protectionists. Their spokesman, the hitherto little-known Benjamin Disraeli, denounced him not so much for seeking to abolish the Corn Laws as for betraying his position as head of a great party. If Peel, he declared, believed in the measure he should resign, as a large section of his party was traditionally pledged to oppose it. The wilful destruction of a great party by its leader was a political crime, for the true working of English politics depended on the balance of parties and if a leader could not convince his colleagues he should withdraw. Thus Disraeli. But Peel maintained that his duty to the nation was higher than his duty to his party, and he believed it was his mission to carry the abolition of the Corn Laws. His private letters reveal his bitterness against the Protectionist wing of the Tories. "Protectionists indeed!—to close their eyes to the result of every commercial experiment that has been made, to find every one of their predictions falsified, to disregard the state of public opinion, to call the Corn Laws a labourer's question, and yet listen to the appalling facts as to the condition of the labourers in Dorsetshire for years past; . . . to be willing to encounter the tremendous risks of two bad harvests and the recurrence of such a state of things in Paisley and Stockport as was witnessed in the winters of 1841–42; nor to see that the Corn Laws would . . . be swept away with dishonour on the demand of a starving population—this is to be a Protectionist! Thank God I am relieved for ever from the trammels of such a party."

On June 25, 1846, with the help of Whig and Irish votes, the Corn Laws were repealed. Disraeli immediately had his revenge. Turmoil in Ireland destroyed Peel's Government, and by a vote on the same night the great Ministry, one of the strongest of the century, came to an end. Peel had been the dominating force and personality in English politics since the passing of the great Reform Bill. Whether in Opposition or in office, he had towered above the scene. He was not a man of broad and ranging modes of thought, but he understood better than any of his contemporaries the needs of the country, and he had the outstanding courage to change his views in order to meet them. It is true that he split his party, but there are greater crimes than that. The age over which he presided was one of formidable industrial advance. It was the Railway Age. By 1848 some five thousand miles of railroads had been built in the United Kingdom. Speed of transport and increasing output were the words of the day. Coal and iron production had doubled. Engineering was making great, though as yet hesitating, strides. All the steps were being taken, not by Government, but by enterprisers throughout the country, which were to make Britain the greatest industrial Power of the nineteenth-century world. Peel had a practical sense of these vast developments. Free trade, he knew, was no cure-all for the pangs and anguish of a changing society. But the days of the land-owning predominance were doomed. Free trade seemed essential to manufacture, and in manufacture Britain was entering upon her supremacy. All this Peel grasped. His Government set an example of initiative which both the Conservative and Liberal Parties honoured by imitation in the future. Of his own methods of government he once said, "The fact is, people like a certain degree of obstinacy and presumption in a Minister. They abuse him for dictation and arrogance, but they like being governed." High words perhaps, but they fitted the time.

Early in 1850, after he had watched with restraint and composure the totterings of his Whig successors, Peel fell from his horse while riding in the Green Park and was fatally injured. So died one of the great shapers of British politics in the Victorian Age.

The Crimean War

TOWARDS the middle of the nineteenth century political life in England was still following its long-accustomed habits, which had so far been only slightly changed by the acceptance of the great Reform Bill. The Whigs were in power under Lord John Russell, whose family had served the State since the days of Henry VII. After three and a half centuries of generally smiling fortune the Russells and their friends and connections had acquired an assurance that they knew best how to govern the country in its true interests. Whatever novel agitations might spread among working men in the industrial towns, who as yet enjoyed few votes, the Whig leaders pursued their reasonable, moderate, and un-democratic courses. Lord John's Government, with a few upsets, survived for six years. It achieved little of lasting note, but it piloted Britain through a restless period when elsewhere in Europe thrones were overturned and revolutions multiplied.

The Tories for their part were irreconcilably split. The faithful followers of Peel and Free Trade, who included in Aberdeen and Gladstone two future Prime Ministers, were content to let the Whigs bear the heat of the day. The Liberal Party, which would presently arise from the coalition of Whigs, Peelites, and Radicals, was not yet foreseen. The opponents of the Peelites, the old Tories, were led by Lord Stanley, soon to be Lord Derby, whose forbears had played a rôle in the kingdom for even longer than the Russells. Derby was in-creasingly assisted in the House of Commons by his lieutenant Disraeli, whose reputation for brilliance was growing rather faster than his capacity for inspiring trust. It was Disraeli's gradual task over these years to persuade the Tories to abandon their fidelity to the Corn Law tariff and to work out a new and more broadly based Conservative policy.

While party affairs at Westminster dwelt gently in flux, Europe succumbed to an anguished spasm. In February 1848 the French monarchy fell. The rule of King Louis Philippe had given prosperity to France, or at least to her middle classes, but it had never been accepted by the adherents of the elder Bourbon line, and it appealed neither to staunch Republicans nor to the Bonapartists, who were still dazzled by the remembered glories of the Empire. A few days of rioting sufficed to eject Louis Philippe, and a Government of romantic outlook and Socialist complexion briefly took control. This in turn collapsed, and by the end of the year a Bonaparte had been elected President of France by an overwhelming majority. Thus, after half a lifetime spent in plotting, exile, and obscurity, Prince Louis Napoleon, nephew of the great Emperor, came to power. He owed his position to the name he bore, to the ineptitude of his rivals, and to the fondness of the French for constitutional experiment. For more than twenty years this amiable, dreamy figure was to play a striking and not always ineffective part upon the European scene.

The peoples of Italy had also broken into revolt against both their own rulers and the Austrian occupiers of Lombardy and Venetia. High hopes were cherished that a united Italian nation might emerge from this commotion. Pope Pius IX, who was also the temporal ruler of Central Italy, was a liberal man of patriotic feeling. To him many of his fellow Italians looked up for guidance and inspiration. But his holy office forbade him to direct a purely national crusade against the Catholic Power of Austria. Popes before had fought for local issues. Pius IX was a wiser man. His duty was not to unify a nation, but to head a universal Church. Political leadership for Italy had to come from elsewhere. In the Italian provinces enthusiastic conspirators soon found that they could not hold their own against the organised forces of Austria and her allies, nor could the army of the kingdom of Sardinia, which was the only wholly independent Italian state, make much impression on Austrian might. The Italian revolt ended in failure, but not without arousing a widespread sympathy in Britain, which was benevolently exercised when the next attempt at unity was made.

North of the Alps revolutionary nationalism was also stirring in Germany, Austria, and Poland. The Austrian Chancellor, Metternich, who had dominated Central Europe for forty years, was forced to resign by a revolution in Vienna. This aged pillar of Continental absolutism found refuge in an obscure hotel in the England of the Whigs. The Emperor was obliged to abdicate, leaving the Habsburg throne to a young Archduke, Francis Joseph, destined to live through many tribulations and witness the opening years of the First World War. Czechs, Poles, and Hungarians in turn all took up arms, and their gallant risings were eventually suppressed only with the cordial help of the Czar of Russia. In Germany itself the minor monarchs were thrown into disarray, and some into exile, by rebellions and demonstrations. A Parliament met at Frankfurt, and after lengthy debate offered the crown of a united Germany to the King of Prussia. This sovereign and his military advisers preferred repressing revolutionaries to accepting favours from them, and the offer was declined. Little came of the events of 1848–49 in Germany, except a powerful impetus to the idea of German unity, and a growing conviction that it could only be achieved with the backing of Prussian arms.

The turmoil in Europe was viewed in England with sympathetic interest, but it went unmatched by any comparable disturbance. The Chartist movement, for some time languishing, took fresh courage from the Republican example in France. It was also stirred by a new economic crisis at home. There was half-hearted talk of revolution, but in the end it was decided to present a new petition to Parliament, reiterating all the old Chartist demands. A meeting was called in April 1848 on Kennington Common, a mile to the south of Westminster Bridge. From there the Chartist leaders proposed to lead an impressive march upon the Houses of Parliament. The Government took precautions. Troops were called out and special constables enrolled; but in the event no undue strain was placed upon their services. As Wellington remarked —still an imperturbable Commander-in-Chief at the age of seventy-eight—the English are "a very quiet people." This is especially so when it is raining. More spectators than Chartists assembled on that wet spring day at Kennington. When the police forbade the proposed march the demonstrators quietly dispersed. Their petition was conveyed to the Commons in three cabs. Such was the measure of revolutionary feeling in London in 1848.

*   *   *   *   *

In the same year Thomas Babington Macaulay, who had been a Minister of the Crown and served the Government of India in high office, published the first volumes of his *History of England*. This great work, with all its prejudiced opinions and errors of fact, provided the historical background for the sense of progress which was now inspiring Victorian Britain. Macaulay set out to show that the story of England since the Whig Revolution of 1688 was one of perpetual and limitless advance. In his opening chapter he wrote: "The history of our own country in the last hundred and sixty years is eminently the history of physical, moral, and intellectual improvement." This was a heartening note, much appreciated by contemporary readers. Optimism reigned throughout the land. An even more shining future, Macaulay implied, lay before the United Kingdom. So indeed it did. His views were widely shared, and were soon given form in the Great Exhibition of British achievement which justly gratified the nation.

Prince Albert sponsored the idea. There had already been small exhibitions of manufactures, in which he had taken an interest. In 1849, after opening the new Albert Dock in Liverpool, the Prince had been so much impressed by the surging vigour of British industry, and its maritime cause and consequence, that he adopted with enthusiasm a plan for an exhibition on a far larger scale than had ever been seen before. It would display to the country and the world the progress achieved in every field. It would also be international, proclaiming the benefits of free trade between nations and looking forward to the universal peace which it was then supposed must inevitably result from the unhampered traffic in goods. Few people foresaw the war with Russia that was soon to break out.

For two years, against considerable opposition, the Prince headed a committee to further his project. In 1851 the Great Exhibition was opened in Hyde Park. Nineteen acres were devoted to the principal building, the Crystal Palace, designed by an expert glasshouse gardener, Joseph Paxton. Housing most of the exhibits, and enclosing whole trees within its glass and iron structure, it was to be the marvel of the decade. In spite of prophecies of failure, the Exhibition was a triumphant success. Over a million people a month visited it during the six months of its opening. Nearly fourteen thousand exhibits of industrial skill and craft were shown, of which half were British. The Prince was vindicated, and the large profit made by the organisers was invested and put to learned and educational purposes. Queen Victoria described the opening day as "one of the greatest and most glorious in our lives." Her feelings were prompted by her delight that Prince Albert should have confounded his critics, ever ready to accuse him of meddling in national affairs, but there was more to it than that. The Queen paid many visits to the Crystal Palace, where her presence aroused in the scores of thousands of subjects with whom she mingled a deep loyalty and a sense of national pride. Never had the Throne been so firmly grounded in the affections of the people. Prosperity, however unevenly its blessings fell, gave Britain a self-assurance that seemed worth more than social legislation and further reform. From mills and mines and factories flowed the wealth that was making life easier for the country. And this the country recognised.

The mid-century marks the summit of Britain's preponderance in industry. In another twenty years other nations, among whom industrial progress had started later, had begun to cut down her lead. Until 1870 Britain had mined more than half the world's coal, and in that year her output of pig-iron was still greater than the rest of the world's put together. Foreign trade stood at a figure of nearly 700 millions sterling, as compared with 300 for the United States, 340 for France, and 300 for Germany. But the proportions were rapidly changing. Railways greatly assisted the growth of industry in Germany and America, where coal and iron resources were separated from each other by considerable distances. A challenge was also presented to British agriculture, now that prairie-grown American wheat could be carried to American ports by railroad and shipped across the ocean to European markets. Nevertheless there was no slowing down of industry in Britain. Textiles, the backbone of British exports, filled an insatiable demand in Asia, and the future of the mighty steel and engineering industries seemed assured for a long time to come. In England the rapidly expanding Midlands and North were blackened by the smoke and dust of the pits and forges.

Critics were not wanting of the age of mass production that was now taking shape. Charles Dickens in his novels revealed the plight of the poor, holding up to pity the conditions in which many of them dwelt and ridiculing the State institutions that crudely encompassed them. John Ruskin was another. In the midst of his long life he turned from the study of painting and architecture to modern social problems. His heart lay in the Middle Ages, which he imagined to be peopled by a fraternity of craftsmen harmoniously creating works of art. Peering out upon the Victorian scene, this prophetic figure looked in vain for similar accomplishment. Bad taste in manufacture, bad relations between employers and men, aroused his eloquent wrath. His was a voice that cried the way both to new movements in the arts and to socialism in politics.

*   *   *   *   *

Foreign affairs and the threat of war now began to darken the scene. Turkey had troubled the statesmen of Europe for many years. Preoccupation with the conflicts and intrigues of Court and harem had so distracted the Sultans at Constantinople and their chief advisers from the duties of government, and event of defence, that the military empire, which for three centuries had dominated the Eastern world from the Persian Gulf to Budapest, and from the Caspian to Algiers, seemed now on the edge of disruption and collapse. What then would become of its vast territories? To whom would fall the wide, fertile Turkish provinces in Europe and Asia? The urgency and imminence of such questions were sharpened by the evident determination of Russia to seize the Danubian lands, Constantinople, and the Black Sea. England could not ignore the threat: the shadow of Russia, already a formidable

Asiatic Power, appeared to be creeping over India. The anxiety and apprehension of the governing circles of England marched with a widespread and hearty dislike of the whole political system of which Nicholas I—the "icy Muscovite" and "o'ergrown Barbarian of the East," in Tennyson's phrases —was the principal prop and pillar in Europe. The contemporaries of Palmerston looked upon the police state of the Czar as "the corner-stone of despotism in the world," the oppressor of the Poles, the ally of reactionary Austria, a fatal obstacle to the liberation of nations and the realisation of the great hopes which had sprung from the Liberal revolutions of 1848.

The need to resist Russia was plain to most British observers, though Radicals like Cobden strongly opposed this view. British diplomacy was confused about the best way of achieving its aims. For it was also necessary to keep an eye on the French, who had ambitions for extending their influence in the Levant. Canning had planned to head Russia off from South-East Europe, not by direct opposition, but by founding on the ruins of the Turkish Empire a *bloc* of small independent states who would stand firm and if necessary fight for the sake of their own survival. With such a programme of emancipation he had hoped to associate not only France, but Russia herself. The creation of the kingdom of Greece was the first and only result of his efforts. But twenty years had gone by and the ruling politicians of England had forgotten the example of Byron, who had died for Greek freedom. They reversed the policy of Canning, and now attempted to check Russian expansion by the opposite method of propping up the decaying system of Turkish rule in South-East Europe. In the execution of this plan the Government was much assisted by Stratford Canning, later Lord Stratford de Redcliffe, the British Ambassador at Constantinople in the

1840's. He was a cousin of George Canning, with a wider knowledge of Turkey, which he had first visited in 1808, than any other Englishman of his day. Proud, difficult, quick-tempered, he enjoyed immense authority with the Turks. He had no illusions about the character of the Ottoman Empire, which he described as "hastening to its dissolution," but he hoped to induce the Sultan to make such reforms as would "retard the evil hour" when it would finally collapse; and so postpone a general war for possession of its territories. For years Stratford struggled with the laziness, corruption, and inefficiency of the Turkish administration. Whether he was wise to do so is another matter, since any tightening up of central authority would have increased tension between Constantinople and the provinces. It was the very laxity of the régime that made it bearable by the subject peoples. Stratford however was unconvinced of this, and when he left Constantinople in 1852 he had little hope that the "evil hour" could be delayed much longer.

The immediate source and origin of the conflict which now came to a head between Turkey and Russia lay in Jerusalem, where the Greek Orthodox and Roman Catholic Churches disputed the custody of certain shrines. The quarrel would have been unimportant had not the Czar supported the Greek pretensions, and Louis Napoleon, now the Emperor Napoleon III, been anxious to please French Catholics by championing the Latins. After long negotiation the Czar sent his envoy Menschikoff to Constantinople to revive his claims for a general protectorate over the Christians in the Turkish Empire. This, if granted, would have given Russia authority over the many millions of Rumanians, Serbs, Bulgarians, Greeks, and Armenians within the Ottoman domains. The balance of power, for which British Governments always sought in the Near East, as elsewhere, would have been destroyed.

Menschikoff was tactless and his demands angered the Turks. The electric telegraph, recently invented, only reached to Belgrade. Upon Stratford, once more British Ambassador, much depended. He was the man on the spot, with considerable freedom from Cabinet control and with strong views on the Russian danger and the need to support Turkey. At home Lord Derby, after a brief spell in office, had been succeeded by Lord Aberdeen, who presided over a coalition Government of Whigs and Peelites, far from united in their opinions. The Prime Minister himself and his Foreign Secretary, Lord Clarendon, were hesitant and favoured appeasement. But Stratford could count on Palmerston, the most popular man in the Cabinet, and on the general hostility in England towards the Russians. Stratford's dispatches do not support the charge that he exceeded his instructions: he recommended the Turks to continue negotiations and not to take too stiff an attitude. But the Turks knew their man, they knew they had his sympathy, and they knew that in the last resort the British Fleet would protect Constantinople and stop Russia seizing the Straits. They accordingly rejected the Russian demands, and on June 2, 1853, the Russian attitude had become so menacing that the Cabinet ordered the British Fleet to Besika Bay, outside the Dardanelles. Napoleon III, eager for British approval and support, agreed to provide a French squadron.

The Fleet reached Besika Bay on June 13. In early July Russian troops crossed the river Pruth and entered Turkish Moldavia. The British Cabinet was still divided, and neither warned the Russians nor promised help to the Turks. The Turks ended the matter by rejecting an offer of mediation by a council of ambassadors. Stratford disapproved of this proposal, known as the Vienna Note, but there is no evidence that he failed to carry out his instructions to advise the Turks to yield.

This they could not do since feeling ran so high at Constantinople that the Sultan had little choice but to refuse.

War was not yet certain. The Czar, alarmed at Turkey's resistance, sought a compromise with the help of Austria, but by September Aberdeen and his Cabinet had become so suspicious that they rejected the offer. On October 4 the Sultan declared war on Russia, and soon afterwards attacked the Russians beyond the Danube. Such efforts as Aberdeen and Stratford could still make for peace were extinguished by a Russian onslaught against the Turkish Fleet off Sinope, in the Black Sea. Indignation flared in England, where the action was denounced as a massacre. Palmerston sent in his resignation in December on a domestic issue, but his action was interpreted as a protest against the Government's Eastern policy and Aberdeen was accused of cowardice. Thus England drifted into war. In February 1854 Nicholas recalled his ambassadors from London and Paris, and at the end of March the Crimean War began, with France and Britain as the allies of Turkey. To the last Aberdeen vacillated. "I still say that war is not inevitable," he futilely wrote to Clarendon in February, "unless, indeed, we are determined to have it; which, for all I know, may be the case."

The operations were ill-planned and ill-conducted on both sides. With the exception of two minor naval expeditions to the Baltic and the White Sea, fighting was confined to Southern Russia, where the great naval fort of Sebastopol, in the Black Sea, was selected as the main Allied objective. The necessity for this enterprise was questionable: the Turks had already driven the Russians out of the Danube valley, there was little danger of an attack upon Constantinople, and it was folly to suppose that the capture of Sebastopol would make much impression on the vast resources of Russia. However, the British expeditionary force was encamped in Turkish territory and some use had to be made of it. Orders from London dispatched it to the Crimea against the wishes of its commander, Lord Raglan. The Allied fleet sailed close by Sebastopol harbour and ceremonial salutes were exchanged between the belligerents. A landing was made at the small town of Eupatoria, to the north-west. The Russian Governor declared that the armies might land, but according to regulations ought immediately to be placed in quarantine. Nobody took any notice of this precaution.

Sebastopol might have been entered by an immediate attack from the north, yet after an initial victory on the Alma in September 1854 the French commander, St Arnaud, who was a sick man and a political appointment, insisted on marching round to the south and beginning a formal siege. With this step Raglan reluctantly concurred; it was against his better judgment. The Russians were thus permitted to bring up reinforcements, and strengthen the fortifications under the direction of the famous engineer Todleben. Unable to complete their investment of the town, the Allies had to beat off fresh Russian field armies which arrived from the interior. The British Army, holding the exposed eastern wing of the lines, had twice to bear the brunt. At Balaclava in October the British cavalry distinguished themselves by two astonishing charges against overwhelming odds. The second of these was the celebrated charge of the Light Brigade, in which 673 horsemen, led by Lord Cardigan, rode up the valley under heavy fire, imperturbably, as if taking part in a review, to attack the Russian batteries. They captured the guns, but only a third of the brigade answered the first muster after the charge. Lord Cardigan calmly returned to the yacht on which he lived, had a bath, dined, drank a bottle of champagne, and went to bed. His brigade had performed an inspiring feat of gallantry. But it was due, like much else in this war,

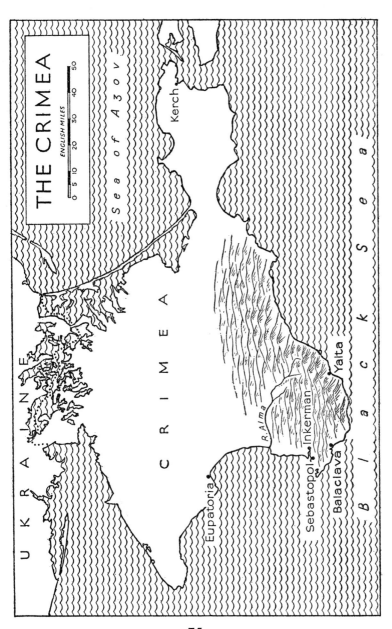

THE CRIMEA

ENGLISH MILES

0 5 10 20 30 40 50

Sea of Azov

Kerch

UKRAINE

CRIMEA

R. Alma

Eupatoria

Sebastopol

Inkerman

Balaclava

Yalta

Black Sea

· 75 ·

to the blunders of commanders. Lord Raglan's orders had been badly expressed and were misunderstood by his subordinates. The Light Brigade had charged the wrong guns.

The Battle of Inkerman followed, fought in the mists of a November dawn. It was a desperate infantry action, in which the British soldier proved his courage and endurance. Russian casualties were nearly five times as many as those of the Allies. But Inkerman was not decisive. The Russians out-numbered the Allies by two to one, and it became plain that there was no hope of taking Sebastopol before the spring of 1855. Amid storms and blizzards the British Army lay, without tents, huts, food, warm clothes, or the most elementary medical care. Cholera, dysentery, and malarial fever took their dreadful toll. Raglan's men had neither transport nor ambulances, and thousands were lost through cold and starvation because it did not occur to the Government of the greatest engineering country in the world to ease the movement of supplies from the port of Balaclava to the camp by laying down five miles of light railway. Nearly half a century of peace had dimmed the glory of the army which defeated Napoleon. Its great chief, Wellington, had died amid national mourning in 1852. During his long reign as Commander-in-Chief at the War Office nothing had changed since Waterloo. Nor could his successors in office see any need for reforming the Army which the Duke had led. The conditions of service were intolerable; the administration was bad, the equipment scanty, the commanders of no outstanding ability. The French and British between them had only 56,000 troops in the Crimea in the terrible winter of 1854–55. Nearly 14,000 of them went to hospital, and many died for want of medical supplies. Most of these casualties were British. The French were much better provided for, while the Russians, who accepted official mismanagement as a matter of course, perished in uncounted numbers of the long route marches through the snow southwards to the Crimea. Fighting the war for the sake of Sebastopol imposed a heavy burden upon the Government of the Czar. He might have been wiser to have withdrawn his troops into the interior of Russia, as his brother had done in the days of Napoleon's invasion. But neither side in the Crimean War was inspired by large strategic views.

*　　*　　*　　*　　*

Even the War Office was a little shaken by the incompetence and suffering. *The Times,* under its great editor J. T. Delane, sent out the first of all war correspondents, William Russell, and used his reports to start a national agitation against the Government. Aberdeen was assailed from every quarter, and when Parliament reassembled in January a motion was introduced by a Private Member to appoint a commission of inquiry into the state of the army before Sebastopol. It was carried by a majority so large that when the figures were announced they were greeted, not with the usual cheers, but with surprised silence, followed by derisive laughter. The Government had been condemned, as a contemporary wrote, "to the most ignominious end of any Cabinet in modern days." Aberdeen resigned, and was succeeded by Palmerston, who accepted the commission of inquiry. Palmerston did not at first command wide confidence, and it was at this moment that Disraeli wrote privately of him, "he is an impostor, utterly exhausted, and at the best only ginger-beer and not champagne, and now an old painted pantaloon." Disraeli was wrong. Palmerston soon proved himself the man of the hour. The worst mistakes and muddles were cleared up, and at the War Office Sidney Herbert struggled manfully to reform the military administration.

By the summer of 1855 the Allied armies had been reinforced and were in good heart. An assault on Sebastopol was mounted in June, but it failed. This was too much for Raglan. Worn out by the responsibilities of the campaign, he resigned, and ten days later he died. Raglan had been ill-served by his Government and by his quarrelsome subordinates, and he too readily let his good judgment be overridden. This disciple of Wellington, who had lost an arm at Waterloo, deserves a higher niche in military history than is sometimes accorded him. He was brave, loyal, and had the misfortune frequently to be right when others took the wrong decision.

The victory that should have been his due was won by his successor, Sir James Simpson, in conjunction with the French Marshal Pélissier. In September Sebastopol at last fell. The futility of the plan of campaign was now revealed. It was impossible to invade Russia from the Crimea. What should the next move be? France by now had four times as many troops in the field as England, and Napoleon III was threatening to withdraw them. A peace party in Paris was making its views felt. The French Emperor was inclined to negotiate, meanwhile reducing operations against Russia to a mere blockade. If the war were to continue, he felt, other Powers would have to be drawn in, and an appeal made to the national sentiments of Poles, Swedes, and other hereditary enemies of the Czar. This was too grandiose even for Palmerston. He privately denounced the French peace party as "a cabal of stock-jobbing politicians," but he realised the war must stop. Threatened by an Austrian ultimatum, Russia agreed to terms, and in February 1856 a peace conference opened in Paris.

The Treaty of Paris, signed at the end of March, removed the immediate causes of the conflict, but provided no permanent settlement of the Eastern Question. Russia surrendered her grip on the mouths of the Danube by abandoning Southern Bessarabia; her claims to a protectorate over the Turkish Christians were set aside; the Dardanelles were closed to foreign ships of war during peace, as they had been before the war; and Turkey's independence was guaranteed by the Powers, in return for a promise of reforms not worth the paper on which it was written. Russia accepted the demilitarisation of the Black Sea, but repudiated her undertaking when Europe was absorbed by the Franco-Prussian War of 1870. For the time being her expansion was checked, but she remained unappeased. Within twenty years Europe was nearly at war again over Russian ambitions in the Near East. The fundamental situation was unaltered: so long as Turkey was weak so long would her empire remain a temptation to Russian Imperialists and an embarrassment to Western Europe.

With one exception few of the leading figures emerged from the Crimean War with enhanced reputations. Miss Florence Nightingale had been sent out in an official capacity by the War Minister, Sidney Herbert. She arrived at Scutari on the day before the Battle of Inkerman, and there organised the first base hospital of modern times. With few nurses and scanty equipment she reduced the death-rate at Scutari from 42 per hundred to 22 per thousand men. Her influence and example were far-reaching. The Red Cross movement, which started with the Geneva Convention of 1864, was the outcome of her work, as were great administrative reforms in civilian hospitals. In an age of proud and domineering men she gave the women of the nineteenth century a new status, which revolutionised the social life of the country, and even made them want to vote. Miss Nightingale herself felt that "there are evils which press much more hardly on women than the want of the suffrage." Lack of education was one, and she favoured better girls' schools and the founding of women's colleges. To these objects she devoted her attention, and by her efforts half the Queen's subjects were encouraged to enter the realms of higher thought.

Palmerston

PALMERSTON, though now in his seventies, presided over the English scene. With one short interval of Tory government, he was Prime Minister throughout the decade that began in 1855. Not long after the signing of peace with Russia he was confronted with another emergency which also arose in the East, but this time in Asia. India had been basking under the administration of the East India Company, with only a moderate degree of supervision from London. The Company had its critics in Parliament and elsewhere, but their words had little effect upon its practices. Suddenly there occurred a disturbing outbreak against British rule.

The Indian Mutiny made, in some respects, a more lasting impact on England than the Crimean War. It paved the way for Empire. After it was over Britain gradually and consciously became a world-wide Imperial Power. The causes of the Mutiny lay deep in the past. About the beginning of the nineteenth century a new generation of British administrators and soldiers appeared in India, austere, upright, Bible-reading men, who dreamed of Christianising and Europeanising the sub-continent, and for a while gained a brief promise of success. Hitherto the English, like the Romans in the provinces of their empire, had a neutral policy on religion and no policy at all on Indian education. Regiments held ceremonial parades in honour of Hindu deities, and Hindu and Muslim holidays were impartially and publicly observed. But in England missionary zeal was stirring, and respect for alien creeds gradually succumbed to the desire for proselytisation. For a time enlightened Hindu opinion seemed not unreceptive to elements of the Christian faith. *Suttee,* the burning of widows, *Thugee,* the strangling of travellers by fanatics who deemed it a religious duty, and female infanticide were suppressed. Largely owing to Macaulay, when he was a member of the Governor-General's council, measures were taken to make English learning available to the higher-ranking and more wealthy Indians. All this was unsettling, and played its part in the terrible events which now occurred.

A more immediate cause of the rising was a series of defeats and reverses suffered by the British. The Russian threat to India had begun to overhang the minds of Englishmen. It was in fact a gross exaggeration to suppose that Russian armies could have crossed the ranges of the Hindu-Kush in force and arrived in the Indus valley. But the menace seemed real at the time. When it was learnt that a small body of Russians had penetrated into the fringes of Afghanistan a British expedition was dispatched in 1839 to Kabul and a British candidate placed on the Afghan throne. The result was disaster. The country rose up in arms. In December 1841, under a promise of safe-conduct, the British garrison of some four thousand troops, accompanied by nearly three times as many women, children, and Afghan camp-followers, began to withdraw through the snow and the mountain passes. The safe-conduct was violated, and nearly all were murdered or taken prisoners. A single survivor reached India on January 13. A second expedition avenged the treachery in the following year, but the repute of European arms was deeply smitten and the massacre resounded throughout the peninsula.

Another defeat soon followed in the Punjab, the most northerly of the Indian provinces at that time. Here the warrior Sikhs, a reformed Hindu sect, forbidden to touch tobacco or cut their hair above the waist, had long held sway. Encouraged by the news from Afghanistan, and restless after the death of their great leader, Ranjit Singh, who had hitherto held them in check, they resolved to try their hand at invading the Company's territory. In 1845 they crossed the boundary river of the Sutlej, and were met and repulsed two hundred miles north of Delhi. The British installed a regency. Three years later the Sikhs tried to overthrow it. There was a desperate drawn battle deep within the province at Chilianwala, in which three British regiments lost their colours. Shortly afterwards the British forces redeemed their name and the Sikh army was destroyed. The Punjab was pacified by John and Henry Lawrence. These famous brothers ruled with absolute power, untrammelled by the Company and splendidly resourceful. They made landowners take a threefold oath: "Thou shalt not burn thy widow, thou shalt not kill thy daughters, thou shalt not bury alive thy lepers." They sent the Koh-i-noor diamond to Queen Victoria, and gained from the formidable warriors of the province an affection and loyalty for the British Crown which was to endure for nearly a century. One of their subordinates, John Nicholson, who was to be for ever famous as the liberator of Delhi, was even worshipped by some Punjabis as a deity. Nevertheless, among the ill-informed and ill-disposed in other regions of India "Remember Chilianwala!" became a battle-cry and a bloodstained slogan in the upheaval which was to come.

This was a period of confident expansion in India, generally undertaken by men on the spot and not always approved by opinion in Britain. Two other major annexations completed the extension of British rule. Possession of Sind, in the lower Indus valley, had been judged necessary to safeguard the command of the north-west coast. It was conquered by Sir Charles Napier, a veteran who had fought at Corunna and in the American war of 1812. In England the magazine

Punch commented sourly on this operation. It represented Napier as reporting the matter in a one-word telegram, "Peccavi" ("I have sinned"). Napier, unperturbed, proceeded to rule with absolute and benevolent power. He dealt with widow-burning by the simple expedient of placing a gibbet beside every pyre. "When men burn women alive we hang them" he said. Like the Punjab, Sind remained peaceful for many years. The other annexation was that of Oudh, on the borders of Bengal, where an Indian king had long oppressed his subjects. The Marquis of Dalhousie, appointed Governor-General at the age of thirty-five, had no doubts about the benefits conferred on India by British rule and British skill. During his eight years of office he added principalities to the Company's dominion by applying what was called the "doctrine of lapse." This meant that when an Indian ruler died without an heir of his own blood his territory was forfeited. Adopted heirs were not allowed to inherit, though this had long been Hindu custom. In Oudh Dalhousie was more forthright. He bluntly declared that "the British Government would be guilty in the sight of God and man if it were any longer to aid in sustaining by its countenance an administration fraught with suffering to millions." He deposed the king and seized his province in 1856. Next year came the Mutiny, and much of the blame for provoking it was laid at Dalhousie's door.

* * * * *

The East India Company's army of Bengal had long been of ill-repute. Recruited mainly in the North, it was largely composed of high-caste Hindus. This was bad for discipline. Brahmin privates would question the orders of officers and N.C.O.s of less exalted caste. Power and influence in the regiments frequently depended on a man's position in the religious rather than the military hierarchy. The Company's

British officers were often of poor quality, for the abler and more thrusting among them sought secondment to the more spacious fields of civil administration. Many of those who remained at regimental headquarters were out of touch with their men, and showed no desire to improve matters. Troops were needed for a war with Burma, but if they crossed the high seas they lost caste. Dalhousie nevertheless made recruits liable for service anywhere in the world. There were grievances about pay and pensions. Other developments, unconnected with this military unrest, added their weight. By the 1850's railways, roads, posts, telegraphs, and schools were beginning to push and agitate their way across the countryside, and were thought by many Indians to threaten an ancient society whose inmost structure and spirit sprang from a rigid and unalterable caste system. If everyone used the same trains and the same schools, or even the same roads, it was argued, how could caste survive? Indian monarchs were apprehensive and resentful of the recent annexations. Hatred smouldered at the repression of *Suttee*. Unfounded stories spread that the Government intended to convert India forcibly to Christianity. The disasters in Afghanistan and the slaughter of the Sikh wars cast doubt on the invincibility of British arms. Many of the sepoys, or Indian soldiers, considered themselves equal or superior to European troops. Thus a legacy of troubles confronted Dalhousie's successor, Lord Canning. He had been in India little more than a year when the introduction of a new type of ammunition provided a spark and focus for the mass of discontent.

In the year of the centenary of Plassey rumours began to flow that the cartridges for the new Enfield rifle were greased with the fat of pigs and cows, animals which Moslem and Hindu respectively were forbidden to eat. The cartridges had to be bitten before they could be inserted in the muzzle. Thus sepoys of both religions would be defiled. There was some truth in the story, for beef-fat had been used in the London arsenal at Woolwich, though it was never used at the Indian factory at Dum-Dum, and as soon as the complaints began no tainted missiles were issued. Nevertheless the tale ran through the regiments in the spring of 1857 and there was much unrest. In April some cavalry troopers at Meerut were court-martialled and imprisoned for refusing to touch the cartridges, and on May 9 they were publicly stripped of their uniforms. An Indian officer told his superiors that the sepoys were planning to break open the jail and release the prisoners. His warning was disbelieved. Next night three regiments mutinied, captured the prison, killed their British officers, and marched on Delhi.

There was nothing at hand to stop them. South of the Punjab fewer than eleven full-strength battalions and ancillary forces, comprising in all about forty thousand British soldiers, were scattered across the vast peninsula, and even these were not on a war footing. The Indian troops outnumbered them by five to one and had most of the artillery. The hot weather had started, distances were great, transport was scarce, the authorities were unprepared. Nevertheless, when the British power was so weak, and India might have been plunged once again into the anarchy and bloodshed from which she had been gradually and painfully rescued most of the populace remained aloof and at peace, and none of the leading Indian rulers joined the revolt. Of the three armies maintained by the Company only one, that of Bengal, was affected. Gurkhas from Nepal helped to quell the rising. The Punjab remained loyal, and its Sikhs and Moslems respected the colours and disarmed wavering regiments. The valley of the Ganges was the centre of the turmoil.

But at first all went with a rush. The magazine at Delhi

was guarded by two British officers and six soldiers. They fought to the last, and when resistance was hopeless they blew it up. The mutineers killed every European in sight, seized the aged King of Delhi, now living in retirement as the Company's pensioner, and proclaimed him Moghul Emperor. The appeal failed and few Moslems rose to support it. For three weeks there was a pause, and then the mutiny spread. British officers would not believe in the disloyalty of their troops and many were murdered. At Cawnpore, on the borders of Oudh, the garrison left the citadel to guard the road. They trusted to the loyalty of the Nana Sahib, the dispossessed adopted son of an Indian ruler, but still a powerful figure. They were mistaken, and a terrible fate was soon to befall them. At Lucknow, the capital, Henry Lawrence prepared the Residency for what was to be a long and glorious defence. Meanwhile, rightly perceiving that the key to the revolt lay in Delhi, the British mustered such forces as they could and seized the ridge overlooking the city. They were too few to make an assault, and for weeks in the height of summer three thousand troops, most of whom were British, held the fifty-foot eminence against an enemy twenty or thirty times their number. Early in August Nicholson arrived with reinforcements from the Punjab, having marched nearly thirty miles a day for three weeks. Thus animated, the British attacked on September 14, and after six days' street-fighting, in which Nicholson was killed, the city fell. The poor King was sent to Burma. His two sons were taken prisoners, and shot after an attempt had been made to rescue them. This created a fresh grievance in Indian eyes.

At Cawnpore there was a horrible massacre. For twenty-one days nine hundred British and loyal Indians, nearly half of them women and children, were besieged and attacked by three thousand sepoys with the Nana Sahib at their head. At length, on June 26, they were granted safe-conduct. As they were leaving by boat they were fired upon, and all the men were killed. Such women and children as survived were cast into prison. On the night of July 15 a relieving force under Sir Henry Havelock, a veteran of Indian warfare, was barely twenty miles away. The Nana Sahib ordered his sepoys to kill the prisoners. They refused. Five assassins than cut the captives to death with knives and threw the bodies into a well. Two days later Havelock arrived. "Had any Christian bishop visited that scene of butchery when I saw it," wrote an eyewitness long afterwards, "I verily believe that he would have buckled on his sword." Here and elsewhere the British troops took horrible vengeance. Mutineers were blown from the mouths of cannon, sometimes alive, or their bodies sewn up in the skins of cows and swine.

The rebels turned on Lucknow. Here also there was a desperate struggle. Seventeen hundred troops, nearly half of them loyal sepoys, held the Residency, under Henry Lawrence, against sixty-thousand rebels, for in Oudh, unlike most of India, the population joined the revolt. Food was short and there was much disease. On September 25 Havelock and Outram fought their way in, but were beset in their turn, Havelock dying of exhaustion a few days later. In November the siege was raised by Sir Colin Campbell, the new Commander-in-Chief appointed by Lord Palmerston. Campbell had seen service against Napoleon and had a distinguished record in the Crimean War. A fresh threat to Cawnpore compelled him to move on. Outram, reinforced, continued to hold out, and Lucknow was not finally liberated till the following March. No one knows what happened to the Nana Sahib. He disappeared for ever into the Himalayan jungle.

Elsewhere the rising was more speedily crushed. The recapture of Delhi had destroyed all semblance and pretence that the mutiny was a national revolt. Fighting, sporadic but often fierce, continued in the Central Provinces until the end of 1858, but on November 1 the Governor-General, "Clemency" Canning, derisively so called for his mercifulness, proclaimed with truth that Queen Victoria was now sovereign of all India. The first Viceroy, as Canning became, was a son of the renowned Foreign Secretary and Prime Minister. The rule of the East India Company, which had long ceased to be a trading business in India, was abolished. This was the work of the short Conservative Government of Derby and Disraeli. Thus, after almost exactly a century the advice which Clive had given to Pitt was accepted by the British Government. Henceforward there were to be no more annexations, no subsidiary treaties, no more civil wars. Religious toleration and equality before the law were promised to all. Indians for a generation and more were to look back on the Queen's Proclamation of 1858 as a Magna Carta.

The scale of the Indian Mutiny should not be exaggerated. Three-quarters of the troops remained loyal; barely a third of British territory was affected; there had been risings and revolts among the soldiery before; the brunt of the outbreak was suppressed in the space of a few weeks. It was in no sense a national movement, or, as some later Indian writers have suggested, a patriotic struggle for freedom or a war of independence. The idea and ideal of the inhabitants of the sub-continent forming a single people and state was not to emerge for many years. But terrible atrocities had been committed by both sides. From now on there was an increasing gulf between the rulers and the ruled. The easy-going ways of the eighteenth century were gone for ever, and so were the missionary fervour and reforming zeal of the early Victorians and their predecessors. The English no longer looked on India as "home," or themselves as crusaders called to redeem

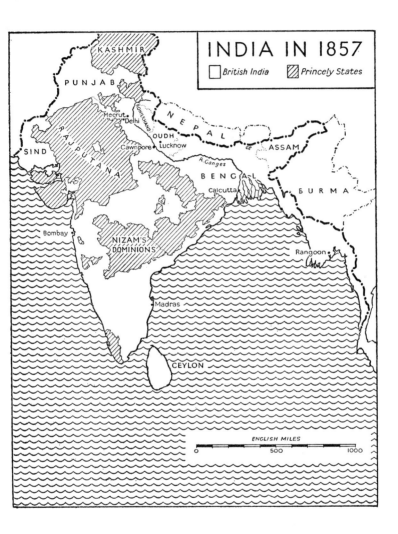

INDIA IN 1857

☐ British India ▧ Princely States

KASHMIR

PUNJAB

Meerut
Delhi
Cawnpore
Lucknow

OUDH

R A J P U T A N A

SIND

NEPAL

ASSAM

R.Ganges

BENGAL

Calcutta

BURMA

Bombay

NIZAM'S
DOMINIONS

Rangoon

Madras

CEYLON

ENGLISH MILES

0   500   1000

and uplift the great multitudes. British administration became detached, impartial, efficient. Great progress was made and many material benefits were secured. The frontiers were guarded and the peace was kept. Starvation was subdued. The population vastly increased. The Indian army, revived and reorganised, was to play a glorious part on Britain's side in two world wars. Nevertheless the atrocities and reprisals of the blood-stained months of the Mutiny left an enduring and bitter mark in the memory of both countries.

* * * * *

While these events unrolled in India the political scene in England remained confused. Issues were not clear-cut. Peel's conversion to Free Trade had destroyed the party lines which he had done much to draw, and for twenty years in England Governments of mixed complexion followed one another. Disraeli and Derby, having broken Peel, found that it took a long time to muster the remnant of the former Tory Protectionists into an effective political party. Rising men like Gladstone, who remained faithful to the Peel tradition, would have nothing to do with them, though on at least one occasion Disraeli tried hard to enlist Gladstone's co-operation. It is an interesting speculation what might have happened had these two bitter opponents and future Prime Ministers at this stage joined hands. The Whigs, under Russell and Palmerston, felt that their main aims had already been accomplished. Palmerston was willing to make improvements in government, but large-scale changes were not to his mind. Russell hankered after a further measure of electoral reform, but that was the limit of his programme. Both conceived of themselves as guardians of the system that they had the fortune to head. In this attitude the two leaders, and Palmerston especially, were probably in harmony with mid-Victorian opinion. Radicalism in these years made little appeal to the voters. Prosperity was spreading through the land, and with it went a lull in the fiercer forms of political agitation. Dignity and deference were the values of the age. If the gentleman was still the admired ideal, the self-made man was also deeply respected. The doctrine of industrious self-help, preached by Samuel Smiles, was widely popular in the middle classes and among many artisans as well. The lessons of the Chartist failure had been learnt, and educating the manual labourer began to seem more important than rousing him to revolution. With this view large numbers of working men happily concurred. All this made for a feeling of stability, with which a sense of steady progress was allied.

Religion in its numerous varieties cast a soothing and uplifting influence on men's minds. Many millions, more than half the total population, were regular attenders at church or chapel, though church-goers were fewer among the very poor. Religious debate was earnest, sometimes acrimonious, but the contests it bred were verbal. Civil strife for the sake of religion was a thing of the past. The virtues of toleration had been learnt, though toleration did not mean lukewarmness. The churches and sects, and their flocks, took leave to disapprove of one another, occasionally with vigour. When the Roman Catholic Church re-established its hierarchy of bishops in England there was vehement commotion and protest in London, but nothing amounting to riot.

The Church of England, earlier in the century, had been stirred from slumber by Evangelical zeal and the lofty ideals of the Oxford Movement. The Low Church and High Church parties, as they were called, strove eloquently for men's souls. About half the church-goers of England were members of the Anglican communion. Dissent also flourished, and Methodist, Baptist, Presbyterian, Congregational, and Unitarian preachers gained a wide allegiance. The Church of Rome in

England had revived under the impulse of Catholic Emancipation, and was reinforced by the accession of a number of High Anglican clergy, including John Henry Newman, a profound and subtle thinker, later created a Cardinal.

Religious preoccupations were probably more widespread and deeply felt than at any time since the days of Cromwell. But thinking men were also disturbed by a new theory, long foreshadowed in the work of scientists, the theory of evolution. It was given classic expression in *The Origin of Species*, published by Charles Darwin in 1859. This book provoked doubt and perplexity among those who could no longer take literally the Biblical account of creation. But the theory of evolution, and its emphasis on the survival of the fittest in the history of life upon the globe, was a powerful adjunct to mid-Victorian optimism. It lent fresh force to the belief in the forward march of mankind.

Palmerston seemed to his fellow-countrymen the embodiment of their own healthy hopes. He had lost none of his old vigour in chastising foreign Governments, and his patriotic sentiments appealed to the self-confidence of the nation. They did not always appeal to the Queen and Prince Albert, who resented his habit of sending off sharply worded dispatches without consulting them. But it was Palmerston's desire, for all his strong language and sometimes hasty action, to keep the general peace in Europe. For this reason the Liberal movements in foreign countries which engaged his sympathy also sometimes gave him reason for anxiety.

The greatest of the European movements in these years was the cause of Italian unity. This long-cherished dream of the Italian peoples was at last realised, though only partially, in 1859 and 1860. The story is well known of how the Italians secured the military aid of Napoleon III for the price of ceding Nice and Savoy to France, and how, after winning

Lombardy from the Austrians, the French Emperor left his allies in the lurch. Venice remained unredeemed; still worse, a French army protected the rump of the Papal State in Rome, and for ten years deprived the Italians of their natural capital. But as one small Italian state after another cast out their alien rulers, and merged under a single monarchy, widespread enthusiasm was aroused in England. Garibaldi and his thousand volunteers, who overturned the detested Bourbon Government in Sicily and Naples with singular dash and speed, were acclaimed as heroes in London. These bold events were welcome to Palmerston and his Foreign Secretary, Russell. At the same time the British leaders were suspicious of Napoleon III's designs and fearful of a wider war. Congratulation but non-intervention was therefore their policy. It is typical of these two old Whigs that they applauded the new Italian Government for putting into practice the principles of the English Revolution of 1688. Russell in the House of Commons compared Garibaldi to King William III. History does not relate what the Italians made of this.

*　　*　　*　　*　　*

In home politics meanwhile a sublime complacency enveloped the Government. Palmerston, like Melbourne before him, did not believe in too much legislation. Good-humour and common sense distinguished him. As the novelist Trollope well said, he was "a statesman for the moment. Whatever was not wanted now, whatever was not practicable now, he drove quite out of his mind." This practical outlook found no favour among the younger and more thrusting Members of the House of Commons. Disraeli, chafing on the Opposition benches, vented his scorn and irritation on this last of the eighteenth-century politicians. "His external system," he once told the House, "is turbulent and aggressive that his rule at home may be tranquil and unassailed. Hence arise excessive expenditure, heavy taxation, and the stoppage of all social improvement. His scheme of conduct is so devoid of all political principle that when forced to appeal to the people his only claim to their confidence is his name." Peel's disciples and followers were no less despairing and powerless. So long as leadership remained in the hands of Palmerston, Russell, and the Whig nobility there could be little hope of advance towards the Liberalism of which they dreamed. "The Whigs," said Sidney Herbert at a moment when they were temporarily out of office, "are incurable in their superstitions about ducal houses. I see no prospect of the formation of an efficient party, let alone Government, out of the chaos on the Opposition benches. No one reigns over or in it but discord and antipathy. The aristocratic Whigs seem to be nearly used up, and the party produces no new men, but at the same time complains of the old ones. Middle-aged merchants, shrewd men of business, feel their vanity hurt that they have not the refusal of office."

The Tories were little better off. Their nominal head was Lord Derby, who could be brilliant in debate, but was apt to regard politics as an unpleasant duty imposed upon the members of his class. His real interest lay in horse-racing, and he also produced an excellent translation of Homer. Disraeli had become the leader of his party in the House of Commons. His struggle for power was hard and uphill. A Jew at the head of a phalanx of country gentlemen was an unusual sight in English politics. After the repeal of the Corn Laws protection was not only dead, but, as Disraeli himself said, damned, and he and Derby had agreed to discard it as a party principle. But the search for a new theme was long, painful, and frustrating. Meanwhile he had to play the part of Derby's lieutenant, and their spells of office in 1852 and 1858 were brief and uneventful. Disraeli more than once sought an alliance with the Radicals, and promised them that he would oppose armaments and an aggressive foreign policy. Colonies, he even declared, were "millstones round our necks." But their chief spokesman, John Bright, was under no illusions. The shrewd Quaker was not to be caught. "Mr Disraeli," he said, "is a man who does what may be called the conjuring for his party. He is what among a tribe of Red Indians would be called the medicine-man." And that was the end of that. Thus foiled, Disraeli returned to his attack on the Whigs. He was convinced that the only way to destroy them was by extending the franchise yet further so as to embrace the respectable artisans and counter the hostility of the middle classes. Patiently he worked on Derby and his colleagues. In his youth he had dreamed of uniting the two nations, the rich and the poor, as the world of his novel *Sybil* shows, and the 1850's saw the slow emergence of a practical doctrine of Tory democracy. But Disraeli's ideas took time to find acceptance.

Standing apart both from the Whigs and Derby's Tories were the Peelites, of whom the most notable was William Gladstone. Having started his Parliamentary career in 1832 as a strict Tory, he was to make a long pilgrimage into the Liberal camp. The death of Peel had destroyed his allegiance to Toryism and he too was in search of a new theme. The son of a rich Liverpool merchant with slave-owning interests in the West Indies, Gladstone came from the same class as his old leader, and believed, like him, in the new arguments for Free Trade. Though admired as an administrator and an orator, his contemporaries considered him wanting in judgment and principle, but in fact, as Palmerston perceived, he was awaking to the political potentialities of the English middle class. "He might," he said, "be called one of the people; he wished to identify himself with them; he possessed religious enthusiasm, and made it powerful over others from the force of his own intellect." Despite his preoccupations with theology, he comprehended the minds of the new voters better than his colleagues and understood the workings of party better than Peel. "Oxford on the surface, but Liverpool underneath"—such was a contemporary judgment. But, like Disraeli, his progress was slow. He was Chancellor of the Exchequer at the beginning of the Crimean War; then he faded into Opposition. It was fortunate for him that supreme power did not come too soon. Peel had been frustrated by early experience of high office, which prevented him from putting his ideas to the test. Long years of waiting made Gladstone sure of himself.

In 1859, at the age of fifty, Gladstone joined the Whigs and the pilgrimage was over. His decision was made on an issue of foreign policy, but he again concentrated on finance. As Chancellor of the Exchequer under Palmerston his golden period began—great Budget speeches in the House of Commons, a superb handling of administrative detail, a commercial treaty with France, which opened a new era in Free Trade, and demands for retrenchment in military affairs, which brought him into conflict with his Prime Minister. His finance was a remarkable success. Three brilliant Budgets reduced taxation. Trade was rapidly expanding, and it was soon apparent who would succeed to the leadership of the party. In 1865, in his eighty-first year Palmerston died. "Gladstone," he declared in his last days, "will soon have it all his own way, and whenever he gets my place we shall have strange doings." The old Whig was right. The eighteenth century died with him. The later Victorian age demanded a new leader, and at long last he had arrived. When Gladstone next appeared before his electors he opened his speech by saying, "At last, my friends, I am come among you, and I am come among you unmuzzled." But the Whigs still hesitated. Gladstone, like Disraeli, wanted to extend the franchise to large sections of the working classes: he was anxious to capture the votes of the new electorate. He prevailed upon the Government, now headed by Russell, to put forward a Reform Bill, but the Cabinet were so divided that they resigned. A minority administration under Derby and Disraeli followed, which lasted for two and a half years.

Disraeli now seized his chance. He introduced a fresh Reform Bill in 1867, which he skilfully adapted to meet the wishes of the House, of which he was Leader. There was a redistribution of seats in favour of the large industrial towns, and nearly a million new voters were added to an existing electorate of about the same number. The Tories were nervous at this startling advance from their original plan. In many towns the working classes would now be in the majority at elections. Derby called it "a leap in the dark." The recent civil war in America seemed a poor recommendation for democracy, and even the Radicals were anxious about how the uneducated masses would behave. But this immediately became clear. The carrying of the second Reform Bill so soon after the death of Palmerston opened a new era in English politics. New issues and new methods began to emerge. As Walter Bagehot, the banker and economist, said, "A political country is like an American forest; you have only to cut down the old trees and immediately new trees come up to replace them." In February 1868 Derby resigned from the leadership of the party and Disraeli was at last Prime Minister—as he put it, "at the top of the greasy pole." He had to hold a General Election. The new voters gave their overwhelming support to his opponents, and Gladstone, who had become leader of the Liberal Party, formed the strongest administration that England had seen since the days of Peel.

The Migration of the Peoples

I: CANADA AND SOUTH AFRICA

OCCUPATION of the empty lands of the globe was violently accelerated by the fall of Napoleon. The long struggle against France had stifled or arrested the expansion of the English-speaking peoples, and the ships and the men who might have founded the second British Empire had been consumed in twenty years of world war. A generation of men and women had toiled or fought in their factories or on their farms, in the fleets and in the armies, and only a very few had had either the wish or the opportunity to seek a new life and new fortunes overseas. Their energies and their hopes had been concentrated on survival and on victory. There had been no time for dreams of emigration, and no men to spare if it had been possible. Suddenly all this was changed by the decision at Waterloo. Once again the oceans were free. No enemies threatened in Europe. Ships need no longer sail in convoy, and the main outlines of the continents had been charted. Once more the New World offered an escape from the hardships and frustrations of the Old. The war was over. Fares were cheap and transport was plentiful. The result was the most spectacular migration of human beings of which history has yet had record and a vast enrichment of the trade and industry of Great Britain.

Of course the process took time to gather way, and at

first the flow of emigrants was very small. But the road had been pointed by the grim convict settlements in Australia, by the loyalists from the United States who had moved to Canada, and by traders, explorers, missionaries, and whalers all over the temperate zones of the earth. News began to spread among the masses that fertile unoccupied and habitable lands still existed, in which white men could dwell in peace and liberty, and perhaps could even better themselves. The increasing population of Great Britain added to the pressure. In 1801 it was about eleven millions. Thirty years later it was sixteen millions, and by 1871 it was ten millions more. Fewer people died at birth or in early childhood, and it has been established by a recent authority that despite the Industrial Revolution, London was a healthier place to live in than rural Prussia or Bourbon Paris. The numbers grew, and the flow began: in the 1820's a quarter of a million emigrants, in the 1830's half a million, by the middle of the century a million and a half, until sixty-five years after Waterloo no fewer than eight million people had left the British Isles.

The motives, methods, and character of the movement were very different from those which had sustained the Pilgrim Fathers and the Stuart plantations of the seventeenth century. Famine drove at least a million Irishmen to the United States and elsewhere. Gold lured hardy fortune-hunters to Australia, and to the bleak recesses of Canada, where they discovered a more practical if less respectable El Dorado than had dazzled the Elizabethan adventurers. Hunger for land and for the profits of the wool trade beckoned the more sober and well-to-do. All this was largely accomplished in the face of official indifference and sometimes of hostility. The American War of Independence had convinced most of the ruling classes in Britain that colonies were undesirable possessions. They did not even have a departmental Secretary of State of their own until 1854. The Government was interested in strategic bases, but if ordinary people wanted to settle in the new lands then let them do so. It might cure unemployment and provide posts for penniless noblemen, but the sooner these communities became completely independent the better and cheaper for the tax-payer in England. Anyway, Greece was more interesting news than New Zealand, and the educated public were much more concerned about the slave-trade than the squalors of the emigrant ships. Thus, as in India, the Second British Empire was founded almost by accident, and with small encouragement from any of the main political parties.

* * * * *

Of the new territories Canada was the most familiar and the nearest in point of distance to the United Kingdom. Her Maritime Provinces had long sent timber to Britain, and rather than return with empty holds the shipowners were content to transport emigrants for a moderate fare. Once they landed however the difficulties and the distances were very great. The Maritime Provinces lived a life very much of their own, and many emigrants chose to push on into Lower Canada, or, as it is now called, the Province of Quebec. Pitt in 1791 had sought to solve the racial problems of Canada by dividing her into two parts. In Lower Canada the French were deeply rooted, a compact, alien community, led by priests and seigneurs, uninterested and untouched by the democratic ideas of liberal or revolutionary Europe, and holding stubbornly like the Boers in South Africa to their own traditions and language. Beyond them, to the north-west, lay Upper Canada, the modern Province of Ontario, settled by some of the sixty thousand Englishmen who had left the United States towards the end of the eighteenth century rather than live under the American republic. These proud folk had out of devotion to the British Throne abandoned most of their possessions, and been rewarded with the unremunerative but honourable title of United Empire Loyalists. The Mohawk tribe, inspired by the same sentiments, had journeyed with them. They had hacked a living space out of the forests, and dwelt lonely and remote, cut off from Lower Canada by the rapids of the St Lawrence, and watchful against incursions from the United States. Then there was a vast emptiness till one reached a few posts on the Pacific which traded their wares to China.

These communities, so different in tradition, character, and race, had been rallied into temporary unity by invasion from the United States. French, English, and Red Indians all fought against the Americans, and repulsed them in the three-year struggle between 1812 and 1814. Then trouble began. The French in Lower Canada feared that the immigrants would outnumber and dominate them. The Loyalists in Upper Canada welcomed new settlers who would increase the price of land but were reluctant to treat them as equals. Moreover, the two Provinces started to quarrel with each other. Upper Canada's external trade had to pass through Lower Canada, and there pay taxes, and disputes occurred about sharing the proceeds. Differences over religion added to the irritations. From about 1820 the Assembly in Lower Canada began to behave like the Parliaments of the early Stuarts and the legislatures of the American colonies, refusing to vote money for the salaries of royal judges and permanent officials. French politicians made vehement speeches. In Upper Canada the new settlers struggled for political equality with the Loyalists. Liberals wanted to make the executive responsible to the Assembly and talked wildly of leaving the Empire, and in 1836 the Assembly in which they held a majority was dissolved.

In the following year both Provinces rebelled, Lower Canada for a month and Upper Canada for a week. There were mobs, firing by troops, shifty compromises, and very few executions. Everything was on a small scale and in a minor key, and no great harm was done, but it made the British Government realise that Canadian affairs required attention. The Whig leaders in London were wiser than George III. They perceived that a tiny minority of insurgents could lead to great troubles, and in 1838 Lord Durham was sent to investigate, assisted by Edward Gibbon Wakefield. His instructions were vague and simple, "To put things right," and meanwhile the Canadian constitution was suspended by Act of Parliament. Durham was a Radical, brilliant, decisive, and hot-tempered. Wakefield was an active theorist on Imperial affairs whose misconduct with a couple of heiresses had earned him a prison sentence and compelled him to spend the rest of his public life behind the scenes. Durham stayed only a few months. His high-handed conduct in dealing with disaffected Canadians aroused much criticism of him at Westminster. Feeling himself deserted by Lord Melbourne's Government, with which he was personally unpopular, but which should nevertheless have stood by him, Durham resigned and returned to England. He then produced, or at least lent his name to, the famous report in which he diagnosed and proclaimed the root causes of the trouble and advocated representative government, carried on by Ministers chosen from the popular Assembly, a united Canada, and planned settlement of the unoccupied lands. These recommendations were largely put into effect by the Canada Act of 1840, which was the work of Lord John Russell.

Thereafter Canada's progress was swift and peaceful. Her population had risen from about half a million in 1815 to a million and a quarter in 1838. A regular steamship service with the British Isles and cheap transatlantic postage were established in the same year. There were hesitations and doubts in England at the novel idea of making colonies almost completely free and allowing their democratic Assemblies to choose and eject their own Ministers, but the appointment of Durham's son-in-law, Lord Elgin, as Governor-General in 1847 was decisive. Elgin believed, like Durham, that the Governor should represent the sovereign and remain in the background of politics. He appointed and dismissed Ministers according to the wishes of the Assembly. For this he was blamed or applauded, and even pelted with eggs and stones, according to how it pleased or angered either side. But when he laid down his office seven years later the principle had been firmly accepted by Canadians of all persuasions that popular power must march with popular responsibility, that Ministers must govern and be obeyed so long as they enjoyed the confidence of the majority and should resign when they had lost it. There was hardly any talk now of leaving the Empire or dividing Canada into separate and sovereign units or joining the American Republic. On the contrary, the Oregon Treaty with the United States in 1846 extended the 49th parallel right across the continent as a boundary between the two countries and gave the whole of Vancouver Island to Great Britain. How the treaty was concluded is related elsewhere in this volume.

In the mid-century a movement for the federation of all the Canadian Provinces began to grow and gather support. The Civil War in the United States helped to convince Canadians that all was not perfect in their neighbours' constitution, and the victory of the North also aroused their fears that the exultant Union might be tempted to extend its borders farther still. Canada had already turned her gaze westwards. Between the Province of Ontario and the Rocky Mountains lay

a thousand miles of territory, uninhabited save by a few settlers in Manitoba, a roaming-place for Indians, trappers and
wild animals. It was a temptation, so it was argued, to the
land-hunger of the United States. Discharged Irish soldiers
from the Civil War had already made armed raids across the
border which Congress had declared itself powerless to arrest.
Might not the Americans press forward, occupy these vacant
lands by stealth, and even establish a kind of squatter's right
to the prairies? The soil was believed to be fertile and was
said to offer a living for white men. In 1867 America purchased the remote and forbidding expanse of Alaska from the
Russians for the sum of 7,200,000 dollars, but here, on the
door-step of the Republic, lay a prize which seemed much
more desirable and was very easy of access. No one ruled over
it except the Hudson's Bay Company, founded in the reign of
Charles II, and the Company, believing that agriculture
would imperil its fur-trade, was both hostile to settlers and
jealous of its own authority. Eleven years before however
the discovery of gold on the Fraser River had precipitated a
rush of fortune-hunters to the Pacific coast. The Company's
officials had proved powerless to control the turmoil, and the
Government in London had been compelled to extend the
royal sovereignty to this distant shore. Thus was born the
Crown colony of British Columbia, which soon united with
the Island of Vancouver and demanded and obtained self-
rule. But between it and Ontario lay a No-man's-land, and
something must be done if it was not to fall into the hands of
the United States. How indeed could Canada remain separate
from America and yet stay alive?

These considerations prompted the British North America
Act of 1867, which created the first of the self-governing
British Dominions beyond the seas. The Provinces of Ontario,
Quebec, New Brunswick, and Nova Scotia were the founding

members. They adopted a federal constitution of a very different shape from that of the United States. All powers not expressly reserved to the Provinces of Canada were assumed by the central Government: the Governor-General, representing the monarch, ruled through Ministers drawn from the majority in her Canadian House of Commons, and Members of the House were elected in numbers proportionate to the population they represented. Thus the way was made easy for the absorption of new territories and Provinces, and on the eve of her Railway Age and westward expansion the political stability of Canada was assured.

When the Parliament of the new Dominion first met, its chief anxiety was about the Western lands. Its members looked to the future, and it is convenient here to chart the results of their foresight. The obvious, immediate step was to buy out the Hudson's Bay Company. This was done two years later for the sum of £300,000. The Company kept its trading rights, and indeed retains them to this day, but it surrendered its territorial sovereignty to the Crown. The process was not accomplished without bloodshed. There was a brief revolt in Manitoba, where wild Indian half-breeds thought that their freedom was endangered, but order was soon restored. Manitoba became a Province of the Dominion in 1870, and in the next year British Columbia was also admitted. By themselves however these constitutional steps would not have sufficed to bind the broad stretches of Canada together. The challenging task that faced the Dominion was to settle and develop her empty Western lands before the immigrant tide from America could flood across the 49th parallel. The answer was to build a transcontinental railway.

When the Maritime Provinces joined the federation they had done so on condition they were linked with Ontario by rail, and after nine years of labour a line was completed in 1876. British Columbia made the same demand and received the same promise. It proved much more difficult to fulfil. Capital was scarce, investors were timid, politics were tangled, and much of the country was unknown. At length however a Scotsman, Donald Smith, better known as Lord Strathcona, carried out the plan. His Company demanded ten years. Helped by Government funds, they finished their work in half the time, and the Canadian Pacific Railway was opened in 1885. Other lines sprang up, and corn, soon counted in millions of bushels a year, began to flow in from the prairies. Canada had become a nation, and shining prospects lay before her.

* * * * *

South Africa, unlike America, had scanty attractions for the early colonists and explorers. As the half-way house to the Indies many broke their voyage there, but few cared to stay. The Gulf of St Lawrence made it easy to reach the interior of Canada, but the coastline of South Africa, short of natural harbours and navigable rivers, mostly consisted of cliffs and sandhills washed by strong currents and stormy seas. Inland a succession of mountain ranges, running parallel to the coast, barred the way. From the west the ascent was comparatively gradual, but the country was barren and waterless. From the south and east range after range, in many places sheer and precipitous, had to be climbed. Few lands have been more difficult for Europeans to enter than South Africa, and for them it long remained the "Tavern of the Seas," a port of call on the route to the East.

In the seventeenth century the fleets of the Dutch East India Company, sailing for the Indies or returning home to Amsterdam and Rotterdam, were the most frequent visitors to the Cape, and Table Bay was their halting-place. The establishment of a permanent settlement was discussed, but nothing was done till 1652, when, at the height of their power and in the Golden Age of their civilisation, the Dutch sent Jan van Riebeek, a young ship's surgeon, with three ships to take possession of Table Bay. Colonisation was no part of the plan: they merely wanted to found a port of call for the Company's ships, and almost all the inhabitants were servants of the Company, forbidden to strike out into the new land. After twenty years there were no more than sixty-four free burghers at Table Bay.

The change came at the turn of the seventeenth century, under the Governorship of Simon van der Stel and his son William Adriaan. They encouraged settlers to come out from Holland and take up grants of land, and by 1707 there were over fifteen hundred free burghers. Not all were Dutch; many were Huguenots, Germans, or Swedes, driven into exile by religious persecution; but the Dutch gradually assimilated them. The little community was served and sustained by a local population of Negro slaves.

Throughout the eighteenth century the colony prospered and grew. In 1760 the first European crossed the Orange River, and by 1778 the Fish River had been made its eastern boundary. By the end of the century the population numbered about fifteen thousand, and there were three areas of settlement. Cape Town, or "Little Paris" as the settlers called it, was a town and port of five thousand inhabitants, and the Company's headquarters. The agricultural coast-belt near the Cape peninsula offered the farmers a limited prosperity, and life was easy, though primitive. Finally there was the inland plateau and remoter coast-belt, where dwelt the frontiersmen, restless, hard, self-reliant, narrow-minded, isolated from society, and impatient of the restraints of civilised government—the forerunners of the Trekkers and the Transvaal Boers of the nineteenth century.

But Holland had now been slowly overtaken by Britain, and as the century drew to its close it became clear that the Imperial future lay, not with the Dutch, but either with the British or the French. Napoleon's wars ruined the Dutch trade, swept the Dutch ships from the seas, and overthrew the Dutch state. In 1782 the Dutch East India Company had paid its last dividend, and twelve years later declared its bankruptcy, with a deficit of ten million pounds. The consequences were serious. Holland had no longer the power to protect her possessions, and when the Dutch were defeated by the French, and the puppet-state of the Batavian Republic was established the British seized Cape Colony as enemy territory. It was finally ceded to them under the peace settlement of 1814 in return for an indemnity of £6,000,000.

At first they met with no great hostility. The Dutch company had been unpopular, there was no deliberate policy of Anglicisation, and the Cape kept most of its Dutch customs and traditions. The British dealt forcefully with the eastern frontier, where the settlers were in contact and conflict with a great southward migration of the Bantu peoples from Central Africa. This extended right across the continent, from the Hereros and Damaras in the west to the Nguni coast peoples in the east. There was much cattle-raiding along the line of the Fish River, and fighting between the Dutch and the natives had broken out in 1779. Thus began a long succession of Kaffir wars, lasting for a hundred years. The settlers, scattered in isolated farms over vast stretches of country, found it difficult to defend themselves, and had demanded help from Cape Town. The far-away Dutch authorities had given them no support. It was now the turn of the British.

They decided that the only way to secure the line of the Fish River was to colonise the border with British settlers, and between 1820 and 1821 nearly five thousand of them were brought out from Great Britain. This emigration coincided with a change of policy. Convinced that South Africa was now destined to become a permanent part of the British Empire, the Government resolved to make it as English as they could. English began to replace Dutch as the official language. In 1828 the judicial system was remodelled on the English pattern, Dutch currency was replaced by English, and the English began to dominate the churches and the schools. Thus was born a division which Canada had surmounted. With the same religion, a similar language, a common stock, and kindred political and social traditions, British and Boers nevertheless plunged into racial strife. British methods of government created among the Boers a more bitter antagonism than in any other Imperial country except Ireland.

Anglicisation was not only ill-conceived, it was unsuccesful. The English were to discover, as the Spaniards had learnt in the sixteenth century, that no race has ever clung more tenaciously to its own culture and institutions than the Dutch, and the only result of the new policy in the 1820's and 1830's was to harden those differences of opinion, especially on the native question, which were already beginning to appear. At this time there was much enthusiasm in England for good works, and English missionaries had been active in South Africa since the early years of the century. The missionaries believed and preached that black men were the equals of white men; the settlers regarded the natives primarily as farm-hands and wanted to control them as strictly as possible. When the missionaries got slavery abolished in 1833 the settlers were indignant as such interference, which meant scarcity of labour, a weakening of their authority and prestige, a risk that large numbers of the Bantu would become beggars and vagrants. At first the English settlers agreed with the Dutch, but as soon as the influence of the missionaries, especially Dr John Philip and the London Missionary Society, came to sway the Government and the Colonial Office the Dutch were left alone to nurse their grievances against the English authorities.

The first crisis came in 1834. The settlement of the Fish River area brought no security, and hordes of Bantu swept over the frontier, laying waste the country and destroying the farms. The Governor, Sir Benjamin D'Urban, drove them back, and to prevent another attack he annexed the territory between the rivers Keiskamma and Kei, expelled the native raiders, and compensated the settlers by offering them land in this new province, which was named after Queen Adelaide. This roused the missionaries, and they persuaded the Colonial Secretary, Lord Glenelg, to repudiate D'Urban and abandon the new province. The settlers lost all compensation, and insult was added to injury when it became known that Glenelg considered that the Kaffirs had an ample justification for the war into which they had rushed. Thus was provoked the Great Trek.

In small parties, accompanied by their women and children and driving their cattle before them, about five thousand Boers set out into the unknown, like the Children of Israel seeking the Promised Land. They were soon followed by many others. Some journeyed over a thousand miles to the banks of the Limpopo, many were attacked by the Matabele and the Zulu, all endured thirst and famine, yet in the unyielding spirit of their Calvinist religion they marched on. The Great Trek was one of the remarkable feats of the nineteenth century, and its purpose was to shake off British rule for ever. "We quit this colony," wrote Pieter Retief, one of the Boer leaders, "under the full assurance that the English Government has nothing more to require of us, and will allow us to govern ourselves without its interference in future."

For long their fortunes looked dark. It was the time of the Mfecane, the "crushing" of the other native tribes by the military empire of the Zulus under Chaka and his successor Dingaan. The Zulu massacre of thousands of natives gave the Boers room to move, but they moved in great peril. In many lonely places within the laager of their ox-wagons they faced the wild onslaught of the Zulu warriors, and not until December 1838 did they crush Dingaan's forces in a great battle at Blood River. After their victory they established the Republic of Natal around the little town of Pietermaritzburg, with Andries Pretorius as its first President.

Their freedom was brief. The British refused to recognise the republic, and after a short struggle in 1845 made it a province of Cape Colony. There remained the Voortrekkers on the plateau farther west, now reinforced by many refugees from Natal. Here too the British intervened. In 1848 Sir Harry Smith, a brave and energetic soldier who had served under Wellington, annexed the country between the Orange and the Vaal Rivers, defeated Pretorius at Boomplaats, and left only scattered Boer settlements across the Vaal outside the colony.

Soon afterwards there was trouble with the tribes beyond the Orange River, and in particular with the Basuto. In Natal the problem had been met by creating native reserves and re-establishing the old tribal hierarchies under the indirect supervision of the Government. But the Government in London did not care to extend its responsibilities, and in 1852 it recognised the independence of the Transvaal settlers. Two years later, in accordance with the Convention of Bloemfontein, the

British withdrew from beyond the Orange River and the Orange Free State was formed. Political dissolution went farther: both Queen Adelaide Province and Natal were made into separate colonies administered directly by the Colonial Office. By 1857 there were five separate republics and three colonies within the territory of the present Union of South Africa. The old colony of the Cape meanwhile prospered, as the production of wool increased by leaps and bounds, and in 1853 an Order in Council established representative institutions in the colony, with a Parliament in Cape Town, though without the grant of full responsible government. Here we may leave South African history for a spell of uneasy peace.

The Migration of the Peoples

II: AUSTRALIA AND NEW ZEALAND

AUSTRALIA has a long history in the realms of human imagination. From the days of Herodotus mankind has had its legends of distant lands, seen for a moment on the horizon, inhabited by strange monsters and rich with the fabulous wealth of Solomon's Ophir and Tarshish. The wonder-loving age of the sixteenth century delighted in such tales, and men who made the long voyage to the East round the Cape of Good Hope talked mysteriously of Marco Polo's Malaiur and Locach and the islands of King Solomon. How the ships of the King of Israel in the tenth century before Christ could have reached the South Pacific Ocean is beyond conjecture. But the geographers and navigators of the Renaissance conceived themselves to be inspired by Biblical example. The author of the *Declaration of the Indies,* presented to Henry VIII, prophesied that if the voyagers to the New World pressed on into the Pacific "there may be discovered divers new lands and kingdoms . . . the richest lands and islands of the world, of gold, precious stones, balms, spices, and other things that we here esteem most, which come out of strange countries." In 1526 Spaniards had dispatched Sebastian Cabot to search for Ophir and Tarshish by way of Magellan's Strait. He never reached the Pacific, but the legend persisted, and in the sixteenth-century maps of the Dieppe cartographers a great Southern continent, "Java la Grande," is marked in the Pacific. In 1568 Alvaro de Mendaña and Pedro Sarmienta de Gamboa discovered what they called the Solomon Islands. The name they gave them shows the strength of the belief. Yet the sixteenth century had ended before landfall was made in Australia by Europeans, and the men who found it were hard-headed, unromantic Dutch traders.

Their voyages to Java and Sumatra brought the Dutch close to the northern shores of the newest continent, but despite Tasman's great expedition in 1642 they avoided it when they could. They had no intention of settling there, and they knew it as an evil coast on which their vessels crossing the Indian Ocean were too often driven by a lee wind. The extent of the continent was not accurately known until the middle of the eighteenth century, when Captain James Cook made three voyages between 1768 and 1779, in which he circumnavigated New Zealand, sailed inside the Australian Barrier Reef, sighted the great Antarctic icefields, discovered the Friendly Islands, the New Hebrides, New Caledonia, and Hawaii, and charted the eastern coastline of Australia. Cook was a surveyor trained in the Royal Navy. His reports were official, accurate, and detailed. His news reached Britain at a timely moment. English convicts had long been transported to America, but since the War of Independence the Government had nowhere to send them and many were now dying of disease in the hulks and gaols of London. Why not send the prisoners to the new continent? The younger Pitt's administration shrank from colonial ventures after the disasters in North America, but delay was deemed impossible, and in January 1788 717 convicts were anchored in Botany Bay. A hundred and ninety-seven were women. The Bay had been so named by Sir Joseph Banks, a distinguished amateur of science, who accompanied Cook on one of his voyages. There was not much botany about it now. The convicts were soon moved a few miles north to Port Jackson, within the magnificent expanse of Sydney Harbour. Famine crouched above the settlement, and for long the colony could not supply all its own food. Without training, capital, or the desire to work, the forgers and thieves, poachers and Irish rebels, criminals and political exiles, had neither the will not the ability to fit themselves to the new land. "The convict barracks of New South Wales," wrote an Australian Governor, "remind me of the monasteries of Spain. They contain a population of consumers who produce nothing." The region had been named by Captain Cook after South Wales. He thought he had detected a resemblance in coastline. But hard-working Wales and its antipodean namesake had very little else in common at the time.

There were of course a few free settlers from the first, but the full migratory wave did not reach Australia till the 1820's. Even the future Commonwealth's name was not yet determined. "New Holland" and other titles were bestowed upon it in official documents. Driven by the post-war distress in Great Britain and attracted by the discovery of rich pasture in the hinterland of New South Wales, English-speaking emigrants began to trickle into the empty sub-continent and rapidly transformed the character and life of the early communities. The population changed from about fifteen thousand convicts and twenty-one thousand free settlers in 1828 to twenty-seven thousand convicts and over a hundred thousand free settlers in 1841. Free men soon demanded, and got, free government. Transportation to New South Wales was finally abolished in 1840, and two years later a Legislative Council was set up, most of whose members were elected by popular vote.

Wool founded the prosperity of the country, and in time

ousted Spanish and German supplies from the world's principal markets. In 1797 a retired Army officer, John MacArthur, had obtained a few merino sheep from the Cape of Good Hope, and his breeding experiments in due course established the famous Australian flocks and changed the whole economy of the continent. The turning-point had been the discovery of the Bathurst Plains, beyond the Blue Mountains. Here and to the south of Sydney, and on the Darling Downs to the north, were great sheep-runs, mile after mile of lonely grazing land, open, grassy downs, inhabited only by a few shepherds and thousands upon thousands of silent, soft-footed sheep moving ever farther into the interior. The flocks multiplied swiftly: by 1850 there were more than sixteen million sheep in Australia. This was over sixteen times more sheep than there were men and women. The wool trade for the year was worth nearly two million pounds in sterling.

The British Government however distrusted sheep-farming. Not only did it claim that all land under British rule was Crown property, but the Colonial Office was much influenced by Gibbon Wakefield's advocacy of systematic and concentrated colonisation. Wakefield maintained that settlement, wherever it took place, should be controlled and planned, and that to allow individuals to spread haphazard into the interior would hinder administration and reduce the value of the land already settled. His theories had much to commend them, but were quite unsuited to Australia. A series of Land Acts, designed to make land more difficult to obtain by enforcing a minimum price, soon broke down. "Squatters," who needed thousands of acres for their sheep-runs and neither could nor would pay a pound, or even five shillings, for their grazing, struck out into the emptiness and took what they wanted, arguing with force that the land belonged to the people of the colony and that they should be given every facility to occupy it. The Colonial Office surrendered to the pressure of events. The squatters were there to stay, and soon became the most important section of the community. The British Government first compromised by instituting licences which gave them some legal standing, and in 1847 authorised the granting of pastoral leases for a term of years, at the end of which the squatter was to have the first right to purchase the land at its unimproved value.

*   *   *   *   *

Long before 1850 the settlement of other parts of Australia had begun. The first to be made from the mother-colony of Port Jackson was in the island of Tasmania, or Van Diemen's Land as it was then called; at Hobart in 1804; and two years later at Launceston. Like New South Wales, Tasmania at first encountered many difficulties. The penal settlements at Macquarie Harbour and Port Arthur had evil reputations; rule was by terror and the labour-gang, and many convicts escaped and lived by bushranging, attacking lonely houses at night, and raiding stock-farms when the men were away. Unlike the rest of Australia, where the aboriginal inhabitants, few in number, scattered over vast areas, and, very primitive, scarcely resisted the white settlers, Tasmania had aborigines who were fairly numerous and comparatively advanced. Their defeat was inevitable; their end was tragic. The Black Drive of 1830 was a failure. The entire forces of the colony, organised at a cost of £30,000, attempted in vain to pen the natives in a reserve. But the Tasmanian tribes were extinct by the beginning of the twentieth century.

Tasmania developed in much the same way as New South Wales, and had become a separate colony in 1825. Prosperity came from wool and whaling, and brought a solid upsurge in population. In 1820 there were 6,500 settlers, mostly convicts; twenty years later the population numbered 68,000 and was mostly free. An elected Legislative Council was granted in 1850, and the abolition of transportation three years later placed Tasmania on an equal footing with New South Wales, and enabled her to participate in the general grant of responsible government.

From Tasmania a settlement was made at Port Phillip in 1835. At first it was administered by New South Wales, but the settlers quickly demanded independence, and in 1848 they withdrew all other candidates for the Legislative Council and elected Earl Grey, Secretary of State for the Colonies, as "Member for Melbourne." Grey was the son of the Earl Grey of the Reform Bill. The move succeeded: within a few months the Colonial Office agreed to the separation, and in 1851 the new colony of Victoria, complete with representative institutions, was established, with its capital at Melbourne. The young Queen gave her name to this new offshoot of the English-speaking peoples. Its capital commemorates the Whig Prime Minister whom she had found to be the most agreeable of her advisers, and who was now no more.

The third offspring of New South Wales was Queensland. It grew up round the town of Brisbane, but developed more slowly and did not become a separate colony until 1859. By then two other settlements had arisen on the Australian coasts, both independently of New South Wales and the other colonies. In 1834 a body known as "the Colonisation Commissioners for South Australia" had been set up in London, and two years later the first settlers landed near Adelaide. The city was named after William IV's Queen. South Australia was never a convict settlement. It was organised by a group of men under the influence of Gibbon Wakefield, whose elaborate theories were now put into practice. On the whole they succeeded, though a system of dual control by which responsibility was divided between the Government and the Colonisation, or Land, Commissioners gave so much trouble that the Commissioners were abolished in 1842. Within seven years the colony numbered 52,000 inhabitants, and had been substantially enriched by the discovery of copper deposits. Along with the eastern colonies, it was presently granted representative institutions.

The other colony, Western Australia, had a very different history. Founded in 1829, it nearly died at birth. With much less fertile soil than the eastern colonies and separated from them by vast and uninhabitable desert, it suffered greatly from lack of labour. Convicts, which the other colonies deemed an obstacle to progress, seemed the only solution, and the British Government, once again encumbered with prisoners, eagerly accepted an invitation to send some out to Perth. In 1849 a penal settlement was established, with much money to finance it. Thus resuscitated, the population trebled within the next ten years, but Western Australia did not obtain representative institutions until 1870, after the convict settlement had been abolished, nor full self-government till 1890.

*　　*　　*　　*　　*

In 1848 gold had been discovered in California, and among the prospectors who crossed the Pacific to try their luck was a certain Edward Hargraves. A few months of digging brought him small success, but he noticed that the gold-bearing rocks of California resembled those near Bathurst, in New South Wales. He returned to Australia early in 1851 to test his theory. The first pans of earth proved him right. News of the discovery leaked out, and within a few weeks the Australian Gold Rush had begun.

The gold fever swept the eastern colonies. The whole of Australia seemed to be on the move, marching out to Bathurst, Ballarat, or Bendigo, with picks and shovels on their shoulders, pots and basins round their waists, an excited, feverish crowd, pouring into mining towns that had sprung up overnight, fully equipped with gambling saloons, bars, and brothels. The Victorian goldfields soon had a population of nearly 100,000. Not all were "diggers," as the miners came to be called, and the hotel-keepers, store-keepers, prostitutes, and other toilers usually fared best. A penniless lollipop-seller made £6,000 a year by opening a public-house on the road to Ballarat. When the miners flocked back to Melbourne or Sydney their money vanished in crazy extravagance and ostentation. Horses were shod with golden shoes, men lit their pipes with banknotes, so the stories ran, and a bridal party attended a wedding in bright pink velvet. When fortunes could be made and lost overnight there seemed no point in steady employment. Squatters lost their shepherds, business houses their clerks, ships their crews. Early in 1852 there were only two policemen left in Melbourne; more than fifty had gone off to the goldfields. Wages doubled and trebled; prices rose fantastically, and the values of land changed with bewildering rapidity. The other colonies, including New Zealand, lost great numbers of men to the goldfields. In a single year 95,000 immigrants entered Victoria; in five months 4,000 men out of a total population, including women and children, of 50,000 left Tasmania for Victoria.

Keeping the peace, settling disputed claims, providing transport, housing, and enough food to stop famine was a grievous burden for the new administration at Melbourne, most of whose staff had also deserted to the goldfields. For some time there were no more than forty-four soldiers in the whole of Victoria, and in 1853 fifty policemen had to be sent out from London. The diggers probably enjoyed the turbulence they created in the mining towns, but they had a serious grievance against the Government. As with the squatters, the Crown claimed ownership of the land, and demanded a licence fee.

The fee was fiercely resented and very difficult to collect, and after many threats the diggers exploded into violence.

On October 6, 1854, a digger was killed in a fight near the Eureka Hotel in Ballarat. The hotel-keeper, Bentley, his wife, and a man named Farrell were accused, but acquitted in spite of the evidence. Ten days later the diggers burned down the hotel, and four of their leaders were arrested. The diggers were now in dangerous mood. They formed the Ballarat Reform League, and issued a political programme which demanded the abolition of licence fees and contained four of the six points of the English Chartists. On November 30 a search for unlicensed miners caused a riot. Led by one Peter Lalor, the diggers began to drill and build a stockade. The local military commander, Captain Thomas, acted with speed and wisdom. He determined to attack before the movement spread. With three hundred men, mainly soldiers, he carried the stockade with a bayonet charge, killing thirty rebels and capturing over a hundred and twenty.

Thus ended what might have become a serious rebellion. Licence fees were soon afterwards abolished and replaced by an export duty on gold. The miners were given the franchise and peace was restored. In the next few years independent diggers were replaced by mining companies, which alone had the resources to carry on underground work. Much the same happened in New South Wales, the only other colony where gold was discovered at this time. Between 1851 and 1861 £124,000,000 worth of it was raised. A more permanent enrichment was the increase in Australian population, which now rose to over a million.

Wool and agriculture at first were deeply smitten by the rush for gold, and squatters who lost their shepherds cursed its discovery. But Australia gained in the end. The squatter prospered by the establishment of better roads and more railways. Food was needed, and over a million acres were soon under cultivation. The economy of the country, hitherto far too dependent on wool, thus achieved a balance.

The political repercussions were far-reaching. The increase of population, trade, and revenue made it imperative to reform the makeshift constitutions of 1850, and after long discussion in the colonies a number of schemes were laid before the Colonial Office and approved by the home Government. Between 1855 and 1859 two-chamber Parliaments, elected by popular vote and with Ministers responsible to the Lower House, were introduced in all the antipodean states except Western Australia, where, as already related, self-government came later.

Great changes were still to unroll, and Australia as we now know it was born in 1901 by the association of the colonies in a Commonwealth, with a new capital at Canberra. Federation came late and slowly to the southern continent, for the lively, various, widely separated settlements cherished their own self-rule. No threat or pressure had yet arisen from Asia to the north which would generate an overriding sense of unity. This was to come. Even to-day most of the Australian population dwells in the settlements founded in the nineteenth century. The heart of the country, over a million square miles in extent, has attracted delvers after metals and ranchers of cattle, but it remains largely uninhabited. The silence of the bush and the loneliness of the desert are only disturbed by the passing of some transcontinental express, the whirr of a boomerang, or the drone of a pilotless missile.

* * * * *

Twelve hundred miles to the east of Australia lie the islands of New Zealand. Here, long before they were discovered by Europeans, a Polynesian warrior race, the Maoris, had sailed across the Pacific from the north-east and established a civilisation notable for the brilliance of its art and the strength of its military system. When Captain Cook visited them towards the end of the eighteenth century he judged that they numbered about a hundred thousand. This was probably an overestimate, but here nevertheless was a first formidable obstacle to European colonisation, a cultured people long in possession of the land, independent in spirit and skilled in warfare. Soon after Cook's discovery a small English community gained a footing in the Bay of Islands in the far north, but they were mostly whalers and sealers, shipwrecked mariners, and a few escaped convicts from Australia, enduring a lonely, precarious, and somewhat disreputable existence. They were tolerated by the Maori chiefs, whom they supplied with firearms. They constituted no great threat to Maori life or lands. Resistance to English colonisation was fortified by the arrival of Christian missionaries. In 1814 the Reverend Samuel Marsden set up a mission station in this same Bay of Islands. He was joined by other clerics, and Christianity quickly gained a large ascendancy over the Maoris, many of whom became proselytisers. The missionaries struggled to defeat the power of the traders, and for many years they opposed, in the interests of the Maoris, all schemes for admitting English immigrants. For a time they succeeded, and the Australian colonies had been established for half a century before the first official English settlement was founded. A move to colonise the islands had nevertheless long been afoot in London, impelled by a group of men around Gibbon Wakefield, who had already so markedly influenced the future of Canada and Australia. Wakefield and his friends had founded a New Zealand Association, of which Lord Durham was a member. But the Government was hostile. The missionaries denounced the project as disastrous to the natives, and the Colonial Office refused to sanction its plans.

Wakefield however was resolute, and in 1838 his Association formed a private joint-stock company for the colonisation of New Zealand, and a year later dispatched an expedition under his younger brother. Over a thousand settlers went with them, and they founded the site of Wellington in the North Island. News that France was contemplating the annexation of New Zealand compelled the British Government to act. Instead of sanctioning Wakefield's expedition they sent out a man-of-war, under the command of Captain Hobson, to treat with the Maoris for the recognition of British sovereignty. In February 1840 Hobson concluded the Treaty of Waitangi with the Maori chiefs. By this the Maoris ceded to Great Britain all the rights and powers of sovereignty in return for confirmation in "the full and exclusive possession of their lands and estates."

Then, but not till then, the company received official recognition. Two powers were thus established, the Governor at Auckland at the top of the North Island, which Hobson had chosen as the capital, and the company at Wellington. They championed different interests and opposing policies. The company wanted land, as much and as soon as possible. The treaty and the Colonial Office said it belonged to the Maoris. The two authorities struggled and bickered throughout the forties. The treaty was bitterly denounced by the company's settlers, and in 1843 Joseph Somes, Governor of the company, wrote to the Colonial Secretary: "We have always had very serious doubts whether the Treaty of Waitangi, made with naked savages by a consul invested with no plenipotentiary powers, without ratification by the Crown, could be treated by lawyers as anything but a praiseworthy device for amusing and pacifying savages for the moment." The "naked savages" however were not to be caught. The treaty with Hobson clearly distinguished between the shadow of sovereignty, which they surrendered, and the substance of property, which they retained. The land was their life-blood. "By woman and land are men lost" ran the Maori proverb, and the older chiefs realised that if they lost their land their tribal life would be extinguished. The ingenuity of their laws exasperated settlers who had innocently purchased land for hard cash and found themselves denied possession because the tribe's inalienable rights over the soil were unaffected by private bargains. Nevertheless by 1859 the settlers had occupied seven million acres in the North Island and over thirty-two million acres in the South, where the Maoris were fewer.

The result was the Maori wars, a series of intermittent local conflicts lasting from 1843 to 1869. The scene of the fighting moved from place to place. By the middle of the sixties twenty thousand troops were engaged. The fanatical cult of the Hauhans and the skill of Te Kooti, a guerrilla leader of genius, taxed all the resources of the colony. The Maoris fought magnificently, and the admiration of the Regular officers for their opponents sharpened their dislike of the settlers. But by 1869 the force of the movement was spent and the risings were defeated. Thereafter the enlightened policy of Sir Donald MacLean, the Minister for Native Affairs, produced a great improvement. The settlers gained some security of tenure. The Maoris realised that the British had come to stay. A series of Native Land Acts, passed in the sixties, protected them against extermination; in 1867 they secured direct representation in the New Zealand legislature, and after declining to 37,000 souls in 1871 by the 1951 census they numbered nearly 100,000.

Despite these years of strife the colony continued to expand. Wakefield, anxious to overcome the opposition of the missionaries, ingeniously persuaded both the Free Church of Scotland and the Church of England to co-operate in establishing two new settlements. These, at Otago and Canterbury, were remarkable applications of his theories. Both were in the South Island, and from 1860 until 1906 it was the South Island, prosperous and comparatively immune from the Maori wars, which contained most of the population. By 1868 the British numbered only about a quarter of a million; twelve years later there were nearly twice as many.

Peace brought prosperity. Great flocks of sheep were reared on the famous Canterbury Plains of the South Island, and a native Corriedale cross-breed was evolved. In the eighteen-sixties gold was found in Otago and Canterbury and there was a temporary boom. The Australian gold discoveries and the swift rise in prices in Melbourne and Sydney gave agriculture a flying start. Despite a depression in the eighties, the prosperity of New Zealand has continued to grow ever since. The invention of the refrigerator enabled the colony to compete with European and English producers thirteen thousand miles away. The co-operative movement, especially in dairy-farming, helped small farmers with little capital to build up an industry of remarkable magnitude, and the Dominion of New Zealand soon possessed the highest external trade in proportion to its numbers of any nation in the world.

*   *   *   *   *

New Zealand's political development was no less rapid. Founded in the days of the Durham Report and the first experiments with colonial self-government in Canada, she obtained by the Constitution Act of 1852 a broad measure of independence. Her problems did not, as in the older colonies, centre on the demand for responsible government, but on relations between the central and provincial administrations. Inland travel was so difficult that until late in the nineteenth century the colony remained a number of small, scattered settlements, all differing in the circumstances of their foundation and the character of their interests. This was recognised in the Constitution Act, which set up a number of provincial councils on a democratic basis, each to a considerable extent independent of the General Assembly.

Conflict between the provincial assemblies and the central administration troubled New Zealand politics for twenty years. Some provinces were wealthy, others less so. Otago and Canterbury, stimulated by the discovery of gold, became rich and prosperous, while the settlers in the North Island, harassed by the Maori wars, grew more and more impoverished. At one time Otago and Canterbury wanted to secede. Reform came in 1875, when the constitution was modified, the provinces were abolished, local administration was placed in the hands of county councils, and the powers of the central Government were greatly increased. Thus, on a smaller scale, New Zealand faced and mastered all the problems of federal government thirty years before Australia. Indeed her political vitality is no less astonishing than her economic vigour. The tradition and prejudices of the past weighed less heavily than in the older countries. Many of the reforms introduced into Great Britain by the Liberal Government of 1906, and then regarded as extreme innovations, had already been accepted by New Zealand. Industrial arbitration, old-age pensions, factory legislation, State insurance and medical service, housing Acts, all achieved between 1890 and the outbreak of the First World War, and State support for co-operative production, testified to the survival and fertility, even in the remote and unfamiliar islands of the Pacific, of the British political genius.

BOOK ELEVEN

THE
GREAT REPUBLIC

American Epic

THE year 1815 had marked the end of a period of American development. Up to this time the life of the continent had been moulded largely by forces from Europe, but with the conclusion of the war of 1812 against England America turned in upon herself and with her back to the Atlantic looked towards the West. The years following the Peace of Ghent are full of the din of the Westward advance. In politics the vehement struggles of Federalist and Republican were replaced by what a contemporary journalist called "the era of good feelings." But underneath the calm surface of the first decade lay the bitter rivalry of sectional interests which were soon to assume permanent and organised party forms. As in all post-war periods, the major political issue was that of finance. The ideas of Alexander Hamilton on Protection and banking were reluctantly accepted by the Republican administration under the stress of war conditions. The tariff of 1816 had created a régime of Protection under which New England turned from her shipping interests to manufacture and laid the foundations of her nineteenth-century prosperity. The old suspicions of Jefferson about a Federal banking system were overcome, and in 1816 a charter replacing the one which had expired was issued for the foundation of a new Federal Bank.

The ties with Europe were slowly and inexorably broken. Outstanding disputes between England and America were settled by a series of commissions. The boundaries of Canada were fixed, and both countries agreed to a mutual pact of disarmament upon that storm centre, the Great Lakes. In

1819, after straggling warfare in Spanish Florida, led by the hero of New Orleans, Andrew Jackson, the Spanish Government finally yielded the territory to the United States for five million dollars. Spain had withdrawn from the Northern continent for ever.

But the turmoils of European politics were to threaten America once again for the last time for many years to come. The sovereigns of the Old World were bound together to maintain the principle of monarchy and to co-operate in intervening in any country which showed signs of rebellion against existing institutions. The policy of this Holy Alliance had aroused the antagonism of Britain, who had refused to intervene in the internal affairs of Italy in 1821. The new crisis came in Spain. Bourbon France, burning to achieve respectability in the new Europe, sent an army across the Pyrenees to restore the Spanish monarchy. Russia would have liked to go farther. The Czar of Russia had world-wide interests, including large claims to the western coastline of North America, which he now reaffirmed by Imperial decree. Rumours also spread to Washington that the reactionary Powers of Europe, having supported the restoration of the Bourbons in Spain, might promote similar activities in the New World to restore Bourbon sovereignty there. In Southern America lay the Spanish colonies, which had in their turn thrown off the yoke of their mother country.

The British Government under Canning offered to co-operate with the United States in stopping the extension of this threatening principle of intervention to the New World. Britain announced that she recognised the sovereignty of the Latin republics in South America. Meanwhile President Monroe acted independently and issued his message to Congress proclaiming the principles later known as the Monroe Doctrine. This famous Doctrine, as has been related, was at once a warning against interference on the part of any European Powers in the New World and a statement of the intention of America to play no part in European politics. With this valedictory message America concentrated upon her own affairs. A new generation of politicians was rising. The old veterans of the days of the Constitution had most of them vanished from the scene, though Jefferson and Madison lingered on in graceful retirement in their Virginian homes.

*　　*　　*　　*　　*

Westward lay the march of American Empire. Within thirty years of the establishment of the Union nine new states had been formed in the Mississippi valley, and two in the borders of New England. As early as 1769 men like Daniel Boone had pushed their way into the Kentucky country, skirmishing with the Indians. But the main movement over the mountains began during the War of Independence. The migration of the eighteenth century took two directions: the advance westward towards the Ohio, with its settlement of Kentucky and Tennessee, and the occupation of the north-west forest regions, the fur-traders' domain, beyond Lake Erie. The colonisation of New England and the eastern coastline of America had been mainly the work of powerful companies, aided by the English Crown or by feudal proprietors with chartered rights. But here in the new lands of the West any man with an axe and a rifle could carve for himself a rude frontier home. By 1790 there were thirty-five thousand settlers in the Tennessee country, and double that number in Kentucky. By 1800 there were a million Americans west of the mountain ranges of the Alleghenies. From these new lands a strong, self-reliant Western breed took its place in American life. Modern American democracy was born and cradled in the valley of the Mississippi. The foresight of the first independent Congress of the United States had proclaimed for all time the principle that when new territories gained a certain population they should be admitted to statehood upon an equality with the existing partners of the Union. It is a proof of the quality and power of the Westerners that eleven of the eighteen Presidents of the United States between 1828 and 1901 were either born or passed the greater part of their lives in the valley of the Mississippi. Well might Daniel Webster upon an anniversary of the landing of the Pilgrim Fathers declaim the celebrated passage: "New England farms, houses, villages, and churches spread over and adorn the immense extent from the Ohio to Lake Erie and stretch along from the Alleghanies [*sic*] onwards beyond the Miamis and towards the falls of St Anthony. Two thousand miles westward from the Rock where their fathers landed may now be seen the sons of pilgrims cultivating smiling fields, rearing towns and villages, and cherishing, we trust, the patrimonial blessings of wise institutions, of liberty and religion. . . . Ere long the sons of the pilgrims will be upon the shores of the Pacific."

America was swelling rapidly in numbers as well as in area. Between 1790 and 1820 the population increased from four to nine and a half millions. Thereafter it almost doubled every twenty years. Nothing like such a rate of growth had before been noted in the world, though it was closely paralleled in contemporary England. The settlement of great bodies of men in the West was eased by the removal of the Indian tribes from the regions east of the Mississippi. They had been defeated when they fought as allies of Britain in the war of 1812. Now it became Federal policy to eject them. The lands thus thrown open were made available in smaller units and at lower prices than in earlier years to the incoming colonists—for we might as well use this honourable word about them, unpopular though it may now be. Colonisation, in the true sense, was the task that engaged the Western pioneers. Farmers from stony New England were tilling the fertile empty territories to the south of the Great Lakes, while in the South the Black Belt of Alabama and Mississippi proved fruitful soil for the recent art of large-scale cotton cultivation.

But this ceaseless expansion to the West also changed the national centre of gravity, and intense stresses arose of interest as well as of feeling. The Eastern states, North and South alike, presently found their political power challenged by these settler communities, and the lure of pioneering created the fear of a labour shortage in the Eastern factories. In fact the gap was filled by new immigrants from Europe. As the frontier line rolled westward the new communities rising rapidly to statehood forced their own problems and desires upon the exhilarated but also embarrassed Federal Government. The East feared the approaching political dominance of the democratic West. The West resented the financial and economic bias of the Eastern moneyed classes. The forces of divergence grew strong, and only the elasticity of the Federal system around the core of state rights prevented the usual conflict between a mother country and its sturdy children.

The political history of these years between 1815 and 1830 is confused through the lack of adequate national party organisations to express the bitter sectional conflicts and hatreds in the North, South, and West. By 1830 the situation cleared and the great parties of the future stood opposed. With the growth of Federal legislation and the creation of a national economic framework of tariffs, banks, and land policies the Union felt the stress of state jealousies and rival interests. The expansion to the West tilted the political balance in favour of the new Western states, and strenuously the older forces in the North and South resisted the rising power of democracy within the Federal State. They had to confront not only the desires of the West, but also those of the small planters in the

South and of the working men in the industrial North. Many of these people now for the first time began to receive the vote as universal manhood suffrage was more widely adopted. The electorate was expanding and eager to make its voice heard. At the same time the convention system was introduced into American politics. Candidates for the Presidency and for lesser public office in the states gradually ceased to be nominated by restricted party caucuses. Instead they were selected at meetings of delegates representing a variety of local and specialised opinion. This obliged the would-be President and other public office-holders to be more responsive to the divergences of popular will. Politicians of conservative mind like Henry Clay and John C. Calhoun feared the menacing signs of particularism and the consequent threat to the Union. These men formulated what they called the "American System." But their policy was merely a re-expression of the ideas of Hamilton. They sought to harmonise economic interests within a Federal framework. As Calhoun had said in 1817, "We are greatly and rapidly—I was about to say fearfully—growing. This is our pride and our danger, our weakness and our strength. . . . Let us then bind the Republic together with a perfect system of roads and canals. Protection would make the parts adhere more closely. . . . It would form a new and most powerful cement."

Public works were set on foot; steamboats appeared upon the Mississippi, and the concentration of trade in the Gulf of Mexico roused alarm in the Atlantic states, who saw themselves being deprived of profitable markets. But they hastened themselves to compete with this increasing activity. In 1817 the state of New York began the construction of the Erie Canal, which was to make New York City the most prosperous of the Eastern seaports. The great Cumberland high-road across the Ohio to Illinois was built with Federal money, and a network of roads was to bind the eager West to the Eastern states. But the history of the American nineteenth century is dominated by the continually threatened cleavage of East and West, and, upon the Atlantic seaboard, of the Northern and Southern states. In the early years of the century the keynote of politics was the rival bidding of Northern and Southern politicians for the votes and support of the Western states.

*   *   *   *   *

The issue of slavery was soon to trouble the relations of the North and South. In 1819 a Bill was tabled in Congress to admit Missouri as a state to the Union. This territory lay inside the bounds of the Louisiana Purchase, where the future of slavery had not so far been decided by Federal law. As the people of Missouri proposed to allow slavery in their draft constitution the Northerners looked upon this Bill as an aggressive move to increase the voting power of the South. A wild campaign of mutual recrimination followed. But with the increasing problem of the West facing them both, North and South could not afford to quarrel, and the angry sectional strife stirred up by this Bill ended in a compromise which was to hold until the middle of the century. Missouri was admitted as a slave-holding state, and slavery was prohibited north of latitude 36° 30′ within the existing territories of the Union which did not yet enjoy statehood. As part of the compromise Maine, which had just severed itself from Massachusetts, was admitted as a free state, making the division between slave and free equal, being twelve each. Far-seeing men realised the impending tragedy of this division. John Quincy Adams noted in his diary, "I considered it at once as the knell of the Union. I take it for granted that the present question is a mere preamble—a title-page to a great, tragic volume."

It was this cultured New Englander, son of the second President of the United States, who succeeded Monroe in 1825.

The so-called era of good feelings was coming to a close, and the four years of his Presidency were to reveal the growth of lively party politics. All the political and economic interests of the Eastern states were forced on to the defensive by the rapid expansion of the West.

The West grouped itself around the figure of the frontier General Andrew Jackson, who claimed to represent the true Jeffersonian principles of democracy against the corrupt moneyed interests of the East. Adams received the support of those classes who feared majority rule and viewed with alarm the growing power of the farmers and settlers of the frontier. The issue between the two factions was joined in 1828, when Jackson stood as rival candidate against Adams's re-election. In the welter of this election two new parties were born, the Democrats and the National Republicans, later called the Whigs. It was the fiercest campaign since Jefferson had driven the elder Adams from office in 1800. As the results came in it was seen that Adams had won practically nothing outside New England, and that in the person of Andrew Jackson the West had reached controlling power. Here at last was an American President who had no spiritual contacts whatever with the Old World or its projection on the Atlantic shore, who represented at the White House the spirit of the American frontier. To many it seemed that democracy had triumphed indeed.

There were wild scenes at Washington at the inauguration of the new President, dubbed by his opponent Adams as "the brawler from Tennessee." But to the men of the West Jackson was their General, marching against the political monopoly of the moneyed classes. The complications of high politics caused difficulties for the backwoodsman. His simple mind, suspicious of his opponents, made him open to influence by more partisan and self-seeking politicians. In part he was guided by Martin Van Buren, his Secretary of State. But he relied even more heavily for advice on political cronies of his own choosing, who were known as the "Kitchen Cabinet," because they were not office-holders. Jackson was led to believe that his first duty was to cleanse the stables of the previous régime. His dismissal of a large number of civil servants brought the spoils system, long prevalent in many states, firmly into the Federal machine.

Two great recurring problems in American politics, closely related, demanded the attention of President Andrew Jackson —the supremacy of the Union and the organisation of a national economy. Protection favoured the interests of the North at the expense of the South, and in 1832 the state of South Carolina determined to challenge the right of the Federal Government to impose a tariff system, and, echoing the Virginia and Kentucky resolutions of 1798, expounded in its most extreme form the doctrine of state rights. In the party struggles which followed the votes of the Western states held the balance. Their burning question was the regulation of the sale of public land by the Federal Government. As the historian S. E. Morison puts it, "It was all a game of balance between North, South, and West, each section offering to compromise a secondary interest in order to get votes for a primary interest. The South would permit the West to plunder the public domain, in return for a reduction of the tariff. The North offered the tempting bait of distribution [of the proceeds from land sales for public works in the West] in order to maintain protection. On the outcome of this sectional balance depended the alignment of parties in the future; even of the Civil War itself. Was it to be North and West against South, or South and West against North?" [1]

The debates on these themes in the American Senate con-

[1] *The Oxford History of the United States* (1927), vol. i, p. 391.

tained the finest examples of American oratory. In this battle of giants the most imposing of them all was Daniel Webster, of Massachusetts, the best speaker of his day. He it was who stated the case for the Union and refuted the case of South Carolina in one of the most famous of American speeches. His words enshrined the new feeling of nation-wide patriotism that was gathering strength, at least in the North. They show that New England in particular was moving away from the sectional views which had prevailed in 1812. A broader sense of loyalty to the Union was developing. "It is to that Union," Webster declared in the Senate, "we owe our safety at home, and our consideration and dignity abroad. It is to that Union that we are chiefly indebted for whatever makes us most proud of our country. That Union we reached only by the discipline of our virtues in the severe school of adversity. It had its origin in the necessities of disordered finance, prostrate commerce, and ruined credit. Under its benign influences these great interests immediately awoke, as from the dead, and sprang forth with newness of life. Every year of its duration has teemed with fresh proofs of its utility and its blessings; and although our territory has stretched out wider and wider, and our population spread farther and farther, they have not outrun its protection, or its benefits. It has been to us all a copious foundation of national, social and personal happiness.

"I have not allowed myself, Sir," he went on, "to look beyond the Union, to see what might lie hidden in the dark recess behind. I have not coolly weighed the chances of preserving liberty when the bonds that unite us together shall be broken asunder. I have not accustomed myself to hang over the precipice of disunion to see whether, with my short sight, I can fathom the depth of the abyss below; nor could I regard him as a safe counsellor in the affairs of this Government, whose thoughts should be mainly bent on considering, not how the Union may be best preserved, but how tolerable might be the condition of the people when it should be broken up and destroyed. While the Union lasts we have high, exciting, gratifying prospects spread out before us, for us and our children. Beyond that I seek not to penetrate the veil. God grant that in my day at least that curtain may not rise! God grant that on my vision never may be opened what lies behind! When my eyes shall be turned to behold for the last time the sun in heaven, may I not see him shining on the broken and dishonoured fragments of a once glorious Union; on states dissevered, discordant, belligerent; on a land rent with civil feuds, or drenched, it may be, in fraternal blood! Let their last feeble and lingering glance rather behold the gorgeous ensign of the Republic, now known and honoured throughout the earth, still full high advanced, its arms and trophies streaming in their original lustre, not a stripe erased or polluted, not a single star obscured, bearing for its motto no such miserable interrogatory as 'What is all this worth?' nor those other words of delusion and folly, 'Liberty first and Union afterwards,' but everywhere, spread all over in characters of living light, blazing on all its ample folds, as they float over the sea and over the land, and in every wind under the whole heavens, that other sentiment, dear to every true American heart—Liberty *and* Union, now and for ever, one and inseparable!"

On the Indiana frontier a young man was moved by this speech. His name was Abraham Lincoln.

President Jackson himself was impressed, and in his warlike approach to politics was prepared to coerce South Carolina by force. But a tactful compromise was reached. The tariff was lowered but rendered permanent, and the Force Act, authorising the President to use the Army if necessary to collect the customs duties, was declared null and void by

South Carolina. Here then for a space the matter was left. But the South Carolina theory of "nullification" showed the danger of the Republic, and with the prophetic instinct of the simple frontiersman Jackson pointed to the future: "The next pretext will be the negro or slavery question."

But the next serious issue was the Federal Bank, whose charter was due to come up for renewal in 1836. The National Republicans, or Whigs, now led by Clay, preferred to force it before the 1832 Presidential election. Jackson had long been expected to attack the moneyed power in politics. The position of the Bank illustrated the economic stresses which racked the American Republic. "It was an economic conflict," wrote Charles Beard, "that happened to take a sectional form: the people of the agricultural West had to pay tribute to Eastern capitalists on the money they had borrowed to buy land, make improvements, and engage in speculation." The contest was joined in the election. The triumphant return of Jackson to power was in fact a vote against the Bank of the United States. It was in vain that Daniel Webster was briefed as counsel for the Bank. Jackson informed the Bank president, "I do not dislike your bank more than all banks, but ever since I read the history of the South Sea Bubble I have been afraid of banks." He refused to consent to the passing of a Bill to renew the charter, and without waiting for the Bank to die a natural death in 1836 he decided at once to deprive it of Government deposits, which were sent to local banks throughout the states. When the charter expired it was not renewed, and for nearly thirty years there was no centralised banking system in the United States. The union of Western and Southern politicians had had their revenge upon the North. The Radicalism of the frontier had won a great political contest. Jackson's occupation of the Presidency had finally broken the "era of good feelings" which had followed the war with Britain, and by his economic policy he had split the old Republican Party of Jefferson. The Radicalism of the West was looked upon with widespread suspicion throughout the Eastern states, and Jackson's official appointments had not been very happy.

The election in 1836 of Jackson's lieutenant, Van Buren, meant the continuation of Jacksonian policy, while the old General himself returned in triumph to his retirement in Tennessee. The first incursions of the West into high politics had revealed the slumbering forces of democracy on the frontier and shown the inexperience of their leaders in such affairs.

*　　*　　*　　*　　*

The westward tide rolled on, bearing with it new problems of adjustment. The generation of the 1840's saw their culmination. During these years there took place the annexation of Texas, a war with Mexico, the conquest of California, and the settlement of the Oregon boundary with Great Britain. Adventurous Americans in search of land and riches had been since 1820 crossing the Mexican boundary into the Texas country, which belonged to the Republic of Mexico, freed from Spain in 1821. While this community was growing, American sailors on the Pacific coast, captains interested in the China trade, established themselves in the ports of the Mexican Province of California. Pioneers pushed their way overland in search of skins and furs, and by 1826 reached the mission stations of the Province. The Mexicans, alarmed at the appearance of these settlers, vainly sought to stem the flood; for Mexican Governments were highly unstable, and in distant Provinces their writ hardly ran. But there appeared on the scene a new military dictator, Santa Anna, determined to strengthen Mexican authority, and at once a revolt broke out. In November 1835 the Americans in Texas erected an autonomous state and raised the Lone Star flag. The Mexicans, under Santa Anna, marched northwards. At the Mission House of the Alamo in March 1836 a small body of Texans, fighting to the last man, was exterminated in one of the epic fights of American history by a superior Mexican force. The whole Province was aroused. Under the leadership of General Sam Houston from Tennessee a force was raised, and in savage fighting the Mexican army of Santa Anna was in its turn destroyed and its commander captured at San Jacinto River. The Texans had stormed the positions with the cry "Remember the Alamo!" The independence of Texas was recognised by Santa Anna. His act was repudiated later by the Mexican Government, but their war effort was exhausted, and the Texans organised themselves into a republic, electing Sam Houston as President.

For the next ten years the question of the admission of Texas as a state of the Union was a burning issue in American politics. As each new state demanded entry into the Union so the feeling for and against slavery ran higher. The great Abolitionist journalist, William Lloyd Garrison, called for a secession of the Northern states if the slave state of Texas was admitted to the Union. The Southerners, realising that Texan votes would give them a majority in the Senate if this vast territory was admitted as a number of separate states, clamoured for annexation. The capitalists of the East were committed, through the formation of land companies, to exploit Texas, and besides the issue of dubious stocks by these bodies vast quantities of paper notes and bonds of the new Texan Republic were floated in the United States. The speculation in these helped to split the political opposition of the Northern states to the annexation. Even more important was the conversion of many Northerners to belief in the "Manifest Destiny" of the United States. This meant that their destiny was to spread across the whole of the North American continent. The Democratic Party in the election of 1844 called for the occupation of Oregon as well as the annexation of Texas, thus holding out to the North the promise of Oregon as a counterweight to Southern Texas. The victory of the Democratic candidate, James K. Polk, was interpreted as a mandate for admitting Texas, and this was done by joint resolution of Congress in February 1845.

It remained to persuade Mexico to recognise this state of affairs, and also to fix the boundaries of Texas. President Polk was determined to push them as far south as possible, and war was inevitable. It broke out in May 1846. Meanwhile a similar train of events was unfolding on the other side of the continent. All this time American penetration of the West had continued, often with grim experiences of starvation and winter snows. Nothing could stop the migration towards the Pacific. The lure of the rich China trade and the dream of controlling the Western Ocean brought the acquisition of California to the fore, and gave her even more importance in American eyes than Texas. In June 1846 the American settlers in California, instigated from Washington, raised the Bear Flag as their standard of revolt and declared their independence on the Texan model. Soon afterwards American forces arrived and the Stars and Stripes replaced the Bear.

The American advance was rapidly gathering momentum. The Mexican army of the North was twice beaten by General Zachary Taylor, a future President. A force under General Winfield Scott was landed at Vera Cruz and marched on Mexico City. The capital fell to the Americans after a month of street fighting in September 1847. On this expedition a number of young officers distinguished themselves. They included Captain Robert E. Lee, Captain George B. McClellan,

Lieutenant Ulysses S. Grant, and Colonel Jefferson Davis.

Mexico sued for peace, and by the treaty which followed she was obliged not only to recognise the annexation of Texas, but also to cede California, Arizona, and New Mexico. Lieutenant Grant confided his impressions to his memoirs: "I do not think there was ever a more wicked war than that waged by the United States on Mexico. I thought so at the time, when I was a youngster, only I had not moral courage enough to resign." But the expansive force of the American peoples was explosive. "Manifest Destiny" was on the march, and it was unfortunate that Mexico stood in the path. The legend of Imperialism and the belief in the right of the United States to exploit both continents, North and South, which sprang from the Mexican War henceforward cast their shadow on co-operation between the South American republics and the United States.

* * * * *

The immediate gains were enormous. While the commissioners were actually debating the treaty with Mexico an American labourer in California discovered the first nugget of gold in that region. The whole economy of a sleepy Mexican province, with its age-old Spanish culture, was suddenly overwhelmed by a mad rush for gold. In 1850 the population of California was about eighty-two thousand souls. In two years the figure had risen to two hundred and seven thousand. A lawless mining society arose upon the Pacific coast. From the cities of the East and from the adjoining states men of all professions and classes of society flocked to California, many being murdered, killed in quarrels, by cold and famine, or drowned in the sea voyage round Cape Horn. The gold of California lured numbers to their death, and a few to riches beyond belief.

Oh! California,
That's the land for me;
I'm off to Sacramento
With my washbowl on my knee.

The anarchy of the gold rush brought an urgent demand for settled government in California, and the old perplexing, rasping quarrel over the admission of a new state was heard again at Washington. For the moment nothing was done, and the Californians called their own state convention and drew up a temporary constitution.

During all this time, farther to the north, another territory had been coming into being. The "Oregon Trail" had brought many men from the more crowded states of the North-East to find their homes and establish their farms along the undefined Canadian frontier to the Pacific. With the prospect of war in the South for the acquisition of Texas and California, the American Government was not anxious to embark upon a quarrel with Great Britain upon its Northern frontier. There was strong opposition by the Southerners to the acquisition of Oregon, where the Northern pioneers were opposed to slavery. Oregon would be another "free soil state." Negotiations were opened with Britain, and in spite of electioneering slogans of "Fifty-four-forty or fight" the boundary was settled in June 1846 by peaceful diplomacy along the forty-ninth parallel. This solution owed much to the accommodating nature of the Foreign Secretary in Peel's Government, Lord Aberdeen. The controversy now died down, and in 1859 the territory of Oregon reached statehood.

Among the many settlements which lay dotted over the whole of the American continent the strangest perhaps was the Mormon colony at Salt Lake City. In the spring of 1847 members of this revivalist and polygamist sect started from the state of Illinois under their prophet leader, Brigham Young, to find homes free from molestation in the West. By the summer they reached the country round Salt Lake, and two hours after their arrival they had begun establishing their homes and ploughing up the soil. Within three years a flourishing community of eleven thousand souls, combining religious fervour, philoprogenitiveness, and shrewd economic sense, had been established by careful planning in the Salt Lake country, and in 1850 the territory received recognition by the Federal Government under the name of Utah. The colony was established in a key position on the trail which led both to Oregon and California. The sale of food and goods to the travellers and adventurers who moved in both directions along this route brought riches to the Mormon settler, and Salt Lake City, soon tainted, it is true, by the introduction of more lawless and unbelieving elements, became one of the richest cities in America.

With the establishment of this peculiar colony the settlement of the continent was comprehensive. The task before the Federal Government was now to organise the Far Western territory won in the Mexican War and in the compromise with Britain. From this there rose in its final and dread form the issue of bond and free.

Slavery and Secession

IN the years following 1850 the prospects of the United States filled America with hope and Europe with envious admiration. The continent had been conquered and nourished. Exports, imports, and, most of all, internal trade, had been more than doubled in a decade. The American mercantile marine outnumbered the ships under the British flag. Nearly £50,000,000 in gold was added to the coinage in the years 1851 and 1852. More than thirty thousand miles of railway overcame the vast distances, and added economic cohesion to political unity. Here democracy, shielded by the oceans and the Royal Navy from European dangers, founded upon English institutions and the Common Law, stimulated by the impulse of the French Revolution, seemed at last to have achieved both prosperity and power. The abounding industrialism of the Eastern states was balanced and fed by an immense agriculture of yeomen farmers. In all material affairs the American people surpassed anything that history had known before.

Yet thoughtful men and travellers had for some years observed the approach of a convulsion which would grip not only the body but the soul of the United States. Of the three races who dwelt in North America, the Whites towered overwhelming and supreme. The Red Men, the original inhabitants, age-long product of the soil and climate, shrank back, pushed, exploited, but always disdainful, from the arms, and still more from the civilisation, of the transplanted European society by which they were ousted and eclipsed. The Black Men presented a problem, moral, social, economic, and political, the like of which had never before been known. It was said that both these races were downtrodden by White ascendancy as truly as animals are mastered, used, or exterminated by mankind. The proud Redskin was set upon his road to ruin by an excessive liberty. Almost all the four million Negroes were slaves.

In regions so wide and varied as those of the Union extreme divergences of interest, outlook, and culture had developed. South of the fortieth parallel and the projecting angle formed by the Mississippi and the Ohio the institution of Negro slavery had long reigned almost unquestioned. Upon this basis the whole life of the Southern states had been erected. It was a strange, fierce, old-fashioned life. An aristocracy of planters, living in rural magnificence and almost feudal state, and a multitude of smallholders, grew cotton for the world by slave-labour. Of the six million white inhabitants of the so-called "slave states" less than three hundred and fifty thousand owned slaves, and only forty thousand controlled plantations requiring a working unit of more than twenty field hands. But the three or four thousand principal slave-owners generally ruled the politics of the South as effectively as the medieval baronage had ruled England. Beneath them, but not dissociated from them, were, first, several hundred thousand small slave-owners, to whom "the peculiar institution," as it had already come to be called, was a domestic convenience; second, a strong class of yeomen farmers similar to that existing in the North; and, thirdly, a rabble of "mean whites" capable of being formed into an army.

There was a grace and ease about the life of the white men in the South that was lacking in the bustling North. It was certainly not their fault that these unnatural conditions had arisen. For two centuries the slave trade in African Negroes with the New World had been a staple enterprise in Spain, in

France, and above all in England. Vast numbers of black men, caught upon the west coast of Africa, had been transported like cattle across the Atlantic to be the property of their purchasers. They had toiled and multiplied. The bulk had become adapted to their state of life, which, though odious to Christian civilisation, was physically less harsh than African barbarism. The average Negro slave, like the medieval serf, was protected by his market value, actual and procreative, as well as by the rising standards of society, from the more senseless and brutal forms of ill-usage.

The planters of the South, and the slaves they owned, had both grown up in wide, unkempt lands without ever having known any other relationship. Now, suddenly, in the midst of the nineteenth century, dire challenge was hurled at the whole system and the society in which it was engrained. A considerable, strongly characterised, and slowly matured community found itself subjected to the baleful and scandalised glare of the Christian world, itself in vigorous and self-confident progress. They had long dwelt comfortably upon the fertile slopes of a volcano. Now began the rumblings, tremors, and exhalations which portended a frightful eruption.

It is almost impossible for us nowadays to understand how profoundly and inextricably Negro slavery was interwoven into the whole life, economy, and culture of the Southern states. The tentacles of slavery spread widely through the Northern "free" states, along every channel of business dealing and many paths of political influence. One assertion alone reveals the powerlessness of the community to shake itself free from the frightful disease which had become part of its being. It was said that over six hundred and sixty thousand slaves were held by ministers of the Gospel and members of the different Protestant Churches. Five thousand Methodist ministers owned two hundred and nineteen thousand slaves;

six thousand five hundred Baptists owned a hundred and twenty-five thousand; one thousand four hundred Episcopalians held eighty-eight thousand; and so on. Thus the institution of slavery was not only defended by every argument of self-interest, but many a Southern pulpit championed it as a system ordained by the Creator and sanctified by the Gospel of Christ.

It had not always been so. During the Revolution against King George III many Southerners had expressed the hope that slavery would eventually be abolished. But as time passed "the peculiar institution" became, in the words of Morison and Commager, "so necessary that it ceased to appear evil." [1] By the 1830's Southerners were ready to defend slavery as a positive good and a permanent basis for society. This was a striking change of opinion for which there were several reasons. The rapid growth of cotton cultivation called for a large labour force which according to Southerners could only be provided by Negroes in a state of slavery. Moreover, widespread fears had been aroused in the South by a number of slave insurrections in which some whites had been massacred. If the Negro were freed, it was asked, would a white man's life be safe? or, to press the question more closely home, a white woman's honour? In earlier times hopeful philanthropists had thought to solve the problem by shipping the Negroes back to Africa and setting them up in their own republic. The state of Liberia had thus come into existence. But attempts to carry this plan further were abandoned. It was too expensive. Besides, the Negroes preferred America. For Southerners there was an alarming example near at hand of what happened when slaves were freed. In the British West Indies, as elsewhere in the British Empire, slavery had been abolished by the Act passed in 1833. This was one of the

[1] *The Growth of the American Republic,* vol. i, p. 246.

great reforms achieved by the Whig Government of Earl Grey. The planters of the West Indies, who led a life much like that of Southern gentlemen, were paid compensation for the loss of their human property. Nevertheless their fortunes promptly and visibly declined. All this could be perceived by men of reflection on the neighbouring American mainland.

Meanwhile the North, once largely indifferent to the fate of slaves, had been converted by the 1850's to the cause of anti-slavery. For twenty years William Lloyd Garrison's newspaper, *The Liberator,* had been carrying on from Boston a campaign of the utmost virulence against the institution of slavery. This public print was not very widely read, but its language enraged the South. At the same time the American Anti-Slavery Society in New York and other humanitarian bodies were issuing vigorous tracts and periodicals. They employed scores of agents to preach Abolition up and down the land. The result was a hardening of sentiment on both sides of the question. It was hardened still further in 1852, when Harriet Beecher Stowe published *Uncle Tom's Cabin.* Her work was frankly propagandist; she used every weapon. In its pages the theoretical and religious arguments are bandied to and fro, but there was one method in which she excelled all other assailants of the evil. She presented to her readers a succession of simple, poignant incidents inseparable from a system of slavery: the breaking up of the Negro's home and family, the parting of husband and wife, the sale of the baby from the breast of its mother; the indiscriminate auction of the slaves on the death of a good employer; the impotence of the virtuous slave-owner, the cruelties of the bad; the callous traffic of the slave-dealers, and the horrors of the remote plantations, the whipping establishments to which fine ladies sent their maids for chastisement for minor faults; the aggravated problem of the quadroon and the mulatto; the almost-white slave girl sold and resold for lust; the bringing into the world of slave children indistinguishable in their colour from the dominant race—all these features of the life of a civilised, educated, modern Christian community, occupying enormous fertile regions of the earth, were introduced with every trapping of art and appeal into her pages.

Such advocacy was devastating. By the end of the year hundreds of thousands of copies of *Uncle Tom's Cabin* had been sold in the United States. In September, it is said, ten thousand copies of it were being supplied every day to a single firm of English booksellers. By the end of 1852 more than a million copies had been sold in England, probably ten times as many as had ever been sold of any other work except the Bible and the Prayer Book. *Uncle Tom's Cabin* rolled round the world in every language and was read with passion and emotion in every country. It was the herald of the storm.

* * * * *

The moral surge of the age had first suppressed, by naval power, the slave trade on the seas, and thereafter—the young Mr Gladstone notwithstanding—abolished the status of slavery throughout the British Empire. The same temper stirred alike the New England states of the Atlantic shore and the powerful, swiftly growing population of the Middle West of the American Union. A gulf of sentiment and interest opened and widened between the Northern and Southern states. Across this gulf there flashed for some years the interchanges of thought, of argument and parley. In the North many of the leaders, religious and secular, felt intensely that the whole future of the noble continent they had won lay under a curse. If it could not at once be lifted, at least it must be prevented from spreading. Nor was this passion in any degree excited, in its earliest phase, by commercial rivalry. There was no doubt that slave labour could not hold its own with free labour in tilling the soil where the climatic conditions were similar. The contrast between the activity and progress of a free state on the Ohio and the stagnation of a slave state on the opposite bank was glaringly apparent to all beholders. It was the contrast between the nineteenth century and the seventeenth. The Northern states were not undersold by the competition of the South. They also needed the cotton crop in which alone slave labour was an economic advantage. The issue was not economic, but moral. It was also social. The slave-owning aristocracy in much of the South felt a class-superiority to the business, manufacturing, and financial society of the North. The Puritan stock of the North regarded the elegant gentry of the South with something of the wrath and censure of Cromwell's Ironsides for Rupert's Cavaliers. Indeed, at many points the grim struggle which impended resembled and reproduced in its passions the antagonisms of the English Civil War.

But the actual occasion of quarrel was political and constitutional. The North held tenaciously to the Federal conceptions of Alexander Hamilton. In the South Jefferson's idea of sovereign state rights was paramount. Many of the Southern Generals, like Joseph E. Johnston, Ambrose P. Hill, and FitzHugh Lee, had never owned a slave. A Virginian colonel of the United States Army serving in Texas, Robert E. Lee, wrote that slavery was "a moral and political evil in any country," as few in an enlightened age could but acknowledge. But upon the constitutional issue all these men of the highest morale and virtue deemed themselves bound to the death to the fortunes and sovereign independence of their states. The North, it was said, was enriching itself at the expense of the South. The Yankees were jealous of a style and distinction to which vulgar commercialism could never attain. They had no right to use the Federal Constitution which the great Virginians Washington and Madison had largely founded, in order to bind the most famous states of the Union to their dictates. They did not understand the totally different conditions of Southern life. They maligned and insulted a civilisation more elevated in manners, if not in worldly wealth, than their own. They sought to impose the tyranny of their ideas upon states which had freely joined the Union for common purposes, and might as freely depart when those purposes had been fulfilled.

The old Missouri compromise of 1820, namely, that latitude 36° 30′ should divide freedom from slavery in the territories of the Louisiana Purchase, no longer satisfied the passions now aroused. By the Mexican War extensive new territories had been acquired; what principle should be applied to them? The Southerners, still dominated by that great figure of the 1812 generation, John C. Calhoun, held that the territories belonged to the states united, not to the United States, that slaves were Common Law property, and that Congress had no right to prohibit slavery in the Territories. The demand of California for admission to the Union precipitated the crisis. Many moderates had wanted to prolong the line of the Missouri compromise across the continent to the Pacific. But in California it did not meet the case. It would have run right through the middle of the state. Besides, the constitution of California prohibited slavery, and its introduction would set a precedent in those states which were to be created out of the conquests from Mexico. In January 1850 the gathering storm-clouds of slavery and secession evoked in the Senate the last of the great oratorical debates in which Calhoun, Clay, and Webster vied with one another. Henry Clay produced his last compromise in resolutions to postpone collision. California should be admitted to the Union immediately as a "free" state;

the territorial Governments in New Mexico and Utah should be organised without mentioning slavery; a stringent Fugitive Slave Law would appease the South, and the assumption of the Texas National Debt by the Federal Government the bond-holders of the North. By these mutual concessions Clay hoped to preserve the political unity of the continent. On this last oc-casion he rose and spoke for nearly two days in the Senate. Cal-houn was dying, and sat grimly silent in the Senate. One of his colleagues spoke his plea for him. "I have, Senators, believed from the first that the agitation of the subject of slavery would, if not prevented by some timely and effective measure, end in disunion. . . . The cords that bind the states together are snapping." Beneath the slavery problem lay the root fear of the Southern states that economically and politically they were being oppressed by the North and losing in the race for allies in the Western states.

Daniel Webster rose three days later: "I speak to-day for the preservation of the Union. Hear me for my cause." The voices of Webster and Clay prevailed and the compromise was adopted. Passions were for the moment stilled by what was called the "principle of popular sovereignty." This meant that when the new Territories became states the settlers should decide for themselves for or against slavery. Calhoun was already dead, and within two years Clay and Webster passed from the scene. They left behind them an uneasy calm. Meanwhile the continent developed at dizzy speed. By 1850 nine thousand miles of railway had been built; by 1861 over thirty thousand. German and Irish immigrants from Europe streamed into the new lands of the West. Agricultural ma-chinery changed the settler type. The prairie farmer replaced the backwoodsman, and the cultivation of the Great Plains began in earnest.

*   *   *   *   *

A fresh cause of divergence sprang from the choice of the transcontinental railway route. The rival interests of North and South were decisively involved, and in the political dispute the North and West drew together. The southern route was the shortest to the Pacific coast, and passed through organised territories from New Orleans to Texas and thence by the Gila valley to San Diego. The northern followed the natural trail of emigration which bound California and Oregon to the states bordering the Great Lakes. In between lay a third route through regions as yet unorganised, but in which Northern capital was invested. Senator Stephen A. Douglas of Illinois, who ardently wished to promote the settlement of the West and was heavily committed to the central line, became the champion of Northern interests. In order to organise this central zone he proposed in January 1854 a Bill establishing the territory of Nebraska. As a bait for Southern votes he included a clause embodying the conception of "popular sovereignty." This changed the issue and aggravated the dispute. People in the North had taken the compromise of 1850 to apply only to the former Mexican territories. Now it was proposed to introduce it into regions where hitherto the line of the Missouri compromise had prevailed. As these areas of the Great Plains were north of latitude 36° 30′ the new Bill implicitly repealed the Missouri Compromise Act. The Southerners wished this to be done explicitly, and Douglas agreed. This might carry slavery north of the line.

The anti-slavery forces in the North, already furious with Douglas, were determined to resist the introduction of slavery into the new territories. In May the Kansas-Nebraska Act was passed by the Senate. The new territories of the Great Plains were to be divided into Kansas and Nebraska, and the principle of "popular sovereignty" was affirmed. This Act was a signal for outbursts of agitation and violence in the Northern states. Under the Fugitive Slave Law Federal agents had already been instructed to arrest and send back to their masters slaves who had escaped into the free states. There had been innumerable minor incidents, but now, on the morrow of the Kansas-Nebraska Act, the patience of the North was at an end. The day after it came into force a Boston mob attempted to rescue a fugitive slave, Anthony Burns, who was detained for deportation to the South. It took a battalion of artillery, four platoons of marines, the sheriff's posse, and twenty-two companies of the militia to line the streets and bring the slave to the ship at Boston wharf. "It cost the United States about a hundred thousand dollars to return the slave to his master. The real bill came later, and it was paid in blood." [1]

In the new territory of Kansas there was murderous faction fighting between the free-soil and pro-slavery partisans. Slavery-men sacked the free-soil town of Lawrence, and three days later John Brown, a Puritanical mystic and militant Abolitionist from Ohio, with his four sons, dragged five slavery-men from their beds and slaughtered them as a reprisal. Over two hundred lives were lost in this local reign of terror, but John Brown escaped. At every point, in every walk of life, the opposing causes came into conflict. A Senator from Massachusetts was beaten over the head with a cane in the Senate by a South Carolina Representative till he was unconscious. All the anti-slavery elements in the North and West had coalesced after the passing of the Kansas-Nebraska Act in a new Republican Party upon the platform of anti-slavery. Feeling ran high in the Presidential elections of 1856. But Democratic influences nominated "a Northern man with Southern principles," James Buchanan of Pennsylvania, and

[1] Morison and Commager, *Growth of the American Republic,* vol. i, p. 622.

for the last time Southern influences had their voice at Washington.

Two days after the inauguration of the new President the Supreme Court published its decision upon the famous case of the slave Dred Scott versus his master, Sanford. Scott had been taken by his master from slave-owning Missouri to the free state of Illinois and then to Wisconsin Territory. He sued for his freedom on the grounds that residence in those two places had made him a free man. The questions before the Court were two. Was Scott a citizen of Missouri, which he needed to be to have the right to bring an action? And had his residence elsewhere changed his established status? The Court decided against him on both points. Chief Justice Taney delivered a judgment which, while it expressed the law as it existed under the Costitution, provoked a storm throughout the North. "The negro," declared Taney, "was not a citizen in the eyes of the Constitution, which was 'made for white men only.'" He could not sue in any court of the United States. The Negroes were regarded as "so far inferior that they had no rights which the white man was bound to respect." The slave was the property of his owner, and the National Government was nowhere given power over the property of the inhabitants of the United States. It had no right to prohibit slavery in the Territories, and the old Missouri compromise, on which Scott had in part relied for his freedom, was constitutionally wrong. Thus the Supreme Court. It is fair to add that Taney remarked it was not within the province of the Court to decide whether the Founding Fathers had been right to regard the Negro in this way. And in fact Dred Scott was immediately freed after the verdict. His had been a case purposefully designed to test the law and inflame opinion. This it certainly did. The Republican Party, which had been launched to prevent slavery spreading into the Territories, saw its whole programme declared unconstitutional. "The people of the United States," cried William H. Seward, a Republican leader, "never can and never will accept principles so abhorrent."

The savage struggle between free-soil and slavery in the Great Plains brought from the backwoods into national politics a new figure. Abraham Lincoln, a small-town lawyer from Springfield, Illinois, was stirred to the depths of his being by the passing of the Kansas-Nebraska Act. He had already served a term in Congress; now he stood for the Senate. He espoused the duty of opposing by the moral force of his personality the principle of slavery. " 'A house divided against itself cannot stand.' I believe this Government cannot endure permanently half slave and half free. I do not expect the Union to be dissolved—I do not expect the house to fall—but I do expect it will cease to be divided. It will become all one thing or all the other. Either the opponents of slavery will arrest the further spread of it, and place it where the public mind shall rest in the belief that it is in the course of ultimate extinction; or its advocates will push it forward till it shall become alike lawful in all the states, old as well as new, North as well as South." In a series of public debates and speeches Lincoln fought Douglas throughout the prairie towns of Illinois in the summer and autumn of 1858, and although he was beaten for the Senatorship he had already become a national figure. He had made slavery a moral and not a legal issue, and he had propounded the disruptive idea of overriding the Supreme Court decision and of outlawing slavery in the new territories. He felt instinctively the weakness and impermanence of this new concession to the susceptibilities of the South. He realised that as the agitation for abolition grew, so the Southerners would demand further guarantees to protect their own peculiar slave society. President Buchanan and the

Democratic circle around the White House talked of conquering Cuba and Nicaragua in the hope of adding new slave-owning territories to the Union. Southern business men urged reopening the slave trade owing to the high price of slaves, while all the time the North, in a series of disturbing incidents, defied the Fugitive Slave Act of 1850.

It needed but a spark to cause an explosion. In October 1859 the fanatic John Brown, with his sons and a dozen followers, seized the Federal arsenal at Harpers Ferry, on the slavery frontier, declared war upon the United States, and liberated a number of bewildered slaves. He was attacked by the Federal marines under Colonel Robert E. Lee, and after some loss of life was captured, severely wounded. He was tried and hanged with four of his adherents. The South, declaring the outrage the work of the Republican Party, was convulsed with excitement. In the North millions regarded John Brown as a martyr. His body lay mouldering in the grave, but his soul went marching on.

The Union in Danger

NOW came the fateful Presidential election of 1860. In February the Southern Senator Jefferson Davis demanded that the Northern states should repeal their Personal Liberty Laws and cease to interfere with the Fugitive Slave Law of 1850. Chief Justice Taney's decision of the Supreme Court must be obeyed. Slavery could not be prohibited by the Federal Government in the Territories of the United States. Rather, Davis demanded, the Federal Government should protect slavery in those areas. Against this, Abraham Lincoln, in New York and elsewhere, unfolded in magnificent orations, calm, massive, and magnanimous, the anti-slavery cause. In this crisis the Democratic Party split. When Douglas, their Presidential candidate, carried a set of compromise proposals in the party meeting at Charleston the Alabama delegation marched out of the hall, followed by those of seven other cotton states. Lincoln would probably in any case have been elected, but the division among the Democrats made his victory certain. The cotton states put forward as their candidate John C. Breckinridge, of Kentucky, who was at that moment Vice-President. He stood as a Southern Rights Democrat. The scene was further complicated by the appearance of a fourth aspirant, Senator John Bell, of Kentucky, who called himself a Constitutional Unionist and was an old-fashioned Whig. Secession was not the issue, though everyone felt that the South would in fact secede if Lincoln won. Slavery was the dominating and all-absorbing topic. Lincoln and the Republicans wanted to reverse the Dred Scott decision, prohibit slavery in the Territories and confine it within its existing limits. Douglas and the official Democrats were for non-intervention in the Territories and "popular sovereignty" by the settlers. Breckinridge and his supporters demanded that slavery in the Territories should be protected by law. Bell tried to ignore the issue altogether in the blissful hope that the nation could be made to forget everything that had happened since the Mexican War. On November 6, 1860, Lincoln was elected. He had behind him only 40 per cent of the voters. Douglas was the runner-up on the popular vote. Breckinridge, who was reputed to be the Secessionist candidate in spite of his assurances of loyalty to the Union, came third. Even in the slave states he failed to win a majority of the votes.

In spite of this great majority against breaking the Union, the state of South Carolina, where the doctrines of Calhoun were cherished, passed by a unanimous vote at Charleston on December 20 its famous Ordinance of Secession, declaring that the Union of 1788 between South Carolina and all other states, Northern and Southern alike, was dissolved. This precipitate and mortal act was hailed with delirious enthusiasm. The cannons fired; the bells rang; flags flew on every house. The streets were crowded with cheering multitudes. The example of South Carolina was followed by the states of Mississippi, Florida, Alabama, Georgia, Louisiana, and Texas. Delegates from the first of these sovereign states, as they regarded themselves, met in Alabama in February and organised a new Confederacy, of which Jefferson Davis was chosen President. A new constitution, similar in almost all respects to that of the United States, but founded explicitly upon slav-

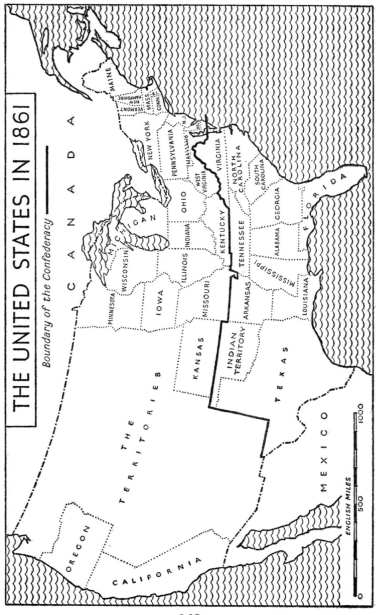

THE UNITED STATES IN 1861

Boundary of the Confederacy

CANADA

MAINE
VERMONT
NEW HAMPSHIRE
MASS.
CONN.
NEW YORK
PENNSYLVANIA
N.J.
MARYLAND
DEL.
WEST VIRGINIA
VIRGINIA
NORTH CAROLINA
SOUTH CAROLINA
GEORGIA
FLORIDA
ALABAMA
MISSISSIPPI
TENNESSEE
KENTUCKY
OHIO
INDIANA
ILLINOIS
MICHIGAN
WISCONSIN
MINNESOTA
IOWA
MISSOURI
ARKANSAS
LOUISIANA
KANSAS
INDIAN TERRITORY
TEXAS
THE TERRITORIES
OREGON
CALIFORNIA
MEXICO

ENGLISH MILES
0   500   1000

· 165 ·

ery, was proclaimed. A Confederate flag—the Stars and Bars—was adopted. President Davis was authorised to raise an army of a hundred thousand men, large sums were voted, and a delegation of three was sent abroad to seek recognition and friendship in Europe. All the leading figures concerned in this decision harboured grave illusions. They thought the North would not try to coerce them back into the Union. If it made the attempt they believed the Yankees would be no match for Southern arms. And if the North imposed a blockade the Confederates expected that the Powers of Europe would intervene on their behalf. They cherished the notion that "King Cotton" was so vital to Britain and France that neither country could peaceably allow its supplies to be cut off.

Buchanan was still President of the United States, and Lincoln, President-Elect, could not take office till March. For four months the dying administration gaped upon a distracted land. Floyd, Secretary of War, an ardent Southerner, showed no particular vigilance or foresight. He tamely allowed muskets which had been sent North for alterations to be returned to the Southern arsenals. Every facility was given to officers of the Regular Army to join the new forces being feverishly raised in the South. Buchanan, longing for release, tried desperately to discharge his duties and follow a middle course. All counter-preparations in the North were paralysed. On the other hand, he refused to recognise the validity of secession. Practically all the Federal posts, with their small garrisons, in the Southern states had passed without fighting into the possession of the Confederacy. But the forts of Charleston harbour, under the command of Major Anderson, a determined officer, continued to fly the Stars and Stripes. When called upon to surrender he withdrew to Fort Sumter, which stood on an island. His food ran low, and when a ship bearing supplies from the North arrived to succour him Confederate batteries from the mainland drove it back by cannon-fire. Meanwhile strenuous efforts at compromise were being made. Many Northerners were prepared for the sake of peace to give way to the South on the slavery issue. But Lincoln was inflexible. He would not repudiate the platform on which he had been elected. He could not countenance the extension of slavery to the Territories. This was the nub on which all turned. In this tense and tremendous situation Abraham Lincoln was sworn President on March 4, 1861. Around him the structure of Federal Government was falling to pieces. Officials and officers were every day leaving for their home states in the South. Hands were clasped between old comrades for the last time in friendship.

The North, for all its detestation of slavery, had by no means contemplated civil war. Between the extremists on both sides there was an immense borderland where all interests and relationships were interlaced by every tie of kinship and custom and every shade of opinion found its expression. So far only the cotton states, or Lower South, had severed themselves from the Union. Missouri, Arkansas, Kentucky, Tennessee, North Carolina, Maryland, Delaware, and above all the noble and ancient Virginia, the Old Dominion, the birthplace of Washington, the fountain of American tradition and inspiration, still hung in the balance. Lincoln appealed for patience and conciliation. He declared himself resolved to hold the forts and property of the United States. He disclaimed all intention of invading the South. He announced that he would not interfere with slavery in the Southern states. He revived the common memories of the North and South, which, like "mystic cords, stretch from every battlefield and patriot grave to every living heart . . . over this broad land." "In your hands," he exclaimed, "my dissatisfied fellow-countrymen, and not in mine, is this momentous issue of civil war. The Government will not assail you. You can have no conflict without yourselves being the aggressors. You have no oath registered in Heaven to destroy the Government, while I shall have the most solemn one to preserve and defend it."

On April 8 Lincoln informed the Governor of South Carolina of his intention to re-victual Major Anderson and his eighty-three men in Fort Sumter. Thereupon President Davis ordered General Beauregard, who commanded seven thousand men at Charleston, to demand the immediate surrender of the fort. Anderson, admitting that famine would reduce him in a few days, nevertheless continued constant. Vain parleys were held; but before dawn on April 12 the Confederate batteries opened a general bombardment, and for two days fifty heavy cannon rained their shells upon Fort Sumter. Anderson and his handful of men, sheltering in their bomb-proof caverns, feeling that all had been done that honour and law required, marched out begrimed and half suffocated on the 14th, and were allowed to depart to the North. No blood had been shed, but the awful act of rebellion had occurred.

The cannonade at Fort Sumter resounded through the world. It roused and united the people of the North. All the free states stood together. Party divisions were effaced. Douglas, Lincoln's rival at the election, with a million and a half Democratic votes at his back, hastened to the White House to grasp Lincoln's hand. Ex-President Buchanan declared, "The North will sustain the administration almost to a man." Upon this surge and his own vehement resolve, Lincoln issued a proclamation calling for "the militia of the Union to the number of seventy-five thousand" to suppress "combinations" in seven states "too powerful to be suppressed by the ordinary course of judicial proceedings." Here, then, was the outbreak of the American Civil War.

* * * * *

Upon Lincoln's call to arms to coerce the seceding states Virginia made without hesitation the choice which she was so heroically to sustain. She would not fight on the issue of slavery, but stood firm on the constitutional ground that every state in the Union enjoyed sovereign rights. On this principle Virginians denied the claim of the Federal Government to exercise coercion. By eighty-eight votes to fifty-five the Virginia Convention at Richmond refused to allow the state militia to respond to Lincoln's call. Virginia seceded from the Union and placed her entire military forces at the disposal of the Confederacy. This decided the conduct of one of the noblest Americans who ever lived, and one of the greatest captains known to the annals of war.

Robert E. Lee stood high in American life. His father had been a colonel in the Revolution. By his marriage with Miss Custis, a descendant of Mrs George Washington, he became the master of Arlington, the house overlooking the national capital which George Custis, Washington's adopted son, "the child of Mount Vernon," as he was called, had built for himself a few miles from Washington's own home. A graduate of West Point, General Scott's Engineer Staff-Officer in the Mexican War, Lee had served for more than twenty-five years in the United States Army with distinction. His noble presence and gentle, kindly manner were sustained by religious faith and an exalted character. As the American scene darkened he weighed carefully, while commanding a regiment of cavalry on the Texan border, the course which duty and honour would require from him. He was opposed to slavery and thought that "secession would do no good," but he had been taught from childhood that his first allegiance was to the state of Virginia. Summoned to Washington during March 1861, he had thus expressed himself to an intimate Northern friend: "If Virginia stands by the old Union, so will I. But if she secedes (though I do not believe in secession as a constitutional right, nor that there is sufficient cause for revolution), then I will still follow my native state with my sword, and if need be with my life."

He reached the capital in the fevered days of March, and General Scott, his old chief, wrestled earnestly with him in a three hours' interview. By Lincoln's authority he was offered the chief command of the great Union army now being raised. He declined at once, and when a day later Virginia seceded he resigned his commission, bade farewell for ever to his home at Arlington, and in the deepest sorrow boarded the train for Richmond. Here he was immediately offered the chief command of all the military and naval forces of Virginia. He had resigned his United States commission on the Saturday, and on the Monday following he accepted his new task. Some of those who saw him in these tragic weeks, when sometimes his eyes filled with tears, emotion which he never showed after the gain or loss of great battles, have written about his inward struggle. But there was no struggle; he never hesitated. The choice was for the state of Virginia. He deplored that choice; he foresaw its consequences with bitter grief; but for himself he had no doubts at the time, nor ever after regret or remorse.

Those who hold that the fortunes of mankind are largely the result of the impact upon events of superior beings will find it fitting that Lee's famous comrade in arms, "Stonewall Jackson," should be mentioned at this point. Lee was fifty-four in the crisis, Jackson but thirty-seven. Like Lee, he was a trained professional soldier who had served gallantly in the

Mexican War. He had devoted himself to the theoretical study of the military art. He was at this time a professor at the Virginia Military Institute. Jackson came of Ulster stock, settled in Virginia. His character was stern, his manner reserved and usually forbidding, his temper Calvinistic, his mode of life strict, frugal, austere. He might have stepped into American history from the command of one of Cromwell's regiments. There burned in him a hatred of Northern domination not to be found in Lee. Black-bearded, pale-faced, with thin, compressed lips, aquiline nose, and dark, piercing eyes, he slouched in his weather-stained uniform a professor-warrior; yet greatly beloved by the few who knew him best, and gifted with that strange power of commanding measureless devotion from the thousands whom he ruled with an iron hand.

Both these men, though they habitually spoke and no doubt convinced themselves to the contrary, loved war as a technical art to which their lives had been given. Their sayings and letters abound with expressions of sorrow at the terrible decrees of which they had now become the servants. But on a long night march to a desprate battle at dawn Jackson muttered to his companion "Delicious excitement!"; and Lee, surveying a field of carnage, observed reflectively, "It is well that war is so horrible—we would grow too fond of it." Against Lee and his great lieutenant, united for a year of intense action in a comradeship which recalls that of Marlborough and Eugene, were now to be marshalled the overwhelming forces of the Union.

*   *   *   *   *

Both sides set to work to form armies. Trained officers and men were few, weapons and munitions scanty. The American people had enjoyed a long peace, and their warfare had been to reclaim the wilderness and draw wealth from the soil. On neither side was there any realisation of the ordeal that lay before them. The warlike spirit ran high in the South, and their gentry and frontier farmers, like the Cavaliers, were more accustomed to riding and shooting than their compeers in the commercial North. The Confederate states were defending hearth and home against invasion and overlordship. Proud and ardent, their manhood rallied to the newly forming regiments, confident that they would conquer, sure at least that they were unconquerable.

The North was at first astonished at the challenge. They could hardly realise that the wordy strife of party politics, the exciting turmoil of electioneering, must now give place to organised slaughter. When they surveyed the vast resources of the North they felt their power incomparable. All were resolved to maintain the Union whatever the cost; and beneath this august constitutional issue there glowed the moral fires of wrath against slavery.

At first sight, to foreign observers, the disparity between the combatants was evident. Twenty-three states, with a population of twenty-two millions, were arrayed against eleven states, whose population of nine millions included nearly four million slaves. But as the Southern states only claimed the right to go their own way their policy would be defensive; the North, which denied this right and was determined to keep them in the Union by force, had to take the offensive. A formidable task confronted the aggressors.

Nothing short of the subjugation of the entire South would suffice. The issue was not to be settled by two or three battles; the whole country would have to be conquered piecemeal. The Confederacy embraced an area which extended eight hundred miles from north to south and seventeen hundred from east to west. The railways were few and badly conditioned; the roads no better. The region was sparsely inhabited, and the invader would have for the most part to bring his own supplies. He would have enormously long lines of communication to guard in his march through a hostile country. Most of the slaves, who might have been expected to prove an embarrassment to the South, on the contrary proved a solid help, tending the plantations in the absence of their masters, raising the crops which fed the armies, working on the roads and building fortifications, thus releasing a large number of whites for service in the field.

In the North it might be suggested that a large proportion of the Democrats would oppose a policy of force. In the struggle of endurance, which seemed the shape which the war would ultimately take, the South might prove more staunch. In a war of attrition the North had the advantage of being a manufacturing community, and her best weapon against Southern agricultural strength, if it could blockade three thousand five hundred miles of Southern coast, might prove to be the Navy. But a resultant cotton famine in Europe might force Great Britain and France into intervention on the side of the South.

The seven states of the Lower South had seceded after Lincoln's election, and set up a Government of their own at Montgomery, Alabama, in February 1861. Lincoln's call for troops after Sumter was followed by the secession of four states of the Upper South, and the Confederate capital was moved to Richmond. There remained the attitude of the border slave states, Kentucky, Missouri, Maryland, and Delaware. Of these Kentucky was the most important on account of its geographical position, and because Missouri was likely to follow its example. Indeed, the issue of the war seemed perhaps to turn upon Kentucky. Lincoln, a Kentuckian by birth, like Jefferson Davis, is reported to have said, "I should like to have God on my side, but I must have Kentucky." But

Kentucky, loyal to the memory of Henry Clay, "the Great Compromiser," tried to remain neutral. Neither combatant could tolerate this attitude for long; yet both feared lest any violent act of aggression might throw the state into the other's arms. Lincoln proved the more astute diplomatist, and by keeping the control of policy in his own hands secured Kentucky for the Union in September. This was the first real victory for the North.

In Missouri, as in the sister state, there was a majority in favour of neutrality; but the extremists on both sides took control and civil war resulted. The Governor was a rabid Secessionist, and, supported by the legislature, endeavoured to take the state out of the Union. The Union leader was one of the powerful Blair family, and his brother a member of the Cabinet. He invoked the aid of General Lyon, commander of the Federal troops in St Louis, and with his help the Governor's separatist designs were defeated, and he himself chased out of Jefferson City, the state capital, into the southwest corner of the state. But the intrusion of Federal troops into a domestic quarrel caused many citizens who had hitherto been neutral to join the ranks of Secession. Although a state Convention deposed the Governor and set up a Provisional Government at St Louis months were to elapse before Missouri was fully brought under Federal control.

In Maryland the issue was more quickly settled. The Secessionists were strong in Baltimore, and gained temporary control of the city. They destroyed the railway bridges on the two northern lines, and for a few days Washington found itself dangerously isolated. Reinforcements from Massachusetts were assaulted in their march through the streets, and a bloody collision occurred. But without help from Virginia the Maryland Secessionists were not capable of making head against the national capital, and the Loyalist Governor gained time, until on May 13 General Butler, with a small Federal force, made a sudden dash, and, taking the Secessionists by surprise, occupied Baltimore. This ended the secession in Maryland. A fourth slave state, Delaware, also stayed in the Union. Its Legislature had Southern leanings, but geography ruled otherwise.

Lincoln not only secured four slavery states as allies, but also detached an important section from the seceding state of Virginia. West Virginia, separated by the Alleghenies from the rest of the state, and geographically and economically a part of the Ohio valley, had long chafed under the oppression of the state Government at Richmond, which ignored its interests and exploited it for the benefit of the "Tidewater" section. It now seized the opportunity to secede from Secession. When in May the popular vote ratified the Ordinance of Secession it broke away, and with the help of its powerful neighbour, Ohio, established its independence under the title of the state of Kanawha, which two years later was formally admitted to the Union as the state of West Virginia.

In the task of preparing for war the Southern President had advantages over his rival. A West-Pointer, he had served in the Regular Army for several years and had fought in the Mexican War; he had afterwards been Secretary of War in President Pierce's administration, and then chairman of the Senate Military Affairs Committee. He had an inside knowledge of the officer corps, and could make the best use of the material at his disposal. Not only did he select with a few exceptions the right men, but he supported them in adversity. The principal Confederate Generals who were in command at the beginning of the war, if not killed, were still in command at its end.

Lincoln, on the other hand, was without military experience; his profession of the law had not brought him in contact with Army officers. His appointments were too often made on purely political grounds. He was too ready, especially at first, to yield to the popular clamour which demanded the recall of an unsuccessful general. Few, having failed once, were given a second chance. After each defeat a change was made in the command of the Army of the Potomac. None of the Generals in command of Federal armies at the end of the war had held high commands at the beginning. The survivors were very good, but the Federal cause was the poorer for the loss of those who had fallen by the way. Others, fearing the President in the rear more than the foe in front, had been too nervous to fight their best. Nor did the War Department make the best use of the junior officers of the Regular Army. Too many were left with their detachments in the Far West instead of being utilised to train and lead the volunteers. But while the North attempted at first to organise its military strength as if it had been a confederacy of states, the Federal Government, gaining power steadily at the expense of the states, rapidly won unquestioned control over all the forces of the Union. The Southern "Sovereign States," on the other hand, were unable even under the stress of war to abandon the principle of decentralisation for which they had been contending. Some State Governors, though loyal to the Confederate cause, were slow to respond to central direction, and when conscription was decided upon by the Confederate Congress in 1862 there was much opposition and evasion by the state authorities.

*　　*　　*　　*　　*

By what paths should the North invade the South to reconquer it for the Union? The Allegheny Mountains divided the Mississippi valley from the broad slopes which stretched eastward to the Atlantic. The Mississippi and its great tributary, the Ohio, with the Cumberland and the Tennessee Rivers, offered sure means of carrying the war into the heart of the Confederacy and rending it asunder. The mechanical and material resources of the North ensured the control of these waterways. The South could not organise any river forces capable of coping with the Federal flotillas. The one lateral line of communication within Confederate territory, the Charleston–Memphis railroad, which passed through the key position of Chattanooga on the Tennessee, at the junction of four railway lines, would be speedily threatened. Waterways could not be cut by cavalry raids; the current of the rivers was with the North, and there was no limit except shipping to the troops and the supplies which could be carried. Old Winfield Scott, the Federal General-in-Chief, saw in this Western theatre the true line of strategic advance. But the initial neutrality of Kentucky confused the Northern view, and when at the end of September Kentucky was gained the main Union forces were differently engaged.

Upon Virginia joining the Confederacy Jefferson Davis made Richmond the Southern capital. It was within a hundred miles of Washington. It controlled, or might control, the estuaries of the James and York Rivers, with their tributaries. It covered the powerful naval base at Norfolk. Between Richmond and the enemy flowed in successive barriers the broad outlets of the Potomac and the Rappahannock, with its tributary the Rapidan. Here, then, upon this advanced battleground, rather than in the interior, must the Confederacy maintain itself or fall. Thus the two capitals stood like queens at chess upon adjoining squares, and, sustained by their combinations of covering pieces, they endured four years of grim play within a single move of capture.

The Confederates hoped at first to defend the line of the Potomac, which marked the northern frontier of Virginia. They had seized the Federal arsenal and army depot at Harpers Ferry, where the Shenandoah joins the Potomac, and for several months, while the Union forces were gathering, Colonel Jackson, and later General Joseph E. Johnston, with a few thousand men, maintained themselves there. In front of the railway junction of Manassas, by the Bull Run stream, only thirty miles from Washington, stood General Beauregard, of Sumter repute, with the main Confederate army. Thus the summer of 1861 came. "How long," cried the politicians in Washington, and the turbulent public opinion behind them in the North, "should the United States tolerate this insolent challenge?" The three-months volunteers whom Lincoln had summoned at the end of April must be made to strike a blow before their time expired. General Scott wished to wait till trained armies were formed. But do not all regulars despise militia and volunteers? Pressed beyond resistance, Scott yielded to the entreaties of Lincoln and his Cabinet. Harpers Ferry had already been recovered, and Joseph E. Johnston, with eleven thousand men, had withdrawn up the Shenandoah, Scott therefore sent fifteen thousand men to hold off Johnston in the valley, while Irvin McDowell, a competent soldier, with thirty-five thousand, moved to attack Beauregard, who mustered twenty-two thousand. The essence of this plan was that Johnston's army, held by superior force, should not join Beauregard before McDowell attacked him. Some have suggested that if Scott, who was still robust of mind, if not in body, could have been conveyed to the field of battle in a litter or ambulance, as Marshal Saxe had been at Fontenoy, the Federal army might have been spared the disaster which overtook it. Knowledge and experience in command outweigh mere physical disability.

The Federal advance had originally been fixed for July 9, but it was not till a week later that it actually began. The two Confederate Generals were both expecting to be attacked by the superior forces on their respective fronts, and each was asking for reinforcements from the other. But the Union General in the valley, Patterson, allowed Johnston to slip away unobserved, and he joined Beauregard with two brigades on the day before the battle. Both McDowell and Beauregard had planned the same manœuvre, to turn the enemy's left flank. McDowell got his blow in first; on the Confederate right orders miscarried and the offensive faltered. With such troops the side standing on the defensive might be expected to hold its ground. But McDowell virtually achieved a surprise, and his much superior force threatened to overwhelm the weak Confederate left before reinforcements could arrive. In this crisis Jackson's brigade, standing "like a stone wall" on the Henry Hill, stopped the Federal advance, until the arrival by rail of another of Johnston's brigades turned the tide of battle.

The combat, though fierce, was confused, and on both sides disjointed. The day was hot, the troops raw, the staffs inexperienced. The Northerners retreated; the Confederates were too disorganised to pursue; but the retreat became a rout. Members of the Cabinet, Senators, Congressmen, even ladies, had come out from Washington to see the sport. They were involved in a panic when thousands of men, casting away their arms and even their coats, fled and never stopped till they reached the entrenchments which surrounded Washington. Not more than five thousand men were killed or wounded on both sides in the action, but the name Bull Run rang far and wide. Europe was astonished; the South was overjoyed; and a wave of fury swept the Union, before which the passions which had followed the attack on Fort Sumter seemed but a ripple.

It is still argued that the Confederates should have struck hot-foot at Washington. But Johnston at the time thought the

Confederate army more disorganised by victory than the Federals by defeat. He had not seen the rout. Jackson and other Confederate Generals were eager to advance on Washington. Who shall say?

*   *   *   *   *

The day after this ignominious affair a new commander replaced McDowell. One of Lee's comrades on Scott's staff in Mexico, General George B. McClellan, a Regular officer with many remarkable qualities, was summoned from West Virginia, where he had been active and forward, to take command. Congress had voted the enlistment of five hundred thousand volunteers and a grant of two hundred and fifty million dollars for the prosecution of the war. A week after his assumption of command McClellan laid before the President the grandiose scheme of forming an army of two hundred and seventy-three thousand men, which, in combination with a strong naval force and a fleet of transports, should march through the Atlantic states, reducing the seaports from Richmond to New Orleans, and then move into the interior and stamp out the remnants of the rebellion. In war matters are not settled so easily. Public opinion, vocal through a thousand channels, demanded quick results. The scythe of Time cut both ways. The Confederacy was becoming consolidated. Every month increased the peril of foreign recognition of the South, or even of actual intervention. However, when at the end of October General Scott retired McClellan became General-in-Chief of all the armies of the Republic, and bent himself with zeal and capacity to forming brigades, divisions, army corps, with artillery, engineers, and supply trains, according to the best European models.

The year 1861 ended with the Confederacy intact and almost unmolested. Along the immense front, with its deep borderlands and debatable regions, more than a hundred and fifty skirmishes and petty actions had been fought without serious bloodshed. Although the Confederate commanders realised that the time would soon come when McClellan would take the field against them with an army vastly superior in numbers, well disciplined and well equipped, they did not dare, with only forty thousand men, however elated, to invade Maryland and march on Baltimore. They did not even attempt to recover West Virginia. Lee, who was sent to co-ordinate defence on this front, could not prevail over the discord of the local commanders. Although he still retained his commission from the state of Virginia, he ranked below both Joseph E. Johnston and Albert Sidney Johnston in the Confederate hierarchy. Beauregard, though junior to him, had gained the laurels. Lee returned from Western Virginia with diminished reputation, and President Davis had to explain his qualities to the State Governors when appointing him to organise the coast defences of the Carolinas.

So far the American Civil War had appeared to Europe as a desultory brawl of mobs and partisans which might at any time be closed by politics and parley. Napoleon III sympathised with the Confederates, and would have aided them if the British Government had been agreeable. Queen Victoria desired a strict neutrality, and opinion in England was curiously divided. The upper classes, Conservative and Liberal alike, generally looked with favour upon the South, and in this view Gladstone concurred. Disraeli, the Conservative leader, was neutral. The Radicals and the unenfranchised mass of the working classes were solid against slavery, and Cobden and Bright spoke their mind. But the Northern blockade struck hard at the commercial classes, and Lancashire, though always constant against slavery, began to feel the cotton famine. The arrest on a British ship, the *Trent,* of the Confederate agents, Mason and Slidell, by a United States cruiser roused a storm. The Foreign Secretary, Lord John Russell, penned a hard dispatch which the Prince Consort persuaded the Prime Minister, Lord Palmerston, to modify. A clause was inserted which enabled the Federal Government without loss of honour to declare their cruiser's action unauthorised. President Lincoln took some persuading, but in the end he sagely remarked "One war at a time," liberated the captives, and all remained in sullen suspense. Blockade-running, both in cotton outwards and arms inwards, developed upon a large scale; but not a single European Government received the envoys of the Confederate states. No one in Europe imagined the drama of terrific war which the year 1862 would unfold. None appraised truly the implacable rage of the antagonists. None understood the strength of Abraham Lincoln or the resources of the United States. Few outside the Confederacy had ever heard of Lee or Jackson.

The Campaign
Against Richmond

THE New Year opened grievously for the South, and a
bitter tide of disillusion chilled its people. In the Cabinet
and headquarters at Richmond, where facts and figures told
their sombre tale, the plight of the Confederacy already
seemed grave. The Union blockade froze the coasts. Hostile
armies, double or triple the numbers the South could muster,
were assuming shape and quality, both in the Atlantic and
Mississippi theatres. The awful weight of the North, with its
wealth and munition-making power, lay now upon the minds
of President Davis, his colleagues and Generals. The Southern
states had no arsenals, little iron and steel, few and small factories from which boots, clothing, equipment could be supplied. The magazines were almost empty. Even flintlock
muskets were scarce. The smooth-bore cannon of the Confederate artillery was far out-ranged by the new rifled guns of
the Union. Nor was there any effectual means by which these
needs could be met. It is upon this background that the military prodigies of the year stand forth.

Disaster opened in the Mississippi valley. Here Albert Sidney Johnston commanded the Confederate forces. Davis believed him to be his finest General. He was certainly a man of
boundless devotion, whose daring was founded upon a thorough knowledge of his art. In the autumn of 1861 he had

advanced to Bowling Green, a railway junction of high strategic value to the south of the Green River, a tributary of the Ohio. Here he stood brazenly, hoping to rouse Kentucky and marshal Tennessee, while to the westward Leonidas Polk, who in peace-time was Bishop of Louisiana, with another small army barred the Mississippi at Columbus. The Federal forces, with their fleets of armoured river gun-boats, descending the Mississippi from St Louis and the Ohio from Louisville, outnumbered both these Confederate Generals by four to one. Still, for months they had remained unmolested in their forward positions, covering enormous territories from whose population and resources much might be drawn. Now with the turn of the year the Union leaders set their men in motion. Masses of blue-clad soldiers began to appear upon the three-hundred-mile front from the great river to the mountain ranges, and all kinds of queer craft cased in steel and carrying cannon and mortars glided slowly down the riverways from the north. The bluff could be played no longer. Polk abandoned Columbus, and Johnston retreated from Bowling Green. This carried the fighting line southwards to the Cumberland and Tennessee Rivers, and to a Confederate fortress called Island No. 10 on the Mississippi.

The Federal General, Henry W. Halleck, who commanded the Western Department was a model of caution. Fortunately among his generals there was a retired Regular officer, Ulysses S. Grant, who since the Mexican War had lived in obscurity, working for a time in his father's leather store in Illinois. The Confederates sought to block the Mississippi at Island No. 10, the Tennessee at Fort Henry, and the Cumberland at Fort Donelson, and their advanced forces garrisoned these armed posts. Fort Henry was weak, and Fort Donelson was an entrenched camp which required a considerable army for its defence. Grant proposed a winter advance up the Tennessee River and an attack upon Fort Henry. Halleck approved. Grant made the advance, and the advance made Grant. Albert Sidney Johnston foresaw with perfect clarity a Federal winter offensive while the rivers were well filled. He clamoured for reinforcements, both to President Davis and the Governors of the Western states. The former could not and the latter did not supply them. In February 1862 Grant seized Fort Henry. It was but ten miles across the tongue of land between the rivers to Fort Donelson, on the Cumberland. Without authority, and in severe frost, Grant struck at Fort Donelson, which was defended by seventeen thousand Confederates under Floyd, the former United States Secretary for War, who in the interval between Lincoln's election and inauguration had allowed the muskets to be transferred to the South. After four days' fighting and confrontation Fort Donelson surrendered, with fourteen thousand prisoners and sixty guns. Floyd, apprehending a charge of treason, escaped the night before. He was probably wise.

The fall of Fort Donelson on February 16 was the first great military disaster of the Confederacy; but others followed quickly in the West. Albert Sidney Johnston, now at last furnished with the beginnings of an army, gathered the remnants of his former front at Corinth, behind the Tennessee, and Polk fell back down the Mississippi to Memphis.

*   *   *   *   *

At Washington McClellan, General-in-Chief, laboured to prepare his army, and resisted by every means the intense political pressures which demanded an advance "on to Richmond." He exaggerated the strength of the enemy, and furnished Lincoln with endless reports from Pinkerton's Private Detective Agency, which he used as his secret service, showing very heavy forces at Richmond and behind Joseph E. Johnston's entrenchments thirty miles away at Centerville.

He strove to gain time to drill his men by repeated promises to advance. As month succeeded month and the swarming Army of the Potomac made no movement the enthusiasm which had greeted McClellan in July 1861 waned. The Radical Republicans began to attack this Democrat General who had been preferred to their own candidate, John C. Frémont. McClellan was known to be opposed to the Radical policy of proclaiming the emancipation of all slaves. Early in December he informed the President that he did not favour a frontal attack on Joseph E. Johnston and a march along the straight road through Fredericksburg to Richmond. He had long been devising a plan for an amphibious movement down Chesapeake Bay to some point on the coast of Virginia close to the rebel capital. He imparted these ideas to Lincoln in general terms early in December. Then in the middle of the month he contracted typhoid fever and was absent for several weeks. The Republican Party leaders had already procured the appointment of a Joint Committee on the conduct of the war, consisting of three Senators and four Congressmen. It was dominated by the Radical enemies of the General-in-Chief. Lincoln and the cabinet, during McClellan's absence from duty, called into council several Generals of the Army, and invited constructive suggestions. But their conferences were abruptly disturbed by the reappearance of McClellan himself. A few days later he explained his plan to the President in detail. Availing himself of sea-power, he proposed to transport an army of a hundred and fifty thousand men down Chesapeake Bay and disembark it at Urbana, on the Lower Rappahannock, where it would be only one day's march from West Point and two more marches from Richmond. He expected to cut off General J. B. Magruder and the Confederate troops defending the Yorktown peninsula, and he hoped to reach Richmond before Johnston could retreat thither.

No one can asperse the principle of this conception. It utilised all the forces of the Union Government; it turned the flank of all the Confederate positions between Washington and Richmond; it struck at the forehead of the Confederacy. Its details were substantially modified on examination. Fortress Monroe, at the tip of the peninsula, between the York and James Rivers, was held by the Union, and was finally chosen as a safe landing-place. President Lincoln had one overpowering objection to the whole idea of a maritime expedition. It would uncover Washington; and Joseph E. Johnston, for the strength of whose army he probably accepted McClellan's own figures, to say nothing of "Stonewall" Jackson, would at once swoop down on the defenceless capital. Hard bargaining ensued upon the number of troops to be left to guard the capital and the mouth of the Shenandoah valley, where at Harpers Ferry the river flows into the Potomac. This was agreed at forty thousand. Eventually on February 27 Lincoln gave a reluctant assent, and everything was set in train for the tremendous enterprise. At the same time Lincoln resolved to keep supreme control, relieved McClellan of the general direction of the United States armies, and restricted him to the command of the Army of the Potomac. For this there were also sound military reasons. Feeling that he required a military adviser, he decided to summon General Halleck from the West. McClellan learnt of his removal from the higher command through the medium of the newspapers before Lincoln's emissary reached him. Thus the President appeared guilty of a grave discourtesy, so unusual in him that the suspicion naturally arose that the "hidden hand" of the Joint Committee was here at work.

It was a far worse mistake not to appoint a new General-in-Chief. All the generals in command of armies were ordered to take their instructions from the Secretary of War. For the last two months this office had been held by Edwin M. Stanton, who had replaced the incompetent and perhaps corrupt Cameron. Stanton, like McClellan, was a Democrat, and during the last days of the Buchanan administration had held the post of Attorney-General. Possibly Lincoln thought that he would be acceptable to McClellan. It was no doubt his intention to reappoint McClellan as General-in-Chief, if he succeeded in his Richmond campaign, and at the time he could think of no one to fill the vacancy, which he hoped would be only temporary. At the outset Stanton had professed unbounded devotion to McClellan, but the General soon began to doubt the sincerity of his professions and thought that he detected a deliberate design to debar him from free access to the President. It was not very long before Stanton appeared to be in collusion with the Joint Committee. The Attorney-General had given the opinion that "the order of the Secretary of War is the President's order." There now began to issue from the Secretary's office a series of orders seriously crippling McClellan's operations. McClellan's scope was reduced by the creation of the Military Departments of the Rappahannock under McDowell, who had commanded at Bull Run, and of the Shenandoah under Nathaniel P. Banks. A whole corps was thus taken from him. He claimed that he was leaving behind him no less than seventy-three thousand men, of whom but thirty-five thousand belonged to Banks's command in the Shenandoah valley. McClellan was justified in regarding this force as available for the protection of the capital. However, he did not clearly explain his arrangements to Lincoln, and his failure to take the President into his confidence had an unfortunate result. For Lincoln in misunderstanding ordered the First Corps, under McDowell, to remain in front of Washington, thus reducing the force on which McClellan had counted by forty thousand men, at the moment of launching his tremendous operation.

*   *   *   *   *

The Confederates lost their best chance of victory when they failed to use the autumn and winter of 1861. Their success at Bull Run proved as injurious as a reverse. Believing with their President that foreign intervention was near at hand, and arrogantly confident that they could beat the North in the field if need arose, they relaxed their efforts. The volunteers who came forward after the first battle could not be armed. Recruiting fell off; the soldiers in the field began to go home. Efforts to fill the ranks by grants of bounties and furloughs were ineffectual. By the beginning of 1862 the position was desperate. Nearly two-thirds of the Confederate Army consisted of one-year volunteers. In May the terms of enlistment of the hundred and forty-eight regiments which they formed would expire. These regiments were the backbone of the Army. Invasion was imminent. Conscription was contrary to the theory of state independence and sovereignty. But the Confederate Congress rose manfully to the occasion, and on April 16 by a vote of more than two to one passed an Act declaring every able-bodied white man between the ages of eighteen and thirty-five subject to military service. The armies were nevertheless filled by volunteers seeking to escape the stigma of serving under compulsion rather than by the Act itself. Indeed, the Act proved unpopular in the States and was difficult to enforce. Full use was made of its exemption clauses by the disaffected in order to escape service.

Throughout this period President Jefferson Davis rigorously adhered to the passive-defensive. He made no attempt to exploit the victories of Bull Run and Wilson's Creek. Determined to keep the control of military operations in his own hands, he devoted his attention to the East, and largely ignored the West, where chaos reigned until Albert Sidney Johnston's appointment to the supreme command in September. He obstinately refused to draw upon the "seasoned soldiers" who formed the garrisons on the Atlantic coastline. Hatteras Inlet, which afforded the best approach to the North Carolina Sounds, and Port Royal and Beaufort in South Carolina, which threatened both Charleston and Savannah, had been captured by small Federal forces and sea-power. Lee after his return from Western Virignia was sent to organise the coast defences. When a large expedition under the Union General Ambrose E. Burnside entered the inland waters of North Carolina the Confederates were ill-prepared, and lost Roanoke Island and New Bern. President Davis was more than ever determined to maintain at their full strength the garrisons in the threatened states. He recalled General Lee from his coastal defence work in the Carolinas, and employed him in a somewhat ill-defined capacity as his chief military adviser at headquarters.

In the middle of March Halleck, who had been appointed to the sole command in the Western theatre, directed Don Carlos Buell, who had occupied Nashville, to march with the greater part of his army to Savannah, on the Tennessee, thirty miles from Corinth, to combine with Grant, who had William T. Sherman with him, on the western bank near Shiloh, and attack Albert Sidney Johnston. But before Buell's men were across the river Johnston struck. In the early morning of April 6 he surprised the advanced Federal troops in their tents near Shiloh, and the largest and most bloody battle yet seen in the war was fought. Johnston at first carried all before him; and Grant, who was late in reaching the field, was by nightfall in grave danger. But Johnston, exposing himself with reckless gallantry at the head of an infantry charge, was wounded and bled to death from a main artery in a few minutes. Whatever results his great personality and wonderful energy could have gained on the morrow were lost. Beauregard, who succeeded him, drew off the Confederate troops, much to the disgust of his subordinate, Braxton Bragg. Each side lost in this furious action ten thousand men; but the proportion of loss was far heavier in the thinner Confederate ranks. The arrival of the cautious Halleck, although he brought Federal reinforcements, stopped any thought of pursuit. Island No. 10 was reduced by General John Pope on April 8, and seven thousand Confederates became prisoners of war. It now seems that a combined naval and military expedition could easily at this time have lunged far to the south and secured the fortress of Vicksburg in Mississippi. But Halleck accommodated himself readily to the President's wish for action in East Tennessee. He moved slowly against Corinth, and spent a month in trying to surround Beauregard, who escaped by a swift and long retreat. By the summer the Union line in the West had moved southwards by two hundred miles on a three-hundred-mile front.

*　　*　　*　　*　　*

The stage was now set for the military drama of the Richmond-Yorktown peninsula. At the beginning of April McClellan's army began to land in large numbers at the Federal Fortress Monroe, which served as a bridgehead. As soon as this movement, about which there could be no secrecy, became evident Joseph E. Johnston, to the surprise and relief of the Federal Government, withdrew from Centreville, abandoned Manassas Junction, crossed the Upper Rappahannock, and stood in the rugged wilderness country behind its tributary the Rapidan. It may seem confusing that there should be two Confederate Generals named Johnston; but after the gallant death of Albert Sidney at Shiloh only one remained.

He was Joseph E. Now behind the Rapidan he was in close touch with Richmond, so that McClellan's strategy, vindicated in principle, was baulked in practice. In the middle of April Johnston, leaving his main army eighty miles to the westward, arrived at Yorktown, and assumed the additional command of the troops in the peninsula. He thus enjoyed interior lines and could concentrate all his forces for the defence of Richmond. The Union Navy, after a heavy combat, found itself unable to face the plunging fire of the batteries on the bluffs of the York River on McClellan's right flank. The Confederate entrenchments, manned by Magruder's troops, stretched before him across the peninsula. He conceived himself outnumbered by the enemy, and if Davis had consented to give Johnston the garrisons of the Atlantic towns he would have been.

In these depressing circumstances McClellan acted with more than his habitual deliberation. He spent a month in a formal siege of Yorktown, incessantly appealing to Lincoln for McDowell's corps. Lincoln, on the other hand, urged him to vigorous action. "I always insisted," he wrote drily, on April 9, "that going down the bay in search of a field instead of fighting at or near Manassas was only shifting and not surmounting a difficulty; that we would find the same enemy, and the same or equal entrenchments, at either place." And a month later: "By delay the enemy will relatively gain upon you—that is, he will gain faster by fortifications and reinforcements than you can gain by reinforcements alone." Eventually, after the surrender of Yorktown, which opened the York River to his ships, McClellan advanced upon the Confederate lines. Magruder, who had only eleven thousand men, made no resistance, and though mauled in a rearguard action at Williamsburg on May 5 extricated himself successfully. By the middle of May McClellan had advanced sixty miles up the York, and arrived at White House, on the Richmond–

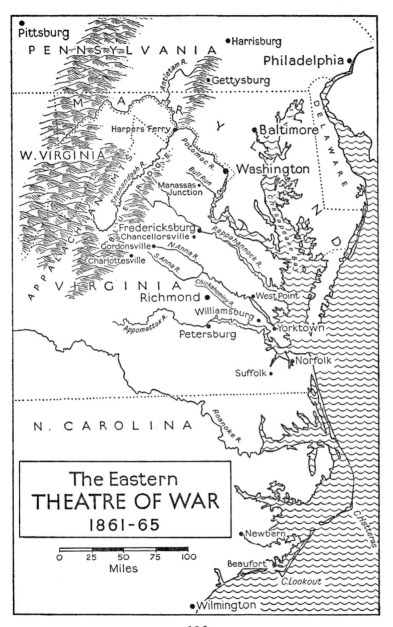

Pittsburg

P E N N S Y L V A N I A

• Harrisburg

Philadelphia •

• Gettysburg

Antietam R.

M A

R

Harpers Ferry

Potomac R.

• Baltimore

W. VIRGINIA

Shenandoah R.

Bull Run

Washington

Manassas
Junction

D
E
L
A
W
A
R
E

Chesapeake Bay

Fredericksburg •

Chancellorsville •

Gordonsville •

N. Anna R.

Charlottesville •

S. Anna R.

Rappahannock R.

Chickahominy R.

V I R G I N I A

Richmond •

West Point •

Appomattox R.

Williamsburg •

Yorktown •

Petersburg •

Norfolk •

Suffolk •

N. C A R O L I N A

Roanoke R.

The Eastern
THEATRE OF WAR
1861-65

0   25   50   75   100
Miles

• Newbern

C. Hatteras

Beaufort •

C. Lookout

• Wilmington

West Point railway, twenty-five miles from the rebel capital. He formed a new base at West Point and became independent of Fortress Monroe. Could he at this moment have brought McDowell from Fredericksburg into his combination the fate of Richmond might well have been sealed.

However, President Davis had in April been persuaded by Lee to reinforce "Stonewall" Jackson for an offensive diversion in the Shenandoah valley. With only sixteen thousand men against four Federal Generals, Banks, Shields, Frémont and Milroy, who disposed of over forty thousand, Jackson fought the brief, brilliant campaign which reinforced his first renown. Striking right and left at the superior forces on either side of him, running daily risks of capture, making enormous marches, sometimes dividing his small force, he gained a series of sharp actions, which greatly perturbed President Lincoln and his advisers. Lincoln had at last promised McClellan McDowell's corps; but six days later, when the Union Army was half across the swampy river Chickahominy, a telegram brought the General the news that McDowell's movement was "suspended." McClellan paused in his advance; violent rains flooded the Chickahominy, and the Union Army found itself divided, with two corps only on the southern side. This was clearly Johnston's opportunity. With his whole force he attacked the two isolated Union corps. President Davis, with Lee at his side, rode out to watch the resulting battle of Seven Pines, or Fair Oaks as it is sometimes called. They had not been consulted by the Commander-in-Chief, who had given all his orders verbally to his Generals. The Confederate attack miscarried. The battle was severe but indecisive, costing each side about six thousand men. McClellan was checked, and heavy rains made him all the more ready to remain inactive. He stood fast with his outposts five miles from Richmond. Lincoln, having learned that Jackson was now in retreat up the valley, again promised McDowell's corps. But when Jackson turned on his pursuers and defeated them on two successive days, June 8 and 9, at Cross Keys and Port Republic, he changed his mind again and would not let McDowell go. It was certainly desirable to guard against any risk of the Federal capital's falling even temporarily into rebel hands, for the effect would have been shattering, though hardly disastrous. But Lincoln's vacillations are a classic instance of the dangers of civilian interference with generals in the field.

Far more important than the fighting was the fact that General Joseph E. Johnston was severely wounded on the first day at Seven Pines, and President Davis on June 1 appointed Lee to command what was henceforward to bear the deathless title of the Army of Northern Virginia.

*　　*　　*　　*　　*

Lee now made the first of his offensive combinations, and immediately his hand was felt in the whole conduct of the war. He procured from Davis the gathering of the Atlantic garrisons which Johnston had been denied. He played upon the fears of Washington by sending seven thousand men to strengthen Jackson in the valley. This ensured the further paralysis of McDowell. Jackson rode in from his army to concert the plans. He was ordered to leave his "enfeebled troops" in the valley, and come secretly with his main force to Ashland, fifteen miles north of Richmond and on the Richmond–Fredericksburg railway. He could thence by advancing turn the flank and the rear of the Union armies and cut their communications with West Point. He was to be ready to act by dawn on June 26. In the interval J. E. B. Stuart, the young Confederate cavalry leader, with twelve hundred horse, made a remarkable reconnaissance of McClellan's right. He actually traversed his communications, and, being unable to return, rode right round the Union Army, arriving south of Richmond with several hundred captives. This was more than Lee had wished, and Stuart's exploit might well have warned the enemy. But McClellan made no change in his array, which still lay in sight of Richmond astride the Chickahominy. Lee's army, counting Jackson, was now over seventy-five thousand strong. McClellan mustered eighty-seven thousand; but of these only the corps of General Fitz-John Porter, twenty-five thousand strong, was now north of the Chickahominy. Lee resolved to move the bulk of his force across that river, and, joined by Jackson, to concentrate fifty-six thousand men against Porter's corps, turn its right flank, destroy it, sever McClellan's communications with West Point, and thereafter cross the Chickahominy in his rear and bring him to ruin. There would be left in the entrenchments defending Richmond only sixteen thousand men under Magruder. It would be open to McClellan, when he saw what was afoot, to march with sixty thousand men straight upon the Richmond lines and assault them with a superiority of nearly four to one. Lee, who knew McClellan well, and judged him rightly, was sure he would not do this. "Anyhow," he said to Davis, "I shall be hard on his heels"—meaning that he would be attacking the Union Army from the rear while it was fighting its way into Richmond. This remark illustrates the agile, flexible grasp which Lee had of war, and how great commanders seem to move their armies from place to place as if they were doing no more than riding their own horses.

During the night of June 25 two Confederate corps crossed the Chickahominy, formed to their right, and fell upon Porter at Mechanicsville. Porter, surprised, made a stubborn resistance. His batteries of rifled cannon wrought havoc in the Confederate ranks. Jackson did not appear upon the scene. The difficulties of the route had delayed him by a day. Porter, hav-

ing inflicted a loss of over two thousand men upon his assailants, was able to fall back upon his reserves at Gaines's Mill,
four miles farther downstream, where the onslaught was renewed with the greatest fury on June 27. Gaines's Mill was
the first battle in which Lee commanded personally. It was
bitterly contested. Again the power of the Union artillery was
manifest. The Confederates were several times repulsed at
all points, and the country on Porter's right was so obstructed
with forest and swamp that when Jackson came into action
in the late afternoon he could not turn the flank. Lee however did not despair. He appealed to his troops. He launched
J. B. Hood's gallant Texans at the centre, and as the shadows
lengthened ordered the whole army to attack. The Texans
broke the centre of Porter's hard-tried corps. The Union
troops were driven from the field. Twenty guns and several
thousand prisoners were already taken when night fell. Where
would Porter go? McClellan had remained immobile opposite Magruder during the two days' fighting. What would he
do? His communications were cut. His right wing was crushed.
Lee's long, swinging left arm, of which Jackson was at last
the fist, must curve completely round the right and rear of
the Federal Army. Surely the stroke was mortal?

But McClellan was a skilful soldier. When his generals met
him at headquarters on the night of Gaines's Mill he informed
them that he had let go his communications with West Point
and the York River; that, using sea-power, he was shifting his
base from the York to the James; that the whole army would
march southwards to Harrison's Landing on that river, where
all supplies would await them. He had, we now know, made
some preparations for such a change beforehand. But he ran
a grave risk in leaving the decision till the last moment. What
was called, from its shape, a "grape-vine bridge" had been
built across the swamps and stream of the Chickahominy,

and by this tortuous, rickety structure Porter made good his escape, while the whole Federal Army prepared to make a difficult and dangerous flank march across the White Oak Swamp to the southern side of the peninsula. It was now Magruder's turn to advance and strike at this vulnerable army. He broke in upon them on the 28th at Savage Station, capturing their field hospitals and large supplies. But Lee could not yet be sure that McClellan was really making for the James. He might as well be retreating by the Williamsburg road on Fortress Monroe. Lee therefore delayed one day before crossing the Chickahominy in pursuit. It was not till the 30th that he brought McClellan to battle at Glendale, or Frayser's Farm. This was the main crisis.

It is almost incredible that McClellan spent the day conferring with the Navy and arranging the new base on the James. He left the battle to fight itself. On the Confederate side many things went wrong. The maps were faulty; the timing failed; the attacks were delivered piecemeal; Jackson, from whom so much had been hoped, appeared in physical eclipse. Out of seventy-five thousand men with whom Lee had proposed to deal the final blow barely twenty thousand were really launched. These, after frightful losses, broke the Union centre; but night enabled the army to continue its retreat. At Malvern Hill, in a position of great strength, with the James River behind them to forbid further retreat, and the fire of the Navy and its gunboats to cover their flanks, McClellan stood at bay. Once again at the end of this week of furious fighting Lee ordered the attack, and his soldiers charged with their marvellous impetuosity. Loud roared the Union cannonade; high rose the rebel yell, that deadly sound *"Aah-ih!"* so often to be heard in these bloody years. But all was in vain. McClellan was saved. Frustrated, beaten, driven into retreat, his whole campaign wrecked, with a loss of enormous masses of stores and munitions, sixty cannon and thirty-six thousand rifles, with Richmond invincible, McClellan and his brave army nevertheless finished the Battle of the Seven Days by hurling back their pursuers with the loss of five thousand men.

Victory in the Seven Days' Battle rested with Lee. The world saw the total failure of the immense Federal plan. This also was the impression at Washington. McClellan, who was undaunted, proposed to move across the James to Petersburg and attack Richmond "by the back door," as Grant was to do in 1865. His proposals were not accepted. But to Lee the adventure was hardly less disappointing. He had failed by a succession of narrow chances, arising largely from the newness of his staffs, to annihilate his foe. He had lost over twenty thousand of the flower of his army, against seventeen thousand on the Union side with its overflowing man-power.

Lincoln and his advisers now sought to return to their original plan of massing overwhelming forces on the overland route between Washington and Richmond and breaking through by weight of numbers. But their armies were divided, and Lee at Richmond stood directly between them. The President ordered McClellan to withdraw from the peninsula and bring his troops up the Potomac to the neighbourhood of Washington. Halleck, who was then credited with the successes gained against his orders in the Western theatre, was appointed General-in-Chief. He brought General Pope, who had done well in the Mississippi valley, to command what was to be called "the Army of Virginia." Pope was a harsh, vainglorious man, puffed up with good fortune in the Western theatre, and speaking in derogatorty terms of the armies of the East and their achievements. He would show them how war should be waged. McClellan was ordered to hand over his troops, who parted from him in outspoken grief, and was relegated to the defence of the Washington lines. Pope now would be the champion of the Union. He signalised his appointment by severities upon the civil population of Western Virginia not yet used in the war. All male inhabitants in the zone of his army must either swear allegiance to the Union or be driven from their homes on pain of death if they returned. Jackson only with difficulty preserved his habitual calm on hearing this news about his beloved native state.

The strategic situation offered advantages to Lee and his lieutenant. Before McClellan's army could be brought round from the Yorktown peninsula they would deal with Pope. How they treated him must be recounted.

* * * * *

An historic naval episode had meanwhile occurred. When in the spring of 1861 the Federal Government had lightly abandoned the Navy yard at Norfolk to the seceding state of Virginia some stores and several vessels of the United States Navy had been burned. One of these, the frigate *Merrimac*, was repaired and refashioned in a curious way. It was given steam-engines to propel it, and above its deck a low penthouse of teak was erected. This was covered with two layers of railway iron hammered into two-inch plates. These layers were riveted transversely upon each other, making an ironclad shelter four inches thick. A heavy metal ram was fastened to the prow, and a battery of ten 7-inch rifled guns, firing through portholes, was mounted in the penthouse. Many had thought of this sort of thing before; now it came upon the scene.

This strange vessel was only finished on March 7, 1862. She had never fired a gun, nor had her engines been revolved, when on March 8 she went into action against the all-powerful Navy of the United States, which from Fortress Monroe was blockading the estuaries of the York and James Rivers.

The engines, described as the worst possible, were found to make only five knots an hour, and the vessel swam and steered like a waterlogged ship. Out she came, and with no hesitation engaged the two nearest ships of the blockading fleet, the *Cumberland* and the *Congress.* These delivered broadsides which would have sunk an ordinary frigate. Besides this, all other United States ships in range and the shore batteries at Sewell's Point concentrated their fire upon her. Without paying the slightest attention to this bombardment, the *Merrimac,* rechristened the *Virginia,* steered straight for the *Cumberland,* and struck her almost at right angles. On board the *Merrimac* the collision was hardly perceptible. The ram broke off; the *Cumberland* heeled over, and, firing her cannon to the last, soon foundered, with most of her crew. The *Merrimac* then turned upon the *Congress,* and at two hundred yards range smashed her to pieces and set her on fire. After an hour the *Congress* hoisted the white flag, and every effort was made by various small Confederate ships to rescue her crew. The *Minnesota,* which was aground, would have shared her fate if the ebb tide had not prevented the *Merrimac,* which drew twenty-two feet of water, from approaching her. Although the *Merrimac* was for a long time under the fire of at least a hundred heavy guns her armour was hardly damaged. Nothing outside the armour escaped. The funnel and two of the muzzles of the guns were shot off. Inside only twenty-one men were killed or wounded by splinters through the portholes. Her triumphant crew lay down by the side of their guns, expecting to destroy the rest of the United States fleet the next morning.

But when daylight came and steam was raised a strange-looking vessel was seen to be protecting the *Minnesota.* "She appeared," wrote one of the *Merrimac's* crew, "but a pigmy compared with the lofty frigate which she guarded." This was

Ericsson's *Monitor,* of which there had been much talk, now at last ready. The *Merrimac* had made the naval revolution, but the *Monitor,* one day later, was a whole lap ahead of her. She carried only two guns; but they were eleven-inch, and mounted in a revolving iron turret nine inches thick. She had a turtle deck, heavily protected, almost flush with the water-line. As she drew only twelve feet of water she had an advantage in manœuvre.

Both these ironclad monsters approached each other, while the stately ships of the United States fleet watched spellbound. They came to the closest quarters, and the *Merrimac,* now ramless, struck the *Monitor.* None of the *Merrimac's* shells pierced the *Monitor's* armour; but when the two eleven-inch guns hit the *Merrimac* amidships the whole side was driven in several inches, and all the guns' crews bled at the nose from concussion. For six hours these two ironclads battered each other with hardly any injury or loss on either side, and both withdrew at close of day, never to meet again. As the *Merrimac* had no armour below the water-line her crew considered her lucky. She returned to the dock-yard to have this defect and many others repaired. The *Monitor,* which was so unseaworthy that she had nearly foundered on the way to the fight, also required attention. As soon as the news reached Europe it was realised that all the war-fleets of the world were obsolete. The British Admiralty, by an intense effort, in the course of a few years reconstructed the Royal Navy so as to meet the altered conditions. But even now there are fools who build large ships to fight at sea with hardly any armour.[1] The combat of the *Merrimac* and the *Monitor* made the greatest change in sea-fighting since cannon fired by gunpowder had been mounted on ships about four hundred years before.

When Norfolk was evacuated by the Confederates efforts

[1] Written in 1939.

were made to take the *Merrimac* up the James River for the defence of Richmond; but although she was so lightened as to become defenceless her draught prevented her escape. By the orders of her captain she was therefore burned and sunk. The joy which her exploit had evoked throughout the Confederacy now turned to grief and anger. But the Confederate court-martial upon the captain declared that "The only alternative, in the opinion of the court, was to abandon and burn the ship then and there; which in the judgment of the court was deliberately and wisely done by order of the accused."

Lee and McClellan

G ENERAL POPE reached the front on August 1, 1862. The new commander's task was plainly to gain as much ground as he could without being seriously engaged until McClellan's army could return from the James River and join him. Aquia Creek, not far south of the capital, was appointed for the landing of this army, and further large reinforcements were moving from Washington, through Alexandria, and along the railroad. Pope had already forty thousand men; in six weeks he would have a hundred and fifty thousand. He was full of energy, and very sanguine. He hoped to capture both Gordonsville and Charlottesville even before his main force arrived, and then finish off Richmond.

As soon as Lee saw that McClellan had no further bite he sent Jackson, in the middle of July, with two divisions (eleven thousand men) to Gordonsville, and raised him by the end of the month to twenty-four thousand. This was a lot for Jackson, who had barely two to one to face. He found Pope's army moving hopefully towards him by the three roads which joined at Culpeper. On August 9 he fell upon General Banks, commanding Pope's leading corps, seven miles south of Culpeper, at Cedar Mountain. He used twenty thousand men against Banks's nine thousand, drove them from the field with the loss of a quarter of their number, and left the rest in no condition to do more than guard the baggage. But before Culpeper he found himself confronted with the other two corps of Pope's army, and in harmony with Lee's conceptions he fell back to Gordonsville.

On August 13 Lee learnt that McClellan's army was being re-embarked at Fortress Monroe. This was the signal for which he was waiting. Before this splendid army could make its weight tell with Pope in Northern Virginia, a period of a month at the outside, he must win a great battle there. He at once ordered General James Longstreet with twelve brigades, the bulk of the Richmond forces, to join Jackson at Gordonsville, and by the 17th he had fifty-five thousand men concentrated in the woods behind Clark's Mountain, within striking distance of Culpeper, where Pope was now established. Pope was unaware of his peril, and might well have been destroyed. But Lee waited a day to bring up his cavalry, and in the meantime a Confederate officer was captured with papers which opened Pope's eyes. Favoured by the morning mist, he retreated forthwith behind the Rappahannock. Lee's first right-handed clutch had failed. He now scooped with the left hand. Jackson crossed the Upper Rappahannock by Sulphur Springs. But the river rose after his first brigade was over, and a second time Pope was saved.

Lee now knew that his brief period of superiority had passed, and that he must expect, in a week or ten days, overwhelming forces to be massed against him. He knew that the leading divisions of McClellan's former army were already ashore at Aquia Creek. How could the Army of Northern Virginia cope with a hundred and fifty thousand men, once they were concentrated? He therefore resolved with Jackson upon a daring and, since it was successful, brilliant manœuvre. In the face of a superior and rapidly growing enemy he divided his army. Before dawn on August 25 Jackson began another of his famous marches. With twenty thousand men, after covering twenty-six miles, he reached Salem, far behind Pope's right flank, and the next day by another twenty-five-mile march through Thoroughfare Gap in the hills he cut the Alexandria-Orange railway, upon which Pope depended for his supplies, a few miles south of Manassas Junction. On the 27th he seized the junction. Here the whole supply of Pope's army was heaped. Food, equipment, stores of every kind, dazzling to the pinched Confederates, fell into his hands. He set guards upon the liquor and let his men take what they could carry. Most of them reclothed themselves. But this booty might be bought at a fatal price. On every side superior Federal forces lay or were approaching. The cutting of Pope's communications was an incident and not the aim of Jackson and his chief. Nothing short of a great battle won was of any use to them. He therefore delivered the junction and its depot to the flames. Looking northwards, Pope perceived the night sky reddened by the immense conflagration. It was Jackson's part to keep him puzzled and occupied till Lee could come round with Longstreet and the main army and join him.

There was now no danger of Pope marching on towards Richmond. He was hamstrung. He must retreat. But with the great forces arriving by every road to join him he would still have a large preponderance. He might even close Thoroughfare Gap to Lee and the rest of the Confederate Army. It was a dire hazard of war. Jackson withdrew from Manassas Junction northward into the woods by Sudley Springs. Pope, believing that he had him in his grip at the Junction, marched upon it from every quarter. The Junction was found in ashes and empty. During the 28th neither side knew all that was happening; but Jackson was aware that Longstreet was thrusting through Thoroughfare Gap with Lee and the main Confederate Army. Pope's orders to his disjointed army were to annihilate Jackson, now located south of Sudley Springs,

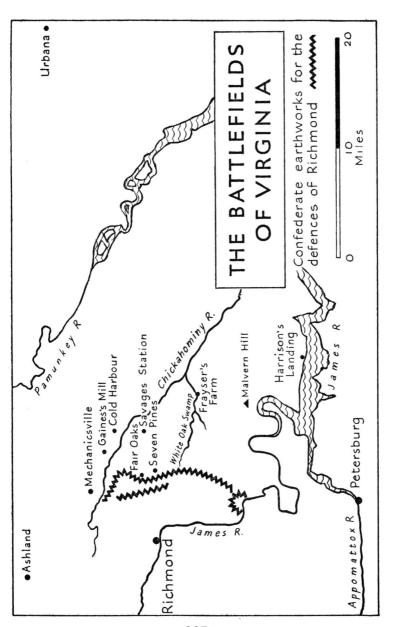

THE BATTLEFIELDS OF VIRGINIA

Confederate earthworks for the defences of Richmond ⌇⌇⌇⌇

0   10   20
Miles

Urbana

Pamunkey R.

Ashland

Mechanicsville

Gaines's Mill

Cold Harbour

Fair Oaks

Savages Station

Seven Pines

Chickahominy R.

White Oak Swamp

Frayser's Farm

▲ Malvern Hill

Harrison's Landing

James R.

Richmond

James R.

Petersburg

Appomattox R.

and for this purpose he set seventy thousand men in motion. He thought only of Jackson. He seemed to have forgotten Longstreet and Lee, who were already massing into line on Jackson's right.

On August 30 began the Second Battle of Bull Run, or Manassas. With great bravery fifty-three thousand Federals in five successive assaults grappled in the open field with Jackson's twenty thousand. To and fro the struggle swayed, with equal slaughter. Longstreet, already in line, but still unperceived, was painfully slow in coming into action. He always wished to look before he leapt; and this sound maxim was far below the level of the event. He was a great war-horse, and Lee would not press him beyond a certain point. On the first day of the Second Manassas Jackson bore the whole brunt alone. As evening came, when his last reserves had delivered their counter-attack, a clergyman with whom he was friendly expressed his fears for the thin-worn Confederate left. "Stonewall," measuring the struggle from minute to minute, took one long look at the field and said, "They have done their worst."

Battle was renewed at dawn on the 31st. Pope had received the support of two new corps, marching up from Aquia. Still unconscious of Longstreet's presence, he ordered the ill-starred General, Porter, to turn Jackson's right, and Porter's troops responded loyally. But now Longstreet, massive once he was in action, threw in the main weight of the Confederate Army. Pope's array was ruptured. On a four-mile front the new, unexpected Confederate Army debouched magnificently from the woods. The two corps of Pope's left, outnumbered and outflanked, retreated. Porter, enveloped, was overwhelmed, and subsequently victimised by court-martial. Although even at the end of the day Pope commanded 70,000 faithful men, he had no thought but to seek shelter behind the Washington entrenchments, into which he also carried with him a final reinforcement of 10,000 men which reached him during the night. Lee had captured thirty guns, 20,000 precious rifles, and 7,000 prisoners, and had killed and wounded 13,500 Federals, at a total cost to the Confederacy of 10,000 men. He had utterly defeated 75,000 Union troops with less than 55,000 in his own hand. It was exactly four months since President Davis had given him command. Then McClellan was within five miles of Richmond. Now Lee's outposts were within twenty miles of Washington. In this decisive manner the tables were turned.

*   *   *   *   *

Ill-treatment was meted out to General McClellan by the Washington politicians and Cabinet, with the cautious, pliant General Halleck as their tool. For this Lincoln cannot escape blame. He wanted an aggressive General who would energetically seek out Lee and beat him. McClellan for all his qualities of leadership lacked the final ounces of fighting spirit. Lincoln with his shrewd judgment of men knew this. But he also knew that McClellan was probably the ablest commander available to him. His instinct had been to stand by his chosen General. Instead he had yielded to political outcry. He had swapped horses in mid-stream. He found he had got a poorer mount. As the different corps of McClellan's army were landed at Aquia they were hurried off to join Pope, until McClellan had not even his own personal escort with him. Yet he was never removed from the command of the Army of Virginia, which had been renamed the Army of the Potomac. He made voluble and justified complaints, to which no attention was paid. But on September 2, when Pope and his beaten army seemed about to collapse upon Washington, and panic lapped around the President, a different attitude was shown. While McClellan was breakfasting that morning he was visited by the President and the General-in-Chief. Halleck declared that Washington was lost, and offered Mc-Clellan the command of all the forces. The flouted commander at once undertook to save the city. As he had never been dismissed officially, he was never reappointed. He had been deprived of all his troops; they were now restored. History has never allowed McClellan to rise above the level of competent and courageous mediocrity; but it must not be forgotten that when he rode out to meet the retreating army they received him with frantic enthusiasm. The long, jaded, humiliated columns of brave men who had been so shamefully mishandled broke their ranks and almost dragged their restored commander from the saddle. The soldiers embraced and kissed his horse's legs. Thus fortified, McClellan restored order to the army and turned its face again to the foe.

Lee, after the second Confederate victory at Manassas, did what ought to have been done after the first. He invaded Maryland to give that state a chance to come over, if it still would or could. Always seeking the decisive and final battle which he knew could alone save the Confederacy, he marched north by Leesburg, crossed the Potomac, and arrived in the neighbourhood of Frederick, abreast of Baltimore. He knew he had never the slightest chance of taking Washington; but there were prizes to be won in the open field. Three Federal garrisons occupied Martinsburg, Winchester, and Harpers Ferry, in the Shenandoah valley. At Harpers Ferry there was a great Union depot of supply. In the three places there were over fifteen thousand men. Halleck had refused to withdraw them while time remained. They became a substantial objective to Lee, and his design was to capture Harpers Ferry, into which the two smaller garrisons withdrew. Accordingly he marched west from Frederick through the range of hills called the South Mountains, sent Jackson looping out by Martinsburg, and on September 13 closed down on Harpers Ferry from all sides.

The Washington politicians, in their hour of panic, had clung to McClellan. They did not mean to sink with him. He was originally given orders only to defend the Washington fortifications. However, on his own responsibility, or, so he later claimed, "with a rope round his neck," he took charge of his old army, quitted "the Washington defences," and set out after Lee, whom he outnumbered by two to one. McClellan's account of this episode is widely contested, for in fact Lincoln discussed with him the Army's movement into Maryland and verbally gave him "command of the forces in the field" as well as around the capital. McClellan's political prejudices may well have coloured his memory. He had reason to feel aggrieved. His innumerable critics in high places never ceased to harry him. Their attitude to the commander in the field at this juncture was dishonouring to them.

McClellan, hoping to save Harpers Ferry, now started after Lee with nearly ninety thousand men, including two fine corps that had not yet suffered at all. By a stroke of luck a Northern private soldier picked up three cigars wrapped in a piece of paper which was in fact a copy of Lee's most secret orders. McClellan learned on the 13th that Lee had divided his army and that the bulk of it was closing on Harpers Ferry. He therefore advanced with very good assurance to attack him. Everything now became a matter of hours. Could Jackson, Walner, and McLaws capture Harpers Ferry before Lee was beaten in the passes of the South Mountains?

McClellan wasted many of these precious hours. But considering that members of the Government behind him could only gape and gibber and that his political foes were avid of a chance to bring him to ruin it is not surprising that he acted with a double dose of his habitual caution. By overwhelming forces Lee was beaten back from the two gaps in the South Mountain range on the 14th. He now had to take a great decision. At first he thought to gather his spoils and laurels and re-cross the Potomac into Virginia. But later, feeling that nothing but victory would suffice, he resolved to give battle behind the Antietam stream, with his back to the Potomac, believing that Jackson would capture Harpers Ferry in the meanwhile and rejoin him in time.

Harpers Ferry surrendered early on the 15th. Seventy-three guns, thirteen thousand rifles, and twelve thousand five hundred prisoners were gathered by Jackson's officers. He was himself already marching all through the afternoon and night to join Lee, who stood with but twenty thousand men against the vast approaching mass of McClellan. This worthy general was unable to free himself from the Washington obsession. Had he been as great a soldier or as great a man as Lee he would have staked all on the battle. But he could not free his mind from the cowardly and personally malignant political forces behind him. To make sure of not running undue risks, he lost a day, and failed to win the battle.

It was not till the 17th that he attacked. By this time Jackson had arrived and was posted on Lee's left, and the rest of the Confederate divisions, having cleaned up Harpers Ferry, were striding along to the new encounter. Lee fought with his back to the Potomac, and could scarcely, if defeated, have escaped across its single bridge by Sharpsburg. This horrible battle was the acme of Federal mismanagement. McClellan, after riding down the line, fought it from his headquarters on what was called "the Commander-in-Chief idea." This meant that he made his dispositions and left the battle to fight itself. But Jackson stood in the line, and Lee rode his horse about the field controlling the storm, as Marlborough, Frederick the Great, and Napoleon were wont to do. The Confederate left, under Jackson, was practically destroyed, but only after ruining double their numbers, two whole corps of the Federal Army. All here came to a standstill, till Jackson was reinforced by Lee from his hard-pressed right and centre. The Union centre then attacked piecemeal, and their leading division was torn to pieces, half falling smitten. Burnside, who with the Union left was to cross the Antietam and cut Lee's line of retreat, would have succeeded but for the arrival of Lee's last division, under A. P. Hill, from Harpers Ferry. Striking the right flank of the assailants from an unexpected direction, he ended this menace; and night fell upon a drawn battle, in which the Federals had lost thirteen thousand men, a fourth of the troops they engaged and one-sixth of those they had on the field, and the Confederacy nine thousand, which was about a quarter.

When darkness fell Lee faced his great lieutenants. Without exception they advised immediate retreat across the Potomac. Even Jackson, unconquerable in action, thought this would be wise. But Lee, who still hoped to gain his indisputable, decisive battle, after hearing all opinions, declared his resolve to stand his ground. Therefore the shattered Confederates faced the morning light and the huge array of valiant soldiers who seemed about to overwhelm them. But McClellan had had enough. He lay still. Before the slightest reproach can fall on him the shabby War Department behind him must shoulder their share. There was no fighting on the 18th. Lee put it hard across Jackson to take the offensive; but when Jackson, after personal reconnaissance with the artillery commander, declared it impossible Lee accepted this sagacious judgment, and his first invasion of Maryland came to an end.

War had never reached such an intensity of moral and physical forces focused upon decisive points as in this campaign of 1862. The number of battles that were fought and their desperate, bloody character far surpassed any events in which Napoleon ever moved. From June 1, when Lee was given the command, the Army of Northern Virginia fought seven ferocious battles—the Seven Days, Cedar Run, the Second Manassas, South Mountain, Harpers Ferry, the Antietam, and later Fredericksburg—in as many months. Lee very rarely had three-quarters, and several times only half, the strength of his opponents. These brave Northerners were certainly hampered by a woeful political direction, but, on the other side, the Confederates were short of weapons, ammunition, food, equipment, clothes, and boots. It was even said that their line of march could be traced by the bloodstained footprints of unshod men. But the Army of Northern Virginia "carried the Confederacy on its bayonets" and made a struggle unsurpassed in history.

* * * * *

Lincoln had hoped for a signal victory. McClellan at the Antietam presented him with a partial though important success. But the President's faith in the Union cause was never dimmed by disappointments. He was much beset by anxieties, which led him to cross-examine his commanders as if he were still a prosecuting attorney. The Generals did not relish it. But Lincoln's popularity with the troops stood high. They put their trust in him. They could have no knowledge of the relentless political pressures in Washington to which he was subjected. They had a sense however of his natural resolution and generosity of character. He had to draw deeply on these qualities in his work at the White House. Through his office flowed a stream of politicians, newspaper editors, and other men of influence. Most of them clamoured for quick victory, with no conception of the hazards of war. Many of them cherished their own amateur plans of operation which they confidently urged upon their leader. Many of them too had favourite Generals for whom they canvassed. Lincoln treated all his visitors with patience and firmness. His homely humour stood him in good stead. A sense of irony helped to lighten his burdens. In tense moments a dry joke relieved his feelings. At the same time his spirit was sustained by a deepening belief in Providence. When the toll of war rose steeply and plans went wrong he appealed for strength in his inmost thoughts to a power higher than man's. Strength was certainly given him. It is sometimes necessary at the summit of authority to bear with the intrigues of disloyal colleagues, to remain calm when others panic, and to withstand misguided popular outcries. All this Lincoln did. Personal troubles also befell him. One of his beloved sons died in the White House. Mrs Lincoln, though devoted to her husband, had a taste for extravagance and for politics which sometimes gave rise to wounding comment. As the war drew on Lincoln became more and more gaunt and the furrows on his cheeks and brow bit deep. Fortitude was written on his countenance.

The Antietam and the withdrawal of Lee into Virginia gave the President an opportunity to take a momentous step. He proclaimed the emancipation of all the slaves in the insurgent states. The impression produced in France and Britain by Lee's spirited and resolute operations, with their successive great battles, either victorious or drawn, made the Washington Cabinet fearful of mediation, to be followed, if rejected, by recognition of the Confederacy. The North was discouraged by disastrous and futile losses and by the sense of being out-generalled. Recruitment fell off and desertion was rife. Many urged peace, and others asked whether the Union was worthy of this slaughter, if slavery was to be maintained. By casting down this final challenge and raising the war to the level of a moral crusade Lincoln hoped to rally British public opinion to the Union cause and raise a new enthusiasm among his own fellow-countrymen.

It was a move he had long considered. Even since the beginning of the war the Radicals had been pressing for the total abolition of slavery. Lincoln had misgivings about the effects on the slave-owning states of the border which had remained loyal. He insisted that the sole object of the war was to preserve the Union. As he wrote to the New York publisher, Horace Greeley, "My paramount object is to save the Union, and is not either to save or to destroy slavery. . . . What I do about slavery and the coloured race, I do because it helps to save the Union; and what I forbear, I forbear because I do not believe it would help to save the Union." Meanwhile he was meditating on the timing of his Proclamation and on the constitutional difficulties that stood in the way. He believed he had no power to interfere with slavery in the border states. He felt his Proclamation could be legally justified only as a military measure, issued in virtue of his office as Commander-in-Chief of the Army and Navy. Its intention was to deprive the Confederacy of a source of its strength. When the Proclamation was published, with effect from January 1st, 1863, it therefore applied only to the rebel states. Slavery in the rest of the Union was not finally abolished until the passing of the Thirteenth Amendment in December 1865. In the South the Proclamation only came into force as the Federal armies advanced. Nor were the broader results all that Lincoln had hoped. In Britain it was not understood why he had not declared Abolition outright. A political manœuvre on his part was suspected. In America itself the war assumed an implacable character, offering to the South no alternative but subjugation. The Democratic Party in the North was wholly opposed to the Emancipation Edict. In the Federal armies it was unpopular, and General

McClellan, who might be expected to become the Democratic candidate for the Presidency, had two months earlier sent Lincoln a solemn warning against such an action. At the Congressional elections in the autumn of 1862 the Republicans lost ground. Many Northerners thought that the President had gone too far, others that he had not gone far enough. Great, judicious, and well-considered steps are thus sometimes at first received with public incomprehension.

The relations between the Washington Government and its General remained deplorable. McClellan might fairly claim to have rendered them an immense service after the panic at Manassas. He had revived the Army, led it to the field, and cleared Maryland. For all the Government knew, he had saved the capital. In fact he had done more. Lord Palmerston in England had decided that summer on mediation. News of the Antietam made him hesitate. This averted the danger to the North that the Confederacy would be recognised by the Powers of Europe. But it was not immediately apparent in the Union. Gladstone, Chancellor of the Exchequer in Palmerston's Government, delivered a speech at Newcastle in the autumn which enraged Northern opinion. He said: "We know quite well that the people of the Northern states have not yet drunk of the cup—they are still trying to hold it from their lips—which all the world sees they nevertheless must drink of. We may have our own opinions about slavery, we may be for or against the South, but there is no doubt that Jefferson Davis and other leaders of the South have made an Army; they are making, it appears, a Navy; and they have made what is more than either, they have made a Nation." Gladstone had not been informed that Palmerston had changed his mind.

Meanwhile between the politicians and the Commander-in-Chief upon the Potomac there was hatred and scorn on both sides. Bitter party politics aggravated military divergence. The President desired a prompt and vigorous advance. McClellan, as usual, magnified Confederate numbers and underrated their grievous losses. He was determined to run no unmilitary risks for a Government which he knew was eager to stab him in the back. Five weeks passed after the battle before he began to cross the Potomac in leisurely fashion and move forward from Harpers Ferry to Warrenton.

Lee withdrew by easy marches up the Shenandoah valley. He had sent "Jeb" Stuart on his second romantic ride round McClellan in mid-October, had harried the Federal communications and acquired much valuable information. He now did not hesitate to divide his army in the face of McClellan's great hosts. He left Jackson in the valley to keep Washington on tenterhooks, and rested himself with Longstreet, near Culpeper Court House. If pressed he could fall back to Gordonsville, where he judged Jackson could join him in time. McClellan however had now at length prepared his blow. He planned to strike Lee with overwhelming strength before Jackson could return. At this moment he was himself taken in rear by President Lincoln. On the night of November 7, 1862, he was ordered to hand over his command to General Burnside, and at the same time Porter, his most competent subordinate, was placed under arrest. The Government had used these men in their desperation. They now felt strong enough to strike them down. McClellan was against the abolition of slavery, and he never changed his view. The dominant Radical wing of the Republican Party was out for his blood. They were convinced that McClellan would never set himself to gain a crushing victory. They suspected him of tender feelings for the South and a desire for a negotiated peace. They also feared that the General would prove to be a potent Democratic candidate for the Presidency. Lincoln allowed himself to be persuaded by the Radical Republicans that McClellan had become a liability to his Government. He had long stood up for his commander against the attacks and whisperings of the politicians. Now he felt he must give way. But it was without animosity, for that viper was never harboured in Lincoln's breast.

There was almost a mutiny in the Union Army when McClellan's dismissal was known. He himself acted with perfect propriety, and used all his influence to place his successor in the saddle. He was never employed again. Thus the General who, as Lee after the war told his youngest son, was by far the best of his opponents disappeared from command. No one can be blind to McClellan's limitations, but he was learning continually from his collisions with Lee and Jackson. His removal was a wrong done to the Union Army, which never gave its love to any other leader. There remained for McClellan a vivid political struggle where numbers, which alone count in such affairs, were found upon the other side. General Porter, although he had rendered good service in the intervening Maryland campaign, was tried by court-martial for his conduct at the Second Manassas, condemned, and dismissed from the United States Army. This injustice was repaired after the lapse of years. A re-trial was ordered and he received honourable acquittal.

We have seen several times in this obstinate war President Lincoln pressing for battle and for frontal attack. "On to Richmond" was his mood; and now at last in Burnside he had found a General who would butt straight at the barrier. Burnside, a charming personality, but a thoroughly bad General, was, to his honour, most reluctant to take command. Once in charge he followed a simple plan. He chose the shortest road which led on the map to Richmond, and concentrated his army along it upon the crossing of the Rappahannock at Fredericksburg.

He took a fortnight in order to do this as well as possible.

Meanwhile Lee brought in Jackson and other reinforce-ments. Hitherto Lee had always fought in the open field; even against the heavy odds of the Antietam he had not used the spade. He now applied the fortnight accorded him to fortify his position above Fredericksburg with every then-known device. Breastworks revetted with logs and stone walls cov-ered by solid earth were prepared. Nearly a hundred and fifty cannon were comfortably sited. Rifle-pits abounded, and good lateral roads were cut through the scrubby forest be-hind the line. On December 11 Burnside occupied Freder-icksburg, crossed the river with a large part of his army, and deployed for battle. He had a hundred and eighteen thou-sand men, against Lee's eighty thousand. On the 13th he delivered his assault. He attacked both the Confederate left wing and its right picccmcal. Then he attacked in the centre. The Northern soldiers showed an intense devotion. Brigade after brigade, division after division, they charged up the slopes under a murderous fire. As evening fell the Union army recoiled with a loss of nearly thirteen thousand men. The Confederate casualties, mostly in Jackson's command, were under six thousand. Burnside, who now thought chiefly of dying at the head of his troops, wished to renew the battle next day. He was restrained by universal opinion at the front and at the capital; and soon after was superseded in chief command by one of his lieutenants, General Joseph Hooker.

Lee had not wished to fight at Fredericksburg at all. The Federal Army was so near its salt-water base at Aquia Creek that no counter-stroke was possible. He had advised Presi-dent Davis to let him meet Burnside thirty miles back on the North Anna River, where there was room for him to use Jackson and Stuart in terrible revenge upon the communica-tions of a repulsed army. But although Davis' relations with the Confederate Generals were on a high plane he had hampered his champion most sadly, cramping him down to a strict defensive, and thus the shattering blow of Fredericksburg had no lasting consequences. If these two Presidents had let McClellan and Lee fight the quarrel out between them as they thought best the end would have been the same, but the war would have been less muddled, much shorter, and less bloody.

* * * * *

In the West nothing decisive had happened up till the end of 1862. By November General Joseph E. Johnston, having recovered from the wounds he got at Seven Pines, was appointed to the chief Confederate command in this theatre, but with only a partial authority over its various armies. In Tennessee General Bragg, with forty-four thousand men in the neighbourhood of Murfreesboro, faced the Federal General William S. Rosecrans, who had forty-seven thousand. General J. C. Pemberton, who commanded the department of the Mississippi, had a field army of about thirty thousand men, apart from the garrisons of Vicksburg and Port Hudson. Lastly, still farther west, in Arkansas, the Confederate General Holmes was encamped near Little Rock with an army raised in that state of fifty thousand men, against whom there were now no active Federal forces. When it was evident that Grant was preparing for the invasion of Mississippi and an attack upon Vicksburg Johnston urged that the Arkansas army should cross the Mississippi and join Pemberton. This would have secured a Confederate superiority. Jefferson Davis vetoed this desirable, and indeed imperative, measure. He knew the violent hostility which an order to the Arkansas forces to serve east of the Mississippi would excite throughout the Western states. No doubt this objection was substantial; but the alternative was disastrous. The President insisted instead that Bragg should send ten thousand men from Chattanooga to strengthen Pemberton in defending Vicksburg. This was accordingly done.

Early in December Grant made a renewed attempt against Vicksburg, sending General Sherman from Memphis, with about thirty thousand men, and Admiral Porter's Naval Squadron, to enter the Yazoo River and occupy the heights to the north of the city. Sherman assaulted the Confederate defences at Chickasaw Bluff on December 29, and in less than an hour was repulsed with the loss of nearly two thousand men, the Confederates losing only a hundred and fifty. He consoled himself with ascending the Arkansas River and capturing a garrison of five thousand Confederates at Arkansas Post. Meanwhile the weakening of Bragg's army in Tennessee brought about, on the last day of the year, a severe battle at Murfreesboro, in which the greatest bravery was displayed by both sides. The Federals, under Rosecrans, lost over nine thousand killed and wounded, as well as nearly four thousand prisoners and twenty-eight guns. But for this Bragg paid over ten thousand men. The Federal hold on Tennessee and its capital Nashville was unshaken. Bragg withdrew his disappointed troops into winter quarters covering Chattanooga.

The armies in the different states still confronted each other on fairly equal terms, and although the Union Navy declared its ability to run the gauntlet of the Confederate batteries when required the great riverway remained barred to Federal transports and traffic. Murfreesboro gave the impression of a drawn battle, and Chickasaw Bluff was an undoubted Confederate success. But now there was to be a profound change in the balance.

Chancellorsville and Gettysburg

THE spring of 1863 found the Army of the Potomac and the Army of Northern Virginia still facing each other across the Rappahannock. Hooker, "Fighting Joe," had distinguished himself as a corps commander at the Antietam. He was not the next senior and had intrigued against his chief. He owed his present advancement to Lincoln, who knew him to be a good fighter and hoped the best of him as a commander. The obvious course, to restore McClellan again, was politically impossible and would have weakened the President's authority. At the end of January, when he was appointed, Hooker found the Federal Army in a sorry plight, which his own previous discontent had fomented. More than three thousand officers and eighty thousand men were either deserters or absent with or without leave. Blows like Fredericksburg are hard to sustain. It was not till April that reorganisation was complete; reinforcements had poured in, and the absentees had returned from their Christmas at home. He was now at the head of over a hundred and thirty thousand men, rested and revived, splendidly equipped, and organised in six army corps. He formed besides a cavalry corps ten thousand strong, and he felt himself able to declare that he led "the finest army on the planet."

In meeting the offensive, which he knew must come, Lee

was gravely hampered by President Davis's policy of the strict defensive and the dispersal of the Confederate troops to cover a number of places. The continued pressure of the war rendered the defence of the ports of Wilmington and Charleston in South Carolina of vital importance, though only blockade-runners could enter them. They and the railways connecting them with Richmond were threatened in the President's eyes by the somewhat near presence of Federal forces which had been landed in March 1862 at New Bern, in North Carolina, and others which had advanced to Suffolk in the estuary of the James River and only seventy-five miles from Richmond. These parties, owing to the nature of the ground near the coast, had been dealt with by local forces. But Lee, also bearing in mind the difficulty of feeding his troops near the Rappahannock, sent first one, then a second and a third detachment, under Longstreet, to deal with them. It was one of Lee's mistakes. Longstreet, who was always striving for an independent command, unnecessarily sat down to besiege Suffolk. Thus Lee's nine divisions were reduced by three, and two of his four cavalry brigades were south of the James to gather forage. His infantry was less than half and his cavalry a quarter of the forces he had to encounter. He therefore abandoned the idea of an offensive into Pennsylvania by way of the Shenandoah valley, which he had had in mind, and awaited events.

Hooker's preponderance enabled him to act with two armies. His plan was, first, a fortnight in advance of the main move, to send his cavalry round Lee's left by the upper fords of the Rappahannock; then to turn Lee's left with three corps, while the two others, under General John Sedgwick, crossed the river below Lee's right at Fredericksburg. Even then he had another corps in reserve. He expected that Lee would be forced to abandon his lines and retreat, in which case he meant to follow him up by the direct road to Richmond. In the middle of April these movements began. The Federal cavalry corps, under a second-rate commander, General George Stoneman, was delayed by floods, and only crossed the Upper Rappahannock simultaneously with the right column of the main army.

At first all went well with Hooker. His three army corps, about seventy thousand strong, crossed the Rappahannock, and, on the morning of April 30, its tributary the Rapidan. As they marched eastward they took in flank and rear the fortified line which Lee had formed. The Confederates guarding United States Ford on the Rappahannock had to retire, and the reserve Federal corps passed over unmolested. By the night of the 30th a Federal army of ninety thousand men was concentrated at or near Chancellorsville behind all these defences. The Federal cavalry, in enormous, though not as it proved overwhelming strength, were already moving towards the Virginia Central Railway, forty-five miles in rear of Lee's army, and one of his main lines of supply, which it was their mission not only to cut but to destroy. At the same time General Sedgwick, commanding the two corps opposite Fredericksburg, crossed the river and deployed to attack Jackson's three divisions under General Jubal A. Early, which held the old trenches of the former battle.

Lee was thus taken in pincers by two armies, each capable of fighting a major battle with him, while at the same time his rear was ravaged and his communications assailed. The advance of either Federal Army would render his position untenable, and their junction or simultaneous action in a single battle must destroy him. Nothing more hopeless on the map than his position on the night of the 30th can be imagined, and it is this which raises the event which followed from a military to an historic level.

The great commander and his trusty lieutenant remained crouched but confident amid this tremendous encirclement. Beset upon both flanks by hostile armies which were for the moment disconnected, and unable to retreat without yielding vital positions, Lee naturally sought to hold off one assailant while striking at the other. Which to choose? Jackson was for falling upon Sedgwick and driving him into the river; but Lee knew that nothing less than the defeat of the main Union army would save him. Hooker had taken command in person of this mighty array, and Lee, as soon as he learned where he was, left only a division to delay Sedgwick and marched at once to attack him. Meanwhile "Jeb" Stuart manœuvred against Stoneman's cavalry over a wide front to such good purpose that though he was outnumbered by four to one he was able to render perfect service to Lee, while the Federal cavalry General, Stoneman, played no part in the battle.

* * * * *

Chancellorsville stands on the edge of a wild region of forest and tangled scrub which still deserves the name of Wilderness. Roads or paths cut through this alone rendered movement possible. On May 1 Hooker, having brought up all his troops, ordered a general advance eastward along the Turnpike and the Plank road. His numerous cavalry were breaking up the Virginia Central Railway at Louisa Court House, thirty miles to the southward. He had three balloons and numerous signal stations, and even a field electric telegraph for communication with Sedgwick. But the mist of the morning lay in fog-banks over the valley of the Rappahannock. The balloons and signal stations could see nothing, and the electric telegraph broke down. As he advanced into the Wilderness he met large enemy forces, who began at once to attack him. These were Stonewall Jackson's corps, handled with its general's usual vigour. Now "Fighting Joe," so famous as a subordinate, bent under the strain of supreme command. He had expected that his well-executed strategy would compel Lee to retreat. He now conceived himself about to be attacked by the whole Confederate Army. He turned at once and fell back upon the entrenched line he had already prudently prepared before Chancellorsville. It was late in the afternoon of the 1st when the advancing Confederates, emerging from the woodland, came within sight of this formidable position with its masses of troops. All the time Sedgwick, at Fredericksburg, receiving no orders by the electric telegraph, and, baffled by Early's brave show on the fatal heights, already dyed with Union blood, although he heard the firing, made no effort. How did he know that Longstreet might not have arrived, as would indeed have been only proper? Thus the night set in.

Lee and Jackson sat together, and knew that they had one day before them. Unless they could beat Hooker at odds of two to one during May 2 they would be attacked front and rear by overwhelming forces. Frontal attack was impossible. Their only chance was to divide their small army and swing round Hooker's right. Search had been made for a road or track for such a movement; and in the small hours one of Jackson's staff officers reported that there was a private road used for hauling wood and ore to a furnace which would serve. Jackson at once proposed to lead his whole corps along it, and Lee after a moment's reflection assented. This meant that Jackson with twenty-six thousand men would march round Hooker's right to attack him, while Lee faced nearly eighty thousand Federals with seventeen thousand.

At 4 A.M. Jackson was on the march. It seemed vital that his movement should be unperceived, but an unexpected gap in the forest revealed about eight o'clock to the Federal troops at Hazel Grove a long column moving towards the right of their wide front. This exposure actually helped the Confederate manœuvre. Two divisions of General Daniel E. Sickles's corps advanced after some delay to strike at these processionists and find out their purpose. They came into contact with Jackson's rearguard, who fought stubbornly, and then vanished in the woods. The two divisions, now joined by Sickles himself, feeling they had a retreating enemy before them, pushed on hopefully, and Sickles thought he had cut the Confederate Army in twain. This was indeed true. Lee and Jackson were now separated, and only victory could reunite them. Had Hooker set his army in motion against Lee he must have driven Lee ever farther from Jackson and ever nearer to Sedgwick, who had now at length forced the heights of Fredericksburg, and, little more than eight miles away, was, with thirty thousand men, driving Early back upon Lee's rear. But Hooker, convinced that he was safe within his fortifications and that his strategy was successful, made no move, while the hours slipped away. It was six o'clock in the evening before Jackson reached the end of his march. He had not only turned Hooker's flank, but was actually in rear of his right-hand corps. He deployed into line, facing Lee about four miles away on the other side of the Federal Army. The surprise was complete. The soldiers of the Eleventh Federal Corps were eating their supper and playing cards behind their defences when suddenly there burst from the forest at their backs the Confederate line of battle. In one hour the Eleventh Corps, attacked by superior forces in this battle, although as a whole their army was two to one, was dashed into rout and ruin.

Night was falling, but Jackson saw supreme opportunity before him. He was within half a mile of the road leading to

United States Ford, the sole line of retreat for Hooker's whole army, and between him and this deadly thrust no organised force intervened. He selected the point which he must gain by night and hold to the death at dawn. The prize was nothing less than the destruction of the main Federal Army. They must either overwhelm him the next day or starve between the Wilderness and his cannon. All this he saw. He rode forward with a handful of officers along the Plank road to the skirmish line to see what he could of the ground. He had often risked his life in this way, and now the forfeit was claimed. As he returned, his own men, Carolinians proud to die at his command, mistaking in the darkness the small party for hostile cavalry, fired a volley. Three bullets pierced the General's left arm and shoulder. He fell from his horse, and when, after an agonising passage, he reached the field hospital he was too much weakened by loss of blood to concentrate his mind. His staff officer, who was to lead A. P. Hill's division to the vital point, had been killed by the same volley. Hill, on whom the command devolved, hastening forward after vainly questioning his swooning chief, was almost immediately himself wounded. It was some hours before Stuart, from the cavalry, could be brought to the scene. No one knew Jackson's plan, and he was now unconscious. Thus on small agate points do the balances of the world turn.

Stuart fought a fine battle during the night, and on May 3, with wild shouts of "Remember Jackson!" the infuriated Confederates assaulted the Federal line. They drove it back. They captured Hazel Grove. They joined hands again with Lee. But the chance of the night was gone for ever. Hooker now had masses of men covering his line of retreat to the ford. He now thought of nothing but retreat. He did not even keep Lee occupied upon his front. He was morally beaten on the 2nd, and during the battle of the 3rd a solid shot hitting the pillar of a house by which he stood stunned him, which was perhaps a merciful stroke.

Lee now turned on Sedgwick, whose position south of the river was one of great peril. He had fought hard during the whole of the 3rd, and found himself on the 4th with the river at his back and only twenty thousand effective men, attacked by Lee, with at least twenty-five thousand. But the Confederate soldiers were exhausted by their superhuman exertions. Sedgwick, though beaten and mauled, managed to escape by his pontoons at Fredericksburg. Here he was soon joined by the Commander-in-Chief and the rest of the magnificent army which nine days before had seemed to have certain success in their path, but now stood baffled and humbled at their starting-point. They were still twice as numerous as their opponents. They had lost 17,000 men out of 130,000 and the Confederates 12,500 out of 60,000.

Chancellorsville was the finest battle which Lee and Jackson fought together. Their combination had become perfect. "Such an executive officer," said Lee, "the sun never shone on. Straight as the needle to the pole, he advances to the execution of my purpose." "I would follow General Lee blindfold" is a remark attributed to Jackson. Now all was over. "Could I have directed events," wrote Lee, ascribing the glory to his stricken comrade, "I should have chosen for the good of the country to be disabled in your stead." Jackson lingered for a week. His arm was amputated. Pneumonia supervened. On the 10th he was told to prepare for death, to which he consented with surprise and fortitude. "Very good, very good; it is all right." Finally, after some hours, quietly and clearly: "Let us cross over the river and rest under the shade of the trees." His loss was a mortal blow to Lee and to the cause of the South.

*   *   *   *   *

Nevertheless in these months the scales of war seemed to turn against the Union. A wave of discouragement swept across the North. Desertion was rife in the Federal ranks. Conscription, called "the draft," was violently resisted in many states. Many troops had to be withdrawn from the front to enforce the law. Many hundreds of lives were lost in New York City in the draft riots. Clement L. Vallandigham, the leader of the peace party, or "Copperheads" as they were called, after a particularly poisonous snake, declared in Congress, "You have not conquered the South; you never will. Money you have expended without limit, blood poured out like water. . . . Defeat, death, taxation, and sepulchres . . . these are your only trophies." The legislatures of Indiana and Illinois threatened to acknowledge the Confederacy. "Everybody feels," wrote Medill, the editor of the *Chicago Tribune,* and a close friend of the President's, "that the war is drawing to a disastrous and disgraceful termination. Money cannot be supplied much longer to a beaten democracy and homesick army." It was indeed the darkest hour. But the heart of Lincoln did not fail him.

Problems on the seas and across the ocean also perplexed and agitated the North. The small Confederate Navy was active and successful in the Gulf of Mexico and on the Atlantic coast. On the high seas Confederate commerce-raiders, built in Britain, were taking a heavy toll of Northern shipping. The most famous of them, the *Alabama,* had stolen out of the river Mersey in June 1862. She sailed under a false name, and in spite of the protests of the American Minister in London. After a glorious career, lasting eleven months, she was brought to bay by a Federal cruiser in the English Channel. A gallant engagement was fought off Cherbourg. It was witnessed by a number of French artists, one of whom, Manet, has left a remarkable painting of the scene. The *Alabama* was outgunned and sunk. The Federal Government pressed Britain hard for compensation for the damage done by the Southern raiders. Negotiations were long and disputatious. They were not concluded until six years after the end of the war, when Gladstone's Government agreed to pay the United States fifteen million dollars.

Throughout the spring and summer of 1863 anxiety grew in Washington because of the building in the British yard which had launched the *Alabama* of two new ironclad Confederate warships. They were fitted with nine-inch rifled guns and formidable underwater rams, thus combining the offensive merits of the *Merrimac* and the *Monitor*. These ships were known as the Laird rams, after their builders. The American Minister bombarded the Foreign Secretary, Lord John Russell, with demands that the Laird rams must not be allowed to escape as the *Alabama* had done. Russell eventually realised that the construction of such vessels by a neutral would set a bad precedent which might work to Britain's disadvantage in future wars. In September he ordered their seizure. Thus was closed the last of the war-time diplomatic crises between Britain and the Union.

*　　*　　*　　*　　*

The initiative in the field now passed to Lee, who resolved to carry out his long-planned invasion of Pennsylvania. But Vicksburg, on the Mississippi, was in dire straits, and unless Joseph E. Johnston could be largely reinforced its fall was imminent. A proposal was made to stand on the defensive in Virginia, to send Lee himself with Longstreet's two divisions to the Mississippi, and other troops to Middle Tennessee to defeat the covering forces under Rosecrans south of Nashville and threaten the commercial cities of Louisville and Cincinnati, perhaps forcing Grant to abandon his campaign against Vicksburg. Lee refused point-blank to go.

Squarely he put the issue before the Council of War: the risk had to be taken of losing Mississippi or Virginia. His view prevailed, and on May 26, three weeks after Chancellorsville, the invasion of Pennsylvania was sanctioned. The Army of Northern Virginia was reorganised in three corps of three divisions each, commanded by Longstreet, Richard S. Ewell, and A. P. Hill. Lee's object in 1863, as in the previous year, was to force the Army of the Potomac to fight under conditions in which defeat would spell annihilation. In this he saw the sole hope of winning Southern independence.

The movement commenced on June 3. Longstreet concentrated his corps at Culpeper, and behind it the other two corps passed into the Shenandoah valley, marching straight for the Potomac. Longstreet meanwhile moved up on the east of the Blue Ridge with his front and flank screened by Stuart's cavalry, eventually entering the valley behind the other two corps through the northern "Gaps." On the 9th, before the movement was well under way, there was an indecisive cavalry battle at Brandy Station, in which the Federal cavalry, under their new commander, Alfred Pleasanton, regained their morale.

At first the campaign went well for Lee. Ewell on the 10th left Culpeper for the valley, and, marching with a speed worthy of "Stonewall" Jackson, cleared the Federal garrisons out of Winchester and Martinsburg, capturing four thousand prisoners and twenty-eight guns, and on the 15th was crossing the Potomac. He established his corps at Hagerstown, where it waited for a week, till the corps in the rear was ready to cross, and his cavalry brigade pushed on to Chambersburg, in Pennsylvania, to collect and send back supplies. On the 22nd he was ordered to advance farther into Pennsylvania and capture Harrisburg, a hundred miles north of Washington, if it "came within his means."

On the 27th Ewell reached Carlisle, and his outposts next day were within four miles of Harrisburg. The other two Confederate corps were at Chambersburg. As far as Chambersburg Lee had been following the Cumberland valley, with his right flank shielded by the South Mountain range, and as yet he knew nothing of Hooker's movements. He accepted Stuart's plan of making a raid through the mountains and joining Ewell in Pennsylvania. Stuart, who started on the 25th, believed that Hooker was still in his encampments on the east side of the mountains, and expected to be able to ride through his camp areas and cross the Potomac near Leesburg. But Hooker had broken up his camps and was marching that same morning for the Potomac. Stuart had to make a third ride round the Federal rear, crossed the Potomac within twenty miles of Washington, failed to make contact with Ewell's right division, and only rejoined Lee with his men and horses utterly exhausted on the afternoon of July 2. Thus for a whole week Lee had been deprived of the "eyes" of his army; and much had happened meanwhile.

As soon as Lee began his movement to the north Hooker proposed to march on Richmond. But Lincoln forbade him, and rightly pointed out that not Richmond but Lee's army was his proper objective. In thus deciding the President did what Lee had expected. After crossing the Potomac Hooker made his headquarters near Frederick, where he covered Washington and threatened Lee's line of communications. Halleck and Stanton had agreed after Chancellorsville that Hooker must not be in command of the army in the next battle. When therefore the General, denied the use of the Harpers Ferry garrison, tendered his resignation it was promptly accepted. Early in the morning of June 28 General George G. Meade, commander of the Fifth Corps, who was now appointed to the chief command, decided to move his whole army by forced marches northwards to the Susquehanna to prevent Lee from crossing that river, and at the same time to cover Baltimore and Washington. Meade was a safe, dogged commander, with no political affiliations. He could be relied upon to avoid acts of folly, and also anything brilliant. Expecting that Lee would come south from the Susquehanna to attack Baltimore, he now prepared to meet him on the line of Pipe Creek, ten miles beyond Westminster.

Lee had been greatly perplexed by Stuart's failure to report, but, having implicit confidence in him, had concluded that Hooker must still be south of the Potomac. On learning the truth during the 28th he ordered a concentration at Cashtown, close to the eastern foot of South Mountain. He did not hurry, and "the march was conducted with a view to the comfort of the troops." At the outset of the campaign he had been in agreement with Longstreet that the strategy should be offensive and the tactics defensive, and he had no intention of fighting a battle except under favourable conditions. But chance ruled otherwise.

On June 30 a brigade of Hill's corps advanced eight miles from Cashtown to Gettysburg, partly to look for shoes, partly to reconnoitre a place through which Ewell's corps might be moving next day. Gettysburg was found in the hands of some Federal cavalry, which had just entered. The Confederate brigade thereupon turned back without ascertaining the strength of the hostile force. Buford, the Federal cavalry commander, who bore the Christian names of Napoleon B., seems to have been the first man in either army to appreciate the strategical importance of Gettysburg, the meeting-place of some dozen roads from all points of the compass. He moved his division to the west of the town, where he found a strong position behind a stream, and called upon the commander of the First Corps to come to his aid with all speed. The First Corps was followed by the Eleventh Corps.

On July 1 severe fighting began with the leading Confederate troops, and presently Ewell, coming down from the north-east, struck in upon the Federal flank, driving the Eleventh Corps through Gettysburg to seek shelter on higher ground three miles southwards, well named Cemetery Ridge. On this first day of battle fifty thousand men had been engaged, and four Confederate divisions had defeated and seriously injured two Federal corps. It now became a race between Lee and Meade, who could concentrate his forces first. Neither Lee nor Meade wished to fight decisively at this moment or on this ground; but they were both drawn into the greatest and bloodiest battle of the Civil War. Lee could not extricate himself and his supply trains without fighting Meade's army to a standstill, and Meade was equally committed to a field he thought ill-chosen.

Lee wished to open the second day of the battle with an attack by Ewell and Hill on Cemetery Ridge, which he rightly regarded as the key to the Federal position. He was deterred by their objections. Longstreet, when he arrived, argued at length for a manœuvre round Meade's left to place Lee's army between Meade and Washington. Such a movement in the absence of Stuart's cavalry would certainly have been reckless, and it is not easy to see how Lee could have provisioned his army in such a position. Finally Lee formally ordered Longstreet to attack the Federal left at dawn. Longstreet, who entirely disapproved of the rôle assigned to him, did not come into action till four in the afternoon. While he waited for an additional brigade two corps joined the Union Army. Lee, who imagined that the Federal left rested upon the Emmetsburg road, expected that Longstreet's advance

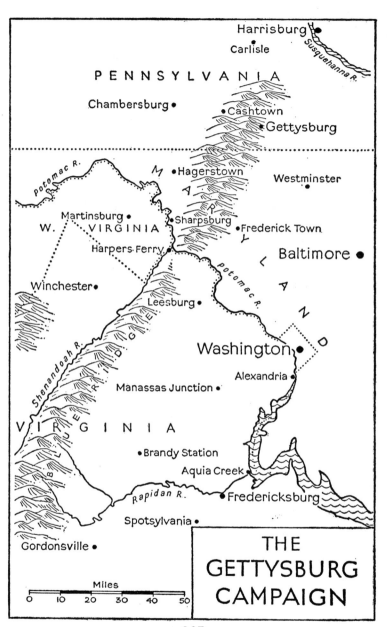

Harrisburg

Carlisle

Susquehanna R.

P E N N S Y L V A N I A

Chambersburg •

•Cashtown

•Gettysburg

Potomac R.

M •Hagerstown

Westminster •

A

Martinsburg •   R   •Sharpsburg

W.   V I R G I N I A   •Frederick Town

Y

Harpers Ferry   L

Baltimore •

Winchester •   A   *Potomac R.*

Leesburg •   N

Washington •   D

Alexandria •

Shenandoah R.   Manassas Junction •

V I R G I N I A

•Brandy Station

Aquia Creek •

Rapidan R.   •Fredericksburg

Spotsylvania •

Gordonsville •

THE
GETTYSBURG
CAMPAIGN

Miles

0   10   20   30   40   50

up this road would roll up the Federal line from left to right. But at this point the Federal corps commander, Sickles, had taken up an advanced position on his own authority, and his flank was not the end of the Federal line. When this was discovered Longstreet obstinately refused to depart from the strict letter of his orders, though he knew that Lee was not aware of the true position. All that he achieved after several hours' fierce fighting was to force Sickles back to Meade's main line. On this day the greater part of Hill's corps took no part in the battle. Ewell, who was to have attacked the north end of the ridge as soon as he heard Longstreet's guns, did not get into action till 6 P.M. There were no signs of any co-ordination of attacks on the Confederate side on July 2. Although Lee had failed to make his will prevail, and the Confederate attacks had been unconnected, the losses of the Federal Army were terrible, and Meade at the Council of War that night was narrowly dissuaded from ordering a general retreat.

The third day began. Lee still bid high for victory. He re-solved to launch fifteen thousand men, sustained by the fire of a hundred and twenty-five guns, against Meade's left cen-tre, at the point where one of Hill's brigades had pierced the day before. Ewell's corps would at the same time attack from the north, and if the assault under General George E. Pickett broke the Federal line the whole Confederate Army would fall on. Again the attack was ordered for the earliest possible hour. It was the Federals however who opened the third day by recapturing in the grey of the dawn some of the trenches vacated the previous evening, and after hard fighting drove the Confederates before noon entirely off Culp's Hill. Ex-hausted by this, Ewell made no further movement. Long-street was still arguing vehemently in favour of a wide turn-ing movement round Meade's left. The heavy losses which his corps had suffered on the 2nd made this more difficult than ever.

The morning passed in utter silence. It was not till one in the afternoon that the Confederates began the heaviest bombardment yet known. Longstreet, unable to rally himself to a plan he deemed disastrous, left it to the artillery commander, Alexander, to give the signal to Pickett. At half-past two the Confederate ammunition, dragged all the way from Richmond in tented wagons, was running short. "Come quick," Alexander said to Pickett, "or my ammunition will not support you properly." "General," said Pickett to Longstreet, who stood sombre and mute, "shall I advance?" By an intense effort Longstreet bowed his head in assent. Pickett saluted and set forty-two regiments against the Union centre. We see to-day, upon this battlefield so piously preserved by North and South, and where many of the guns still stand in their firing stations, the bare, slight slopes up which this grand infantry charge was made. In splendid array, all their battle flags flying, the forlorn assault marched on. But, like the Old Guard on the evening of Waterloo, they faced odds and metal beyond the virtue of mortals. The Federal rifled artillery paused till they were within seven hundred yards; then they opened again with a roar and cut lanes in the steadfastly advancing ranks. On they went, without flinching or disorder; then the deadly sound, like tearing paper, as Lee once described it, rose under and presently above the cannonade. But Pickett's division still drove forward, and at trench, stone wall, or rail fence closed with far larger numbers of men, who, if not so lively as themselves, were at least ready to die for their cause. All three brigadiers in Pickett's division fell killed or mortally wounded. General L. A. Armistead with a few hundred men actually entered the Union centre, and the spot where he died with his hand on a captured cannon is to-day revered by the manhood of the United States.

But where were the reserves to carry through this superb effort? Where were the simultaneous attacks to grip and rock the entire front? Lee at Gettysburg no more than Napoleon at Waterloo could win dominance. The victorious stormers were killed or captured; the rest walked home across the corpses which encumbered the plain amid a remorseless artillery fire. Less than a third came back. Lee met them on his horse Traveller with the only explanation, which they would not accept, "It is all my fault." Longstreet, in memoirs written long afterwards, has left on record a sentence which is his best defence: "As I rode back to the line of batteries, expecting an immediate counter-stroke, the shot and shell ploughed the ground around my horse, and an involuntary appeal went up that one of them would remove me from scenes of such awful responsibility."

But there was no counter-stroke. The Battle of Gettysburg was at an end. Twenty-three thousand Federals and over twenty thousand Confederates had been smitten by lead or steel. As after the Antietam, Lee confronted his foe on the morrow and offered to fight again. But no one knew better that it was decisive. With every personal resource he gathered up his army. An immense wagon train of wounded were jolted, springless, over sixteen miles of crumpled road. "Carry me back to old Virginia." "For God's sake kill me." On the night of the 4th Lee began his retreat. Meade let him go. The energy for pursuit had been expended in the battle. The Potomac was found in flood; Lee's pontoon bridge had been partially destroyed by a raid from the city of Frederick. For a week the Confederates stood at bay behind entrenchments with their backs to an unfordable river. Longstreet would have stayed to court attack; but Lee measured the event. Meade did not appear till the 12th, and his attack was planned for the 14th. When that morning came, Lee, after a cruel night march, was safe on the other side of the river. He carried with him his wounded and his prisoners. He had lost only two guns, and the war.

The Washington Government were extremely discontented with Meade's inactivity; and not without reason. Napoleon might have made Lee's final attack, but he certainly would not have made Meade's impotent pursuit. Lincoln promoted Meade only to the rank of Major-General for his good service at Gettysburg. Lee wended his way back by the Shenandoah valley to his old stations behind the Rappahannock and the Rapidan. The South had shot its bolt.

Up to a certain point the Gettysburg campaign was admirably conducted by Lee, and some of its objects were achieved; but the defeat with which it ended far more than counterbalanced these. The irreparable loss of twenty-eight thousand men in the whole operation out of an army of seventy-five thousand forbade any further attempts to win Southern independence by a victory on Northern soil. Lee believed that his own army was invincible, and after Chancellorsville he had begun to regard the Army of the Potomac almost with contempt. He failed to distinguish between bad troops and good troops badly led. It was not the army but its commander that had been beaten on the Rappahannock. It may well be that had Hooker been allowed to retain his command Lee might have defeated him a second time. Fortune, which had befriended him at Chancellorsville, now turned against him. Stuart's long absence left him blind as to the enemy's movements at the most critical stage of the campaign, and it was during his absence that he made the fatal mistake of moving to the east side of the mountains. Lee's military genius did not shine. He was disconcerted by

Stuart's silence, he was "off his balance," and his subordinates became conscious of this mood. Above all he had not Jackson at his side. Longstreet's recalcitrance had ruined all chance of success at Gettysburg. On Longstreet the South laid the heavy blame.

There was no other battle in the East in 1863, and the armies were left for the winter facing each other on the Rapidan.

*　　*　　*　　*　　*

We must now turn to the West, where great battles were fought, and many fell. But since a decisive victory by Lee's army would have enabled him to march where he pleased, and to hold New York and every great city of the Atlantic coast to ransom or surrender, this secondary though spacious theatre need not be precisely lighted. From the West, it is true, the eventual thrust came which split and devastated the South. But its importance in 1862 and 1863 lay chiefly in the advance of Grant to the supreme unified command of the Union armies. The objective was the clearance or barrage of the Mississippi. In April 1862 Admiral Farragut, a Southerner, who adhered to the Union, had become prominent at the head of the Federal Navy. In April, with a fleet of all kinds of vessels, partly armoured or naked, he had run past the forts guarding the approaches to New Orleans, the largest city and the commercial capital of the Confederacy, which fell next day. He had then continued the ascent of the river, and reached Vicksburg on May 18. Finding no Federal troops at hand to support him, he retired to run the batteries again on June 25, and join hands with the Federal flotilla at Memphis. It was therefore known by the end of 1862 that the Confederate batteries could not stop the Union ships. As for the torpedoes, a new word, of which there was then much talk, Farragut was to say, "Damn the torpedoes!"

and be justified. Thenceforward the Union flotillas could move up and down the great river, through its entire course, by paying a toll. This was a substantial aid to the Federal Army on either bank. Here in the Mississippi valley was almost a separate war. The Western states of the Confederacy claimed a great measure of autonomy from Jefferson Davis and his Government at Richmond, while clamouring for its help. At Washington the Western theatre was viewed in much the same way as was the Eastern front by the Allied and associated Powers in the First World War. It was secondary, but also indispensable. It was not the path to victory, but unless it was pursued victory would be long delayed.

After the failure of the river expedition in December 1862 Grant reassembled his army on the right bank of the Mississippi. Vicksburg was still his first aim, but the floods of the Yazoo basin prevented at this season all operations except by water. Having by numerous feints deceived the Confederate General, Pemberton, who with a field army was defending Vicksburg, Grant successfully ferried forty-five thousand men across the Mississippi below the Grand Gulf batteries thirty-six miles down-stream from Vicksburg. He surprised and drove back Pemberton's troops, and on May 3 established himself at Grand Gulf, in a safe position on the uplands, with his left flank protected by the wide Black River, and in touch with the Federal flotillas. Here he was joined four days later by his third corps, under Sherman. He now began a cautious movement towards Vicksburg and the railway which joined it to the town of Jackson. General Joseph E. Johnston, reinforced too late by President Davis, was hurried, ill though he was, to the scene. His only thought now was to extricate Pemberton's army. He ordered that General to march at once to join him before Grant could interpose his three corps between them. Pemberton resolved to disobey this order. He conceived that a movement across Grant's communications with Grand Gulf would compel a Federal retreat. He not only disobeyed, he miscalculated; for Grant, like McClellan before Richmond in 1862, with his command of the rivers, was not dependent upon any one particular base. Dropping his links with Grand Gulf, he pressed Johnston back with his right hand, and then turned on Pemberton in great superiority. After a considerable battle at Champion's Hill, in which over six thousand men fell, Pemberton was driven back into Vicksburg. With the aid of the flotilla the Union General opened a new base north of the city, and after two attempts to storm its defences, one of which cost him four thousand men, commenced a regular siege. Large reinforcements presently raised his army to over seventy thousand men. Johnston, with twenty-four thousand, could do nothing to relieve Pemberton. Vicksburg was starved into surrender, and its Confederate garrison and field army, more than thirty thousand strong, capitulated on July 4, at the very moment of Lee's defeat at Gettysburg. Five days later Port Hudson, in Louisiana, also reduced by famine, surrendered with seven thousand men to General Banks, and the whole course of the Mississippi was at last in Federal hands. "The Father of Waters," said Lincoln, "again goes unvexed to the sea." These were stunning blows to the South.

*　　*　　*　　*　　*

The main fury of the war was now transferred to the West. Until the fall of Vicksburg was certain the highly competent Rosecrans, with about sixty thousand men, forming the Union Army of the Cumberland, was content from the scene of his success at Murfreesboro to watch Bragg, who stood across the railway line between him and Chattanooga. This city and railway centre, protected by the deep and wide Tennessee

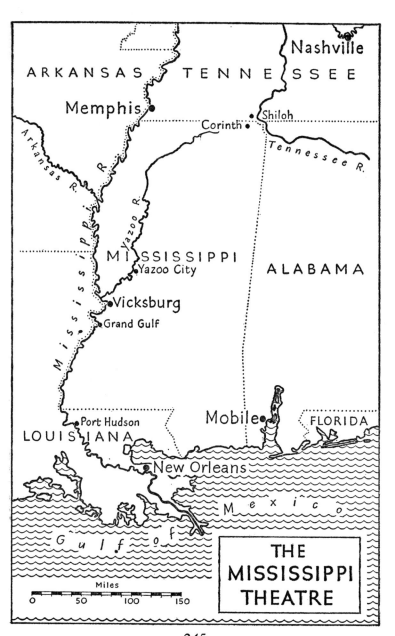

THE
MISSISSIPPI
THEATRE

River on the north and the high ridges of the Appalachian Mountains, a western chain of the Alleghenies, on the south, was the key not only to the mastery of the Mississippi valley, but to the invasion of prosperous, powerful, and hitherto inviolate Georgia. The waiting period was marked by fierce Confederate cavalry raids to break up the railways behind the Union army, and by Federal counter-strokes against important ironworks and munitions factories in the southern part of Tennessee. In these the Confederates had the advantage. But when Rosecrans, at the end of June, advanced along the railway to Chattanooga, and Burnside, with another army of forty thousand men, a hundred miles to the east, struck at Knoxville, great and far-reaching operations were afoot. Burnside captured Knoxville, cutting one of the sinew railways of the Confederacy. Rosecrans manœuvred Bragg out of all his defensive lines astride the Nashville–Chattanooga railway, and by September 4 gained Chattanooga without a battle.

Until this moment Rosecrans had shown high strategic skill. He now made the disastrous mistake of supposing that the resolute, agile army in his front was cowed. Bragg, who was one of the worst generals, hated by his lieutenants, and nearly always taking the wrong decision, was none the less a substantial fighter. South of Chattanooga the mountain ridges spread out like the fingers of a hand. Bragg lay quiet at Lafayette with an army now reinforced to sixty thousand men. By September 12 Rosecrans realised the appalling fact that his three corps were spread on a sixty-mile front, and that Bragg lay in their midst three times as strong as any one of them. Bragg, overbearing and ill-served, missed this opportunity, which Lee or Jackson would have made decisive for the whole of the West. Rosecrans recoiled, and concentrated towards Chattanooga; but he was too late, even against

Bragg, to escape a battle on ground and under conditions far from his choice.

At Chickamauga, across the border of Georgia, on September 18 Bragg fell upon his enemy. Longstreet, from Virginia, with two divisions and artillery, had reached him, together with other heavy reinforcements, so that he had the rare fortune for a Confederate General of the weight of numbers behind him. Seventy thousand Confederates attacked fifty-five thousand Federals. The two days' battle was fought with desperate valour on both sides. Bragg tried persistently to turn the Federal left and cut Rosecrans from Chattanooga, but when this wing of the Union Army, commanded by General George H. Thomas, had drawn to its aid troops from the centre and right, Longstreet, with twenty thousand Virginian veterans, assaulted the denuded parts of the Union front, and drove two-thirds of Rosecrans' army, with himself and the corps commanders, except Thomas, in ruin from the field. Longstreet begged Bragg to put all his spare weight behind a left-handed punch; but the Commander-in-Chief was set upon his first idea. He continued to butt into Thomas, who had built overnight breastworks of logs and railway iron in the woodland. Night closed upon a scene of carnage surpassed only by Gettysburg. Thomas, "the rock of Chickamauga," extricated himself and his corps and joined the rest of the Federal Army in Chattanooga.

The casualties in this battle were frightful. Sixteen thousand Federals and over twenty thousand Confederates were killed, wounded, or missing. The Confederates, who had captured forty guns and the battlefield, and who for the moment had broken the enemy's power, had gained the victory. It might have been Ramillies, or Waterloo, or even Tannenberg. It was Malplaquet.

Bragg now blockaded and almost surrounded Rosecrans

and the Army of the Cumberland in Chattanooga. He held the two heights which dominated Lookout Mountain and Missionary Ridge. For a time he barred all supplies by the Tennessee River. In early October it looked as if the Army of the Cumberland would be starved into surrender. Meanwhile the position of Burnside at Knoxville, against whom Longstreet had been sent, appeared no less deadly.

The Washington Government now began to lean heavily upon General Ulysses Grant. His faults and weaknesses were apparent; but so also was his stature. On the Union side, baffled, bewildered, disappointed, weary of bloodshed and expense, Grant now began to loom vast and solid through a red fog. Victory had followed him from Fort Donelson to Vicksburg. Here were large rebel surrenders—troops, cannon, territory. Who else could show the like? On October 16 Grant was given command of the departments of the Ohio, Cumberland, and Tennessee Rivers, with his lieutenant, Sherman, under him at the head of the Army of Tennessee.

Rosecrans was dismissed. He had lost a great battle, and under the Washington administration no General survived defeat. He had however played a distinguished part in the West, and his military record was clean. Long before Chickamauga he had lost favour with Halleck. That poor figure, who stood at the portals of the grim politics of these days, who sought to tell the armies what the politicians wanted and the politicians as much as they could understand of the military needs, showed his measure clearly when in February 1863 he wrote to Grant and Rosecrans that the vacant Major-Generalship would be given to whoever won the first notable success. Grant left his letter unanswered. Rosecrans wrote in stern rebuke that "a patriot and a man of honour should require no additional incentive to make him do his duty." Thus when he tripped he fell on stony ground.

By a series of intricate measures Grant freed the Tennessee

River, stormed both Missionary Ridge and Lookout Mountain, and drove Bragg and the Confederate Army in thorough disorder away from Chattanooga. At the same time he relieved Burnside at Knoxville. The frontiers of the Confederacy rolled southwards in another long lap. Vicksburg had cut it in two along the line of the Mississippi. Chattanooga cut the eastern half again along the range of the Alleghenies. By December 1863 the Confederates were driven back into Georgia, and the whole Mississippi valley was recovered for the Union. All these convulsive events might have taken a different grip if President Davis had made Lee Supreme Commander of the Confederate Army after Chancellorsville, or, better still, in 1862, and if he had devoted his authority and fine qualities wholly to the task of rallying behind the chief General the loyal, indomitable, but woefully particularist energies of the South. By the end of 1863 all illusions had vanished. The South knew they had lost the war, and would be conquered and flattened. It is one of the enduring glories of the American nation that this made no difference to the Confederate resistance. In the North, where success was certain, they could afford to have bitter division. On the beaten side the departure of hope left only the resolve to perish arms in hand. Better the complete destruction of the whole generation and the devastation of their enormous land, better that every farm should be burned, every city bombarded, every fighting man killed, than that history should record that they had yielded. Any man can be trampled down by superior force, and death, in whatever shape it comes, is only death, which comes to all. It might seem incredible when we survey the military consequences of 1863 that the torments of war should have been prolonged through the whole of 1864 and into 1865. "Kill us if you can; destroy all we have," cried the South. "As you will," replied the steadfast majority of the North.

BOOK ELEVEN · CHAPTER
FOURTEEN

The Victory of the
Union

THE Confederacy was defeated, and the last long phase of the war was one of conquest and subjugation. During the winter of the year which had witnessed Chancellorsville and Gettysburg, Vicksburg, Chattanooga, and Chickamauga, there was a pause. The North gathered its overwhelming strength for a sombre task. The war-leadership of President Davis was gravely questioned in the South. He had kept in his own hands not only the enormous business of holding the Confederacy together and managing its political and economic life, but he had exercised an overriding control upon its military operations. He had obdurately pursued a defensive policy and strategy, against odds which nothing but decisive victory in the field could shorten. This had led logically and surely to ruin. Lee and Longstreet were now asked for a general plan for 1864. They proposed that Beauregard, with twenty thousand men drawn from the forts in South Carolina, should be joined to Longstreet's army in East Tennessee, and, invading Kentucky, strike at the Louisville railway, the sole line of supply for the main Federal Army, which was expected to advance southward from Chattanooga against Joseph E. Johnston. Thereafter Johnston and all Confederate forces in the West would unite, fighting such battles as might be necessary, in a northward march towards

· *250* ·

the Ohio. This, they declared, would rupture all Federal combinations in the West. As for the East, Lee and the Army of Northern Virginia would be answerable. When this great scheme was laid before Davis at a Council of War, Bragg, of all men, pressed an alternative plan, with the result that there was no plan. Johnston must fight as best he could in the West, and Lee would continue to defend Richmond.

On March 9 President Lincoln appointed Ulysses Grant to the command of all the armies of the United States, raising him to the rank of Lieutenant-General. At last on the Northern side there was unity of command, and a general capable of exercising it. Grant's plan was brutal and simple. It was summed up in the word "Attrition." In intense fighting and exchange of lives weight of numbers would prevail. To Meade, who nominally retained the command of the Army of the Potomac, he gave the order, "Wherever Lee goes you will go also." To Sherman, his friend and brother officer, who had risen with him, he confided the command in the West with similar instructions, but with an addition: "To move against Johnston's army, to break it up, and to get into the interior country as far as you can, inflicting all the damage you can against their war resources." If either Johnston or Lee, profiting by interior lines, showed signs of trying to join the other no exertion was to be spared to follow him.

Grant also ordered three secondary operations: an attack, aided by the Navy, upon Mobile, on the Gulf of Mexico; pressure from Fortress Monroe towards Richmond; and the devastation of the Shenandoah valley, the granary of the South, and its oft-used route towards Maryland and Washington. Of these diversions the first two failed, and the Shenandoah plan only succeeded late in the year, when two corps and three cavalry divisions were applied to it under General Philip H. Sheridan.

With the approach of spring Grant, having launched the Union Army, came to grips with Lee on the old battle-grounds of the Rappahannock and the Rapidan, where the traces of Chancellorsville remained and memories of "Stonewall" Jackson brooded. He took the field at the beginning of May with a hundred and twenty thousand men against Lee with sixty thousand. He crossed the Rapidan by the fords which "Fighting Joe" Hooker had used the year before. There in the savage country of the Wilderness was fought a battle worthy of its field. In two days of intricate and ferocious fighting, May 5 and 6, Grant was repulsed with a loss of eighteen thousand men, Lee himself losing about ten thousand, the most part in a vehement counter-stroke. Grant then passaged to his left, and in a series of confused struggles from the 8th to the 19th sought to cut the Confederates from their line of retreat upon Richmond. This was called the Battle of Spotsylvania Court House, in which the Federal armies suffered another loss of over eighteen thousand men, or double that of their opponents. Undeterred by this slaughter, Grant repeated his movement to the left, and prolonged heavy fighting followed in the wild regions of the South Anna stream and afterwards on the Pamunkey River. Grant, for all the courage of his men, could never turn Lee's right flank, and Lee and his devoted soldiers could never overcome odds of two to one. They could only inflict death and wounds in proportion to their numbers. According to Grant's war-thought, this process, though costly, had only to be continued long enough to procure the desired result. "I propose to fight it out on this line," he wrote to Halleck at Washington, "if it takes all summer." But other factors, less arithmetical in their character, imposed themselves.

At Cold Harbour, on the ground of the "Seven Days" in 1862, the Federal Commander-in-Chief hurled his army

through the blasted, undulating woodland against the hag-
gard, half-starved, but elated Confederate lines. It was at this
battle that Lee conversed with the Postmaster-General of the
Confederacy, who had ridden out to see the fighting, and
asked, "If he breaks your line what reserve have you?" "Not
a regiment," said Lee, "and that has been my condition since
the fighting commenced. If I shorten my lines to provide a
reserve he will turn them; if I weaken my lines to provide
a reserve he will break me." But the result of the day ended
Grant's tactics of unflinching butchery. After seven thousand
brave blue-coated soldiers had fallen in an hour or so the
troops refused to renew the assault. More is expected of
the high command than determination in thrusting men to
their doom. The Union dead and wounded lay between the
lines; the dead soon began to stink in the broiling sun, the
living screamed for water. But Grant failed to secure a truce
for burial and mercy. It was not till the third day after the
battle that upon a letter from Lee, saying he would gladly
accord it if asked, formal request was made, and for a few
hours the firing ceased. During the World Wars through
which we have lived no such indulgences were allowed, and
numbers dwarfing the scale of the American Civil War perished in "no-man's-land," in long, helpless agony where they
fell. But in that comparatively civilised and refined epoch in
America Cold Harbour was deemed a horror almost beyond
words.

The Army of Northern Virginia had inflicted upon Grant
in thirty days a loss equal to its own total strength. He now
saw himself compelled to resort to manœuvre. He did exactly
what McClellan had done on this same ground two years
earlier. By a skilful and daring march, which Lee was too weak
to interrupt, he moved his whole army across the peninsula,
and, again using sea-power, crossed the James River and

established a new base on the south bank. He set himself to attack Richmond by the "back-door," as McClellan had wished to do. Repulsed at Petersburg, he laid siege with an army now reinforced to a hundred and forty thousand men to the trench lines covering that stronghold and the lines east of Richmond. He failed again to turn Lee's right flank by movements south of the James, and at the end of June resigned himself to trench warfare attack by spade, mine, and cannon. There was no investment, for Lee's western flank remained open. There static conditions lasted till April 1865. These performances, although they eventually gained their purpose, must be regarded as the negation of generalship. They were none the less a deadly form of war.

* * * * *

Meanwhile, in the West, Sherman, who enjoyed a superiority of almost two to one, had begun in May to fight his way south along the railway from Chattanooga to Atlanta, deep in Georgia. He was faced by Joseph E. Johnston, with three strong Confederate corps. A remarkable duel ensued between skilful adversaries. Sherman avoided frontal attacks, and by flanking movements manœuvred Johnston out of one strong position after another. Fierce fighting was continuous on the outpost lines, and in a minor engagement one of Johnston's corps commanders, General Leonidas Polk, was killed by a cannon-shot. Only at Kenesaw Mountain did Sherman assault. He was repulsed with the loss of two thousand five hundred men. But meanwhile the spectacle of this remorseless advance and his unwillingness to force a battle cost Johnston the confidence of Jefferson Davis. At the moment when he had resolved to stand at Peach Tree Creek he was superseded by John B. Hood. The Confederate Army, impatient of long retreats, acclaimed the change; but military opinion has always regarded the removal of Johnston as one of the

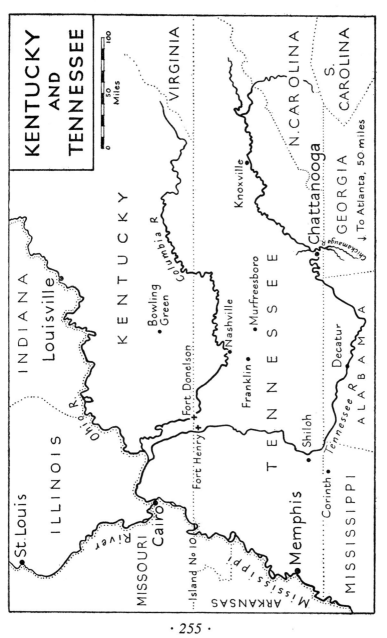

KENTUCKY
AND
TENNESSEE

50 100
0 50
Miles

INDIANA

ILLINOIS

MISSOURI

St.Louis

Louisville

Ohio River

Cairo

Island No.10

Mississippi River

ARKANSAS

Memphis

MISSISSIPPI

Corinth

Shiloh

Fort Henry

Fort Donelson

KENTUCKY

Bowling
Green

Franklin

Nashville

Columbia R

TENNESSEE

Murfreesboro

Tennessee R

Decatur

ALABAMA

Knoxville

VIRGINIA

N. CAROLINA

Chattanooga

Chickamauga R

GEORGIA

↓ To Atlanta, 50 miles

S.
CAROLINA

worst mistakes of President Davis in his anxious office. Hood felt himself under obligation to attack, and at Peach Tree Creek, Decatur, and East Point he gave full range to the passion for an offensive which inspired the Government he served and the army he led. The Confederates, defending their native soil, hurled themselves against the invader, and suffered irreparable losses. At Decatur alone they lost ten thousand men, without inflicting a third of that loss upon the enemy. After East Point, where five thousand Confederates fell, both the Army of the West and the Richmond Government were convinced that Johnston had probably been right. Hood was directed to return to the defensive, and after some weeks of siege was driven from Atlanta. In the four months' fighting Sherman had carried the Union flag a hundred and fifty miles into the Confederacy, with a loss of thirty-two thousand men. The Confederate loss exceeded thirty-five thousand. Thus Sherman could claim a solid achievement.

This victory prepared another. Indeed, the most important conflict of 1864 was fought with votes. It was astonishing that in the height of ruthless civil war all the process of election should be rigidly maintained. Lincoln's first term was expiring, and he must now submit himself to the popular vote of such parts of the American Union as were under his control. Nothing shows the strength of the institutions which he defended better than this incongruous episode. General McClellan, whom he had used hardly, was the Democratic candidate. His platform at Chicago in August was "that after four years of failure to restore the Union by the experiment of war . . . immediate efforts be made for the cessation of hostilities . . . and peace be restored on the basis of a Federal Union of the states." This proposal was known as the Peace Plank. Republicans had no difficulty in denouncing it as disloyal. In fact it represented the views of only a section of the Democrats. The worst that can be said about it is that it was absurd. All knew that the South would never consent to the restoration of the Federal Union while life and strength remained. In Lincoln's own Cabinet Salmon P. Chase, Secretary of the Treasury, a man of proved ability, became his rival for the Republican nomination. This was one of a number of moves made by Republican malcontents to displace their leader by someone whom they imagined would be a more vigorous President. Lincoln's political foes, gazing upon him, did not know vigour when they saw it. These were hard conditions under which to wage a war to the death. The awful slaughters to which Grant had led the Army of the Potomac and the prolonged stalemate outside Richmond made a sinister impression upon the North. But the capture of Atlanta, and a descent by Admiral Farragut upon the harbour of Mobile, the last Confederate open port, both gave that surge of encouragement which party men know how to use. Four million citizens voted in November 1864, and Lincoln was chosen by a majority of only four hundred thousand. Narrow indeed was the margin of mass support by which his policy of the remorseless coercion of the Southern states to reincorporation was carried. This did not mean that all Democrats wanted peace at any price. McClellan had made it plain when he accepted nomination that the South must offer to return to the Union before an armistice could be negotiated. But the founders of the American Constitution, which was now based upon the widest male suffrage, had so devised the machinery that the choice of the President should be indirect; and in the electoral college Lincoln, who carried every Union state except New Jersey, Delaware, and Kentucky, commanded two hundred and twelve delegates against only twenty-one.

In order to placate or confuse the pacifist vote Lincoln had encouraged unofficial peace parleys with the South. Horace Greeley, of the *New York Tribune,* was the President's representative. He met the Southern emissaries in Canada at Niagara Falls. Greeley soon discovered that they had no authority to negotiate a peace. The move would in any case have failed, since Lincoln's conditions now included the abolition of slavery as well as Reunion. The fourth winter of this relentless moral and physical struggle between communities who now respected and armies who had long admired one another came on.

Although Atlanta had fallen Hood's army of forty-four thousand bitter men was still active in the field and free to strike at Sherman's communications. With him were also ten thousand cavalry under Nathan B. Forrest, a new figure who gleamed in the sunset of the Confederacy. Forrest could hardly read or write, but by general account he possessed military qualities of the highest order. His remark that the art of war consists of being "Firstest with mostest" is classic. All these forces were at large around and behind Sherman. On November 12 that General, having persuaded a naturally anxious Washington Cabinet, cast his communications to the winds and began his grim march through Georgia to the shores of the Atlantic. When the Northern blockade had practically stopped the export of cotton from the Confederacy the women, with the slaves, who obeyed and respected them, had sowed the fields with corn. Georgia was full of food in this dark winter. Sherman set himself to march through it on a wide front, living on the country, devouring and destroying all farms, villages, towns, railroads, and public works which lay within his wide-ranging reach. He left behind him a blackened trail, and hatreds which pursue his memory to this day. "War is hell," he said, and certainly he made it so.

But no one must suppose that his depredations and pillage were comparable to the atrocities which were committed during the World Wars of the twentieth century or to the barbarities of the Middle Ages. Searching investigation has discovered hardly a case of murder or rape. None the less a dark shadow lies upon this part of the map of the United States.

Meanwhile Hood, with the Confederate Army of the West, not only tore up Sherman's communications with the United States, so that he was not heard of for a month, but with an army of nearly sixty thousand men struck deep into the Northern conquests. He invaded Tennessee, Thomas, who had been left by Sherman to watch him, retiring. His soldiers, infuriated by the tales of what was happening in their homes, drove the Federals from Franklin, though at the cost of nearly seven thousand men. It looked as if the Confederates might once more break through to the Ohio. But, pressing on, they were defeated and routed by Thomas on December 15 in the Battle of Nashville. Hood returned in much disorder to the South. Sherman, after vicissitudes, reached Savannah on the ocean coast in time to send the news of its fall as a "Christmas present" to the re-established President Lincoln.

*   *   *   *   *

The end was now in sight. Sherman planned for 1865 a more severe punishment for South Carolina than had been inflicted upon Georgia. Here was a state which by its arrogance had let loose these years of woe upon the American people. Here were the men who had fired upon the Stars and Stripes at Fort Sumter. In Lincoln's Cabinet Ministers spoke of obliterating Charleston and sowing the foundations with salt. Sherman marched accordingly with extreme vigour. But meanwhile outside Richmond Lee's powers of resistance were exhausted. He had not been deterred by Grant's arrival on the south bank of the James from sending General Early with a strong detachment into the Shenandoah valley. In July 1864 Early defeated the Federal commanders in the Jackson style, and once again Washington had heard the cannon of an advancing foe. But now the Shenandoah had been cleared and devastated by Sheridan with overwhelming forces. The Petersburg lines before Richmond had long repelled every Federal assault. The explosion of a gigantic mine under the defences had only led to a struggle in the crater, in which four thousand Northerners fell. But the weight which lay upon Lee could no longer be borne.

It was not until the beginning of February 1865, in this desperate strait, that President Davis appointed him Commander-in-Chief. In the same month another attempt was made at negotiation. The Vice-President of the Confederacy, A. H. Stephens, was empowered to meet the President of the United States on board a steamer in Hampton Roads, at the mouth of the James River. It offers a strange spectacle, which has not been repeated since, that two opposed belligerent leaders should thus parley in the midst of war. Moreover, the Southern representative had not so many years ago been an acquaintance of Lincoln's. But neither side had the slightest intention of giving way on the main issue. Jefferson Davis in his instructions spoke of a treaty "whereby our two countries may dwell in peace together." Lincoln offered a wide generosity, but only if the United States were again to be one country. It was as he had predicted. The South could not voluntarily re-accept the Union. The North could not voluntarily yield it.

Lee meanwhile had at once restored Joseph E. Johnston to the command of the Western Army. No rule can be laid down upon the High Command of states and armies in war. All depends upon the facts and the men. But should a great general appear the civil Government would be wise to give him full scope at once in the military sphere. After the Second

Manassas, or after Chancellorsville at the latest, Lee was plainly discernible as the Captain-General of the South. But that was in the spring of '62; it was now the spring of '65. Every Confederate counter-offensive had been crushed. The forces of the North ravaged the doomed Confederacy, and at last Grant closed upon its stubborn capital.

On Sunday, April 2, after the Battle of Five Forks and the turning of the Petersburg lines, President Davis sat in his pew in the church at Richmond. A messenger came up the aisle. "General Lee requests immediate evacuation." Southward then must the Confederate Government wander. There were still some hundreds of miles in which they exercised authority. Nothing crumbled, no one deserted; all had to be overpowered, man by man and yard by yard. Lee had still a plan. He would march swiftly south from Richmond, unite with Johnston, break Sherman, and then turn again to meet Grant and the immense Army of the Potomac. But all this was for honour, and mercifully that final agony was spared. Lee, disengaging himself from Richmond, was pursued by more than three times his numbers, and Sheridan, with a cavalry corps, lapped around his line of retreat and broke in upon his trains. When there were no more half-rations of green corn and roots to give to the soldiers, and they were beset on three sides, Grant ventured to appeal to Lee to recognise that his position was hopeless. Lee bowed to physical necessity. He rode on Traveller to Appomattox Court House to learn what terms would be offered. Grant wrote them out in a few sentences. The officers and men of the Army of Northern Virginia must surrender their arms and return on parole to their homes, not to be molested while they observed the laws of the United States. Lee's officers were to keep their swords. Food would be provided from the Union wagons. Grant added, "Your men must keep their horses and mules. They will need them for the spring ploughing." This was the greatest day in the career of General Grant, and stands high in the story of the United States. The Army of Northern Virginia, which so long had "carried the Confederacy on its bayonets," surrendered, twenty-seven thousand strong; and a fortnight later, despite the protests of President Davis, Johnston accepted from Sherman terms similar to those granted to Lee. Davis himself was captured by a cavalry squadron. The armed resistance of the Southern states was thus entirely subdued.

Lincoln had entered Richmond with Grant, and on his return to Washington learned of Lee's surrender. Conqueror and master, he towered above all others, and four years of assured power seemed to lie before him. By his constancy under many varied strains and amid problems to which his training gave him no key he had saved the Union with steel and flame. His thoughts were bent upon healing his country's wounds. For this he possessed all the qualities of spirit and wisdom, and wielded besides incomparable authority. To those who spoke of hanging Jefferson Davis he replied, "Judge not that ye be not judged." On April 11 he proclaimed the need of a broad and generous temper and urged the conciliation of the vanquished. At Cabinet on the 14th he spoke of Lee and other Confederate leaders with kindness, and pointed to the paths of forgiveness and goodwill. But that very night as he sat in his box at Ford's Theatre a fanatical actor, one of a murder gang, stole in from behind and shot him through the head. The miscreant leapt on the stage, exclaiming, *"Sic semper tyrannis,"* and although his ankle was broken through his spur catching in an American flag he managed to escape to Virginia, where he was hunted down and shot to death in a barn. Seward, Secretary of State, was also stabbed at his home, though not fatally, as part of the same plot.

Lincoln died next day, without regaining consciousness, and with him vanished the only protector of the prostrate South. Others might try to emulate his magnanimity; none but he could control the bitter political hatreds which were rife. The assassin's bullet had wrought more evil to the United States than all the Confederate cannonade. Even in their fury the Northerners made no reprisals upon the Southern chiefs. Jefferson Davis and a few others were, indeed, confined in fortresses for some time, but afterwards all were suffered to dwell in peace. But the death of Lincoln deprived the Union of the guiding hand which alone could have solved the problems of reconstruction and added to the triumph of armies those lasting victories which are gained over the hearts of men.

> Who overcomes
> By force hath overcome but half his foe.

Thus ended the great American Civil War, which must upon the whole be considered the noblest and least avoidable of all the great mass-conflicts of which till then there was record. Three quarters of a million men had fallen on the battlefield. The North was plunged in debt; the South was ruined. The material advance of the United States was cast back for a spell. The genius of America was impoverished by the alienation of many of the parent elements in the life and history of the Republic. But, as John Bright said to his audience of English working folk, "At last after the smoke of the battlefield had cleared away the horrid shape which had cast its shadow over the whole continent had vanished and was gone for ever."

BOOK TWELVE

THE
VICTORIAN AGE

The Rise of
Germany

WHILE the American Republic was entering upon her
ordeal and the restless Napoleon III was consolidating
his rule in France an event of great moment took place beyond the Rhine. In 1861 William I of Prussia ascended the
throne of Frederick the Great, and marked the first years of
his reign with three public appointments whose impact on
European history and modern events is incalculable. Count
von Moltke became Chief of the General Staff, Count von
Roon Minister of War, and—most important of all—Count
Otto von Bismarck was recalled from the Embassy in Paris
to become Minister-President of Prussia. First as Chancellor
of the North German Federation, and finally of the German
Empire, this singular genius presided with a cold passion
over the unification and Prussianisation of Germany, the elim-
ination of Prussia's nearest European rivals, and the eleva-
tion of William to the German Emperor's throne in 1871. He
was to serve, or dominate, William I and his two successors
uninterruptedly until his clashes with the young Emperor
William II finally and acrimoniously ended his tenure in 1890.

Bismarck was well equipped physically, temperamentally,
and by training for the gigantic rôle he played. He had served
in the Prussian Civil Service and the Pomeranian Provincial
Parliament before being appointed Prussian representative at

the Federal Diet at Frankfort. He had travelled widely, and had also gained practical experience by managing the spacious family estates in Pomerania. His last two appointments before becoming Minister-President were at the Prussian Embassies at Petersburg and Paris. He retained from his early career rooted convictions on both ends and means, which he expressed freely and sometimes with brutal frankness. Absolute monarchy was his ideal and aim. Liberalism and Parliamentarianism were anathema. Prussia must be purged of weak and liberal elements so that she could fulfil her destiny of leading and controlling the German-speaking peoples. A decisive struggle with Austria was inevitable.

Before a background of intense, brilliant, and unscrupulous diplomatic activity the three hammer-blows that forged Germany were deliberately prepared and struck. These were the war with Denmark in 1864, by which the Duchies of Schleswig and Holstein were attached to Prussia, the Seven Weeks' War of 1866, in which Austria was crushed and her associates in Germany overrun, and as culmination the war against France in 1870.

To ensure freedom of action in other directions Bismarck had always been convinced that Prussia's eastern frontiers must be secure. "Prussia must never let Russian friendship grow cold. Her alliance is the cheapest among all Continental alliances," he had said in Frankfort. Prussia had stood aside from the Crimean War, and before long she had a further opportunity of demonstrating her calculated friendship for the Czar. In 1863 the Poles rose against Russia in a spasm of the hopeless gallantry that has so often characterised the history of that unhappy people. Bismarck gave the Russians his support and encouragement, and even allowed Russian troops to pursue the rebels over the Prussian frontiers. Polish independence, which he had always disliked and feared, was once more extinguished, and Russia was given a proof of Prussian goodwill and a hint of further favours to come.

In the same year Bismarck seized his chance to expand Prussia north-westwards and gain control of the port of Kiel and the neck of the Danish peninsula. With the death of the King of Denmark, without a direct heir, an old dispute about the succession to the Duchies of Schleswig and Holstein came to a head. For centuries the Danish kings had ruled these Duchies as fiefs of the Holy Roman Empire. The Empire had vanished, but the Duchies remained an ill-defined part of the loose German Confederation created at the Congress of Vienna. Schleswig was half Danish in population and the Danes wished to incorporate it in their kingdom. Holstein was wholly German. The conflict of national feeling was inflamed by dynastic issues. Was the Danish king of the new line entitled to succeed to the Duchies? There was a rival claimant in the field. Mounting German patriotism was determined to prevent the parting of the Duchies from the German fatherland.

Bismarck knew well how to cast his line in these troubled waters. The German Confederation had already clashed with the Danes on the issue, and when the new Danish king assumed sovereignty over the Duchies Hanoverians and Saxons united in a Federal Army and occupied Holstein. At this point Bismarck intervened, dragging with him Austria. Austria was still a member of the German Confederation, and with her remaining Italian possessions in mind was hostile to the triumph of nationalism in outlying provinces. In January 1864 an Austro-Prussian ultimatum was dispatched to Copenhagen, and by July Denmark was defeated and overrun and Schleswig was occupied. That superb weapon, the new Prussian Army, had hardly been extended, and its future victims were scarcely made aware of its power.

Britain played no effective part in this affair. Palmerston would have liked to intervene, for Britain had guaranteed the integrity of Denmark by the Treaty of Berlin in 1852, which he himself had helped to negotiate. Before the blow fell he had said in the House of Commons: "We are convinced—I am convinced at least—that if any violent attempt were made to overthrow [Danish] rights and interfere with that independence those who made the attempt would find in the result that it would not be Denmark alone with which they would have to contend." But the Cabinet was hesitant and divided and was not prepared to back these imprecise assurances. Queen Victoria held fast to the views of the late Prince Consort and favoured the rise of Prussia. Moreover, Palmerston himself, who had started his Ministerial career during the wars against Napoleon I, was suspicious of France. If a general war were unleashed, he feared that Napoleon III might seize the Rhineland and dangerously augment his power in Europe. In fact France turned down tentative British proposals for joint action, conscious that Britain could only put an army of 20,000 on the Continent and that her contribution to a war with Prussia and Austria might well be limited to the easy but indecisive task of naval control of the Baltic. Napoleon III was hoping instead to exact compensations from Prussia, without recourse to war. He was unsuccessful in his double diplomacy. Russia, for her part, was in debt to Bismarck, and with an eye to the future refused to be involved. In these circumstances Palmerston felt he could do no more than press for conferences and mediation. It is not the only time in British history when strength has been lacking to reinforce bold words. Palmerston's words had given the Danes a false sense of security and tempted them to obduracy in an argument where legality did not entirely lie on their side, though some justice did. An ominous precedent was thus set

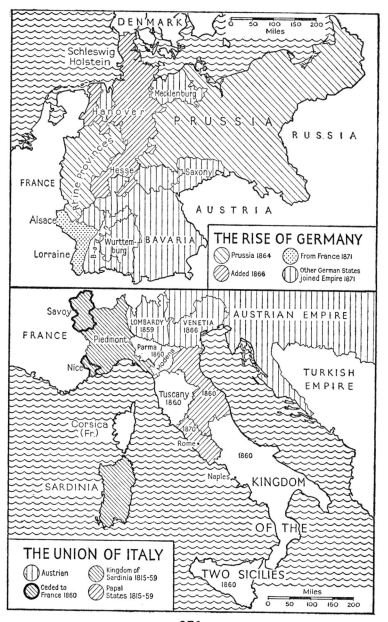

THE RISE OF GERMANY

Prussia 1864
Added 1866
From France 1871
Other German States joined Empire 1871

THE UNION OF ITALY

Austrian
Ceded to France 1860
Kingdom of Sardinia 1815-59
Papal States 1815-59

for what the Germans politely called *Realpolitik,* while Britain and France looked on. *Realpolitik* meant that standards of morality in international affairs could be ignored whenever material advantage might be gained. In this instance Denmark, the small victim, was not extinguished, nor were the peace terms unduly onerous. Then and later Bismarck knew the value of a certain hard magnanimity to the vanquished.

The outcome of the war with Denmark was soon to furnish the pretext and occasion for the next and far more important step of eliminating Austria from the German Confederation and vesting its leadership in Prussia. Schleswig and Holstein had become a condominium of Prussia and Austria. Bismarck played upon the awkwardness of this arrangement, maintaining a screen of protests against the indignant but long-suffering Austrians. At the same time he sought support in other quarters. In 1865 he visited Napoleon III at Biarritz. No accurate record of what was said was kept, but Bismarck presumably reiterated the theme he had for some time been impressing on the French Embassy in Prussia: if Prussia was given a free hand against Austria, France might expect Prussian sympathy in extending herself "wherever the French language was spoken." Belgium was clearly meant. Moreover, France could mediate in the final stages, and might even expect a territorial reward in South Germany. Napoleon promised nothing, but was not unreceptive, and Bismarck went home content. He had not committed himself to paper.

Of equal importance was the friendship of Italy, for she too was moving towards unity. Cavour and Garibaldi, as has been related, had brought almost the whole of the peninsula under the rule of the house of Savoy. But Venice, Trieste, and the Southern Tyrol remained in Austrian hands. For these territories the Italians yearned. In April 1866 King Victor

Emmanuel signed a secret treaty with Prussia agreeing to attack Austria if war broke out within three months.

The stage was set. France was neutralised. Russia was benevolent. Italy was an ally. Britain counted little in the matter, but in any case her sympathies lay with the Italian Liberation movement, and her relations with Austria had not been good for some years. The provocation to war of Austria and her associates in the German Confederation followed with precision.

Within ten days of the outbreak of war Hanover, Hesse, and Saxony were occupied. The King of Hanover, grandson of George III, fled to England and his country was incorporated in Prussia. Thus disappeared the ancient Electorate which had given Britain her Protestant dynasty in 1714. The Hanoverian State funds were later judiciously used among the ruling circles of other German states to mitigate their resentment against Prussia. The main Prussian armies then marched south into Bohemia, while Bismarck's agents stirred up the Hungarians in the Austrian rear. After a week of manœuvring, in which the Prussian staff made a remarkable use of railways as an aid to the strategic concentration of their forces, the decisive battle was joined at Sadowa. Over 200,000 men were engaged on either side. The Prussians used a new breech-loading rifle, and its rapidity of fire was conclusive. The Austrians sought to overcome their disadvantage by coming to close quarters, but their belief in their superiority in the use of the bayonet, a vanity common to many nations, proved unfounded. The years of endeavour of Moltke and his Generals bore fruit. The Austrian Army was shattered.

Three weeks later the Prussians were within reach of Vienna. At Bismarck's vehement insistence the capital was spared the humiliation of occupation and the peace terms were once again lenient. Bismarck's mind was already turned to his next move, and he set store by future Austrian friendship. "So to limit a victory," he said, "is not only a generous but a most wise policy. But for the victor to benefit from it the recipient must be worthy." Austria's only territorial loss was Venetia, granted to Italy, but she was finally excluded from Germany and her future ambitions had inevitably to lie south-eastwards among the Slavs. So ended the Seven Weeks' War. Prussia had gained five million inhabitants and 25,000 square miles of territory in Germany. The balance of Continental power had changed radically. A premonitory shudder went through France.

Napoleon III tried vainly to extract from Prussia some reward for his neutrality—a policy of asking for tips, as it was contemptuously called. But to a French demand for territories in South Germany Bismarck returned a blank refusal, and published both his and Napoleon's Notes, thus raising suspicions of France and consolidating his own position in non-Prussian Germany. Belatedly France came to realise her full danger. In the logic of Bismarck's methodical planning a Franco-Prussian war lay on the close horizon. In desperate haste Marshal Niel, Minister of War, set in train the reform of the French Army, and Napoleon cast about for allies in the forthcoming struggle. All was vain. Distraught by Napoleon's increasing ill-health and diminished powers of decision and driven by the petulant arrogance of her Parliament and Press, France ran headlong on her fate.

The next four years were marked by growing tension, the steady increase of armaments on both sides, and incidents that lipped the brink of war. The position was perfectly plain to British statesmen and they did their best to mediate. Without a firm commitment to France or Prussia such attempts were necessarily doomed. Neither obvious national interest nor a liking for either side was strong enough to sway Britain. Napoleon's unstable ambitions were suspect in London, and Bismarck, in the words of the British Ambassador in Berlin, seemed to have opted for a *politique de brigandage*.

Once again the German Chancellor succeeded in depriving his adversary of allies. In spite of French blandishments Austria stood aloof. Italy had no reason to turn against her Prussian ally of 1866. French troops still held Rome for the Pope, and a French defeat would compel them to withdraw. Russia, at Bismarck's prompting, seized her advantage to break the treaty bonds placed on her movements in and out of the Black Sea. Bismarck was not greatly concerned with Britain. As he had put it some time before, "What is England to me? The importance of a state is measured by the number of soldiers it can put in the field." Nevertheless in 1870 he sent to *The Times* newspaper the text of a draft treaty apparently proposed by the French four years earlier in which they sought to acquire Belgium in return for supporting Prussia. To Britain, a guarantor of Belgian inviolability, this made intervention on the French side even less attractive.

In that summer Bismarck delivered his stroke. A revolution in Spain had driven out the Bourbon dynasty and the Spanish throne had been vacant for nearly two years. The interim Spanish Government cast about for a suitable royal candidate from the great families of Europe, and the choice finally fell on Prince Leopold of Hohenzollern-Sigmaringen, a member of the elder branch of King William of Prussia's family. The Prince declined the offer. Nevertheless, at Bismarck's suggestion the Spaniards renewed their invitation, and this time it was accepted. The French reaction was violent. To the accompaniment of inflammatory speeches in Parliament the French Ambassador in Prussia was instructed to demand a revocation of Prince Leopold's acceptance, which the French Foreign Minister described as "the disturbance to French detriment of the existing equilibrium of the forces of Europe and the endangering of the interests and honour of France." Nowadays he would no doubt have spoken of encirclement. King William received these remonstrances patiently enough. He privately advised Prince Leopold to withdraw, and within forty-eight hours the Prince complied. The French Press exulted. With fatal importunity the French Ambassador was instructed to demand guarantees that the candidature would never again be renewed. This was too much even for King William. He put off the Ambassador courteously but firmly, and as soon as he was officially informed of Prince Leopold's renunciation he sent the Ambassador a message to say that he regarded the matter as closed.

To Bismarck his sovereign's diplomacy was gall. He believed the fruits of his work to be slipping away and his country to be set on a course of humiliation. Dining in dejection with Moltke and Roon in Berlin, he received from the King at Ems a telegram describing the latest events. The King's telegram gave Bismarck discretion to publish the story if he thought it desirable. Bismarck seized the opportunity, and without literal falsehood so abbreviated the account as to give the impression that the French demands had been rejected in the curtest manner and that their Ambassador had been rebuffed. Well aware that the communiqué—now in Bismarck's words "a red rag to the Gallic bull"—made conflict inevitable, the dinner party broke up content. Roon exclaimed exultantly, "Our God of old lives still, and will not let us perish in disgrace." The French declaration of war followed within a week. The picturesque quality of the incident is somewhat marred by subsequent knowledge that the French Cabinet had decided on war in any case, if King William's attitude was anything less than capitulation. Their deficient military intelligence had led some French leaders to the belief that their military preparation surpassed Prussia's. The next forty days were to give a terrible answer to the contrary.

Prussia placed half a million men in the field, with the same number in reserve. Bavaria, which for two hundred years had supported France upon the European scene, now threw 150,000 men against her. The course of the struggle was brief and fierce. The French fought with all their native dash and gallantry and their infantry weapons were fully up to their enemy's standard. But they were outdated and outclassed in the new dialectic of war, in transport, in the supply system, above all in staff work and training.

From the start things went ill for France. The mobilisation scheme, revised by the Emperor himself, was slow and fearfully confused. Officers searched for non-existent units; reservists in Alsace were sent to camps in the Pyrenees to be equipped before they joined formations within a few miles of their point of departure; many were only able, weeks later, to reach their regiments when these were already dispersed or in retreat.

The Germans advanced in three main armies, two, totalling 350,000 men, moving by converging routes on the French fortress of Metz, and the Crown Prince of Prussia, at the head of a force of 220,000, making for Strasbourg. Far in front of the armies drove a cloud of cavalry, blinding and confusing the French and providing their own staffs with accurate information. The greater number of the battles in the open field were joined almost inadvertently by the impetuous advance of the Prussian vanguard, which the excellent organisation of their main forces enabled them to exploit rapidly. On August 4 the Crown Prince defeated part of the

French Army of Alsace under Marshal MacMahon at Wissembourg, and two days later, after a major engagement at Wörth, drove the main French force south towards Châlons. Simultaneously the Army of the Rhine, commanded by the Emperor, was compelled to fall back on Metz. At this fortress Napoleon handed over his command to Marshal Bazaine and joined MacMahon at Châlons.

By mid-August the first and second German armies had contrived to get between Metz and Paris. Bazaine fought three bloody battles, which reached their climax at Gravelotte on August 18, where the German cavalry, at great cost, turned the scales. He then retreated into Metz, where he remained with 180,000 of the best of the French Army, a passive and inglorious spectator of the swift development of Moltke's plans. MacMahon and the Emperor advanced to the relief of Metz. The Crown Prince, who had by-passed Strasbourg, came up with the French near Sedan and forced them to retreat into that ancient fortified town on the Belgian frontier. The Germans, whose artillery had early showed a marked superiority, methodically surrounded the French positions and girded them with a circle of fire. Sedan was ill adapted for defence in modern warfare. As the Germans took possession of the heights above the town the position became untenable. After a desperate struggle Napoleon was forced to capitulate with 130,000 men. Only six weeks after the outbreak of war he surrendered his sword to the King of Prussia. Bismarck was present. Their last meeting had been as fellow diplomatists five years before at Biarritz.

Three weeks later the Germans had surrounded Paris, and within a few days Bazaine, through folly, weariness, or worse, as many Frenchmen believed, unnecessarily surrendered the great fortress of Metz. In 1876 a French court, unable to believe that he had acted on grounds other than of cowardice or treason, condemned him to death, though the sentence was not carried out.

* * * * *

The war seemed over. The French Emperor was a prisoner. The Empress had fled to England. Paris was firmly gripped by the besieging armies. A "Government of National Defence" held on in the capital, but in spite of the spirited efforts of one of its members, Gambetta, who escaped from the city in a balloon to stimulate resistance in the provinces, the last French armies on the Loire and the Swiss frontier were not able to achieve anything effective. In January 1871 the siege of Paris was ended.

Negotiations for an armistice opened in Versailles. This time Bismarck drove a relatively hard bargain and exacted a heavy return for every concession he made. The peace treaty with France was considered in its day to be severe. An indemnity of 5,000 million francs in gold was demanded, which was believed to be sufficient to engage the French economy for a long time. It was paid off in three years. The victorious army paraded through the streets of Paris. Alsace and Eastern Lorraine were ceded to Germany. Bitter indeed were the seeds sown thereby.

The final text of the treaty was not signed for several months. Meanwhile France suffered one of the terrible consequences of a major and disintegrating military defeat. In March revolutionaries seized control of Paris, where the French garrison had been greatly depleted by the terms of the armistice. At first the movement, styled the Commune, was inspired by patriotic motives and called on the people of Paris, humiliated by the sight of the triumphant Prussian Army, to rise and continue the struggle. A half-hearted attempt to quell the insurrection failed, and the Provisional French Government withdrew to Versailles leaving Paris un-

der the red flag. Bismarck released French prisoners of war
to assist in the subduing of the capital, which now became
a full-scale military operation.

As the Government forces under Marshal MacMahon advanced the character of the Commune changed. Its supporters lost interest in repelling the Prussian invaders and
became increasingly vicious and bloodthirsty social revolutionaries. Hostages, including the Archbishop of Paris and
many priests, were shot, and great national buildings were
burned to the ground. MacMahon's troops had to fight their
way through barricade after barricade as they closed on the
centre of Paris amid all the horrors of civil war. Merciless
reprisals were taken on the Communards. By the time order
was restored, after some six weeks' fighting, the dead were
numbered in tens of thousands. Twenty-five thousand alone
are estimated to have been executed as the struggle proceeded.
The movement did not spread to any extent to other cities in
France. It had been hailed by Communists abroad, and Karl
Marx, living in England, saw in it a vindication of the
theories of class-warfare which he had been preaching for
half a lifetime. In lineal descent from the revolutions of 1789
and 1848, the Commune left scars on the French body politic
that are visible to this day.

* * * * *

In the month of the armistice the final touches were put
to the tremendous edifice of German unity. Since the autumn
the German diplomatic staffs had been at work at Versailles,
and on January 18, 1871, in the Hall of Mirrors William I
of Prussia received from his fellow sovereigns the title of
German Emperor. There had been some dispute over the
exact wording of the title. Bismarck, always ready to con-
cede the form for the substance, had decided for the version
most likely to spare the susceptibilities of the smaller states.

As William left the Hall he pointedly ignored the titanic architect of his fortunes. He had wished to be styled Emperor of Germany.

On the day of the Battle of Sadowa Disraeli had addressed his constituents on the virtues of serene detachment from European affairs. He had none the less a true insight, as the sequel will show. Five years later it was still possible for Britain to be a benevolent, distressed, but somewhat distant spectator of the struggle. During the decade ending in 1870 the Royal Navy had been powerfully re-equipped with iron-clad steamships which mounted rifled guns firing shell instead of shot. At sea the age of wood and sail was at long last over. The naval lessons of the American Civil War had been learnt. But on land the regular British Army remained by Continental standards a negligible quantity. The wars of the nineteenth century had not lasted long enough to show the military deployment of which an industrialised country was finally capable.

At Versailles Bismarck's life-work reached its climax. In the face of every obstacle at home and at the cost of the deliberate provocation of three wars Prussia presided over Germany, and Germany had become one of the two most powerful nations on the Continent. The cost was great. France was embittered, determined on revenge and anxious to gain allies to help her. The Concert of Europe, founded at Vienna, was now fatally cracked and flawed. In the years that followed various efforts were made to revive it, sometimes with temporary success. But gradually the Powers of Europe drifted into two separate camps, with Britain as an uneasy and uncommitted spectator. From this division, growing into an unbridgeable chasm, the eruptions of the twentieth century arose. Britain was slow to recognise the transformation of the scene, and Disraeli—though he exaggerated—was in advance of his time when he declared that the victories of Prussian arms meant a German Revolution, "a greater political event," he forecast, "than the French Revolution of the last century." The era of armed peace had opened. Britain however, in the age of Gladstone and Disraeli, was absorbed in home affairs and in the problems of Ireland and Empire. But the days of an apparent disconnection between European and Colonial affairs were drawing rapidly to a close. Nevertheless so long as Bismarck led Germany, he was careful to do nothing to arouse British hostility. Meanwhile colonial quarrels increasingly darkened the Island's relations with France. Not until Kaiser William II had dismissed the great Chancellor and plunged into provocative policies did Britain fully awake to the Teutonic menace.

Gladstone and Disraeli

W E now enter upon a long, connected, and progressive period in British history—the Prime Ministerships of Gladstone and Disraeli. These two great Parliamentarians in alternation ruled the land from 1868 to 1885. For nearly twenty years no one effectively disputed their leadership, and until Disraeli died in 1881 the political scene was dominated by a personal duel on a grand scale. Both men were at the height of their powers, and their skill and oratory in debate gripped and focused public attention on the proceedings of the House of Commons. Every thrust and parry was discussed throughout the country. The political differences between them were no wider than is usual in a two-party system, but what gave the conflict its edge and produced a deep-rooted antagonism was their utter dissimilarity in character and temperament. "Posterity will do justice to that unprincipled maniac, Gladstone," wrote Disraeli, in private, "—extraordinary mixture of envy, vindictiveness, hypocrisy, and superstition; and with one commanding characteristic— whether preaching, praying, speechifying, or scribbling— never a gentleman!" Gladstone's judgment on his rival was no less sharp. His doctrine was "false, but the man more false than his doctrine. . . . He demoralised public opinion, bargained with diseased appetites, stimulated passions, prejudices, and selfish desires, that they might maintain his influence . . .

he weakened the Crown by approving its unconstitutional leanings, and the Constitution by offering any price for democratic popularity." Thus they faced each other across the dispatch-boxes of the House of Commons: Gladstone's commanding voice, his hawk-like eyes, his great power to move the emotions, against Disraeli's romantic air and polished, flexible eloquence.

When Gladstone became Prime Minister in 1868 he was deemed a careful and parsimonious administrator who had become a sound Liberal reformer. But this was only one side of his genius. What gradually made him the most controversial figure of the century was his gift of rousing moral indignation both in himself and in the electorate. In two great crusades on the Balkans and on Ireland his dominant theme was that conscience and the moral law must govern political decisions. Such a demand, strenuously voiced, was open to the charge of hypocrisy when, as so often happened, Gladstone's policy obviously coincided with the well-being of the Liberal Party. But the charge was false; the spirit of the preacher breathed in Gladstone's speeches. He was willing to break his party rather than deny his conscience. Soon after his conversion to Home Rule for Ireland he said to his lieutenant, Sir William Harcourt, "I am prepared to go forward without anybody." It was a spirit which was to mismanage men and split the Liberals, but it won him a place in the hearts of his followers of which Britain had never seen the like.

To face Gladstone Disraeli needed all the courage and quickness of wit with which he had been so generously endowed. Many Tories disliked and distrusted his reforming views, but he handled his colleagues with a rare skill. He has never been surpassed in the art of party management. In all his attitudes there was a degree of cynicism; in his make-up there was not a trace of moral fervour. Large sections of the working classes were held to Church, Crown, Empire, and aristocracy by practical interests which could be turned to party advantage. Or so he saw it. He never became wholly assimilated to English ways of life, and preserved to his death the detachment which had led him as a young man to make his own analysis of English society. It was this which probably enabled him to diagnose and assess the deeper political currents of his age. Long handicapped by his own party, he led it in the end to an electoral triumph, and achieved for a period the power he had always desired.

Nothing created more bitterness between them than Gladstone's conviction that Disraeli had captured the Queen for the Conservative Party and endangered the Constitution by an unscrupulous use of his personal charm. When Gladstone became Prine Minister Victoria was still in mourning and semi-retirement for Prince Albert, who had died in 1861. She deeply resented his attempts to bring the monarchy back into public life, attempts which culminated in a well-intentioned scheme to make her eldest son the Viceroy of Ireland. Gladstone, though always respectful, was incapable of infusing any kind of warmth into his relationship with her. She once said, according to report, that he addressed her like a public meeting. Disraeli did not make the same mistake. "The principles of the English Constitution," he declared, "do not contemplate the absence of personal influence on the part of the Sovereign; and, if they did, the principles of human nature would prevent the fulfillment of such a theory." He wrote to the Queen constantly. He wooed her from the loneliness and apathy which engulfed her after Albert's death, and flattered her desire to share in the formulation of policy. At the height of the Eastern crisis in May 1877 he ended a report on the various views of the Cabinet with the following words: "The policy is that of Your Majesty, and which will be introduced and enforced to the utmost by the Prime Minister." Victoria found this irresistible. She complained that Gladstone, when in office, never told her anything. Had he done so after 1880 it might have been transmitted to the Conservative Opposition. From then on she was not friendly to her Liberal Governments; she disliked Gladstone and detested the growing Radicalism of his party. But in fact little harm was done; Gladstone was careful to keep the person of the Queen out of political discussion and none of their disagreements was known to the public. He grumbled that "the Queen is enough to kill any man," but he scrved her patiently, if not with understanding. In any case the development of popular Government based on popular elections was bound to diminish the personal power of the Crown. In spite of her occasional leanings, Victoria remained a constitutional monarch.

*   *   *   *   *

Gladstone always said that his Cabinet of 1868 to 1874 was "one of the best instruments of government that ever was constructed." Driven by his boundless energy, it put into effect a long-delayed avalanche of reforms. This was the Golden Age when Liberalism was still an aggressive, unshackling force, and the doctrine of individualism and the philosophy of *laissez-faire* were seeking out and destroying the last relics of eighteenth-century government. The Civil Service, the Army, the universities, and the law were all attacked and the grip of the old landed interest began to crumble. The power of what James Mill had called the "sinister interests" shrivelled bit by bit as the public service was gradually but remorselessly thrown open to talent and industry. Freedom was the keynote, *laissez-faire* the method; no undue extension of Government authority was needed; and the middle class at last acquired a share in the political sphere equal to their economic power. Gladstone came in on the flood; a decisive electoral victory and a country ready for reform gave him his opportunity. The Liberal Party, for a rare moment in equilibrium, was united behind him. The scale and scope of his policy, directed at a series of obvious abuses, was such that Radicals, moderate Liberals, and even Whigs were brought together in agreement. He began with Ireland. "My mission," he had said when the summons from the Queen reached him at his country home in Hawarden, "is to pacify Ireland," and, in spite of bitter opposition and in defiance of his own early principles, which had been to defend property and the Anglican faith, he carried, in 1869, the disestablishment of the Protestant Church of Ireland. This was followed next year by a Land Act which attempted to protect tenants from unfair eviction. But Ireland was not so easily to be pacified.

In England the Government found no lack of work to do. After the Electoral Reform of 1867 Robert Lowe, now Chancellor of the Exchequer, had said that "We must educate our masters." Voters ought to know at least how to read and write, and have opened to them the paths to higher knowledge. Thus the extension of the franchise and the general Liberal belief in the value of education led to the launching of a national system of primary schools. This was achieved by W. E. Forster's Education Act of 1870, blurred though it was, like all education measures for some decades to come, by sectarian passion and controversy. At the same time patronage was finally destroyed in the home Civil Service. Entrance to the new administrative class was henceforth possible only through a competitive examination which placed great emphasis on intellectual attainment. Ability, not wealth or family connection, was now the means to advance. In the following year all religious tests at Oxford and Cambridge were abolished. The universities were thrown open to Roman Catholics, Jews, Dissenters, and young men of no belief. The ancient intricacies of the judicial system, so long a nightmare to litigants and a feeding ground for lawyers, were simplified and modernised by the fusion of courts of law and equity. The Judicature Act marked the culmination of a lengthy process of much-needed reform. For centuries litigants had often had to sue in two courts at once about the same matter. Now a single Supreme Court was set up, with appropriate divisions, and procedure and methods of appeal were made uniform. Offices that had survived from the reign of Edward I were swept away in a complete remodelling. All this was accompanied by a generally sound administration, and, what was perhaps closest to Gladstone's own heart, a policy of economy and low taxation.

The sufferings and disgraces of the Crimea had made it evident that the great Duke of Wellington's practices, in the hands of lesser men, had broken down. The Prussian victories in France administered a shock to military and civilian opinion. Reforms were long overdue at the War Office. They were carried out by Gladstone's Secretary of State, Edward Cardwell, one of the greatest of Army reformers. The Commander-in-Chief, the Duke of Cambridge, was opposed to any reform whatever, and the first step was taken when the Queen, with considerable reluctance, signed an Order in Council subordinating him to the Secretary of State. Flogging was abolished. An Enlistment Act introduced short service, which would create an efficient reserve. In 1871 Cardwell went further, and after a hard fight with Service opinion the purchase of commissions were prohibited. The infantry were rearmed with the Martini-Henry rifle, and the regimental system was completely reorganised on a county basis. The War

Office was overhauled, though a General Staff was not yet established.

All this was achieved in the space of six brilliant, crowded years, and then, as so often happens in English history, the pendulum swung back. Great reforms offend great interests. The Anglicans were hit by several measures; the Nonconformists found little to please them in the Education Act. The Army and the Court resented Cardwell's onslaught. The working classes were offered little to attract them apart from a Ballot Act which allowed them to exercise the newly won franchise in secret and without intimidation. The settlement for fifteen million dollars of the *Alabama* dispute with the United States, though sensible, was disagreeable to a people long fed on a Palmerstonian diet. They began to suspect that Gladstone was half-hearted in defending British interests. An unsuccessful Licensing Bill, prompted by the Temperance wing of the Liberal Party, estranged the drink interest and founded an alliance between the brewer and the Conservative Party. Gladstone was soon to complain that he had been borne down from power "in a torrent of gin and beer." Disraeli, now at the height of his oratorical powers, painted this portrait of the Ministry: "Her Majesty's new Ministers proceeded in their career like a body of men under the influence of some deleterious drug. Not satiated with the spoliation and anarchy of Ireland, they began to attack every institution and every interest, every class and calling in the country. . . . As time advanced it was not difficult to perceive that extravagance was being substituted for energy by the Government. The unnatural stimulus was subsiding. Their paroxysms ended in prostration. Some took refuge in melancholy, and their eminent chief alternated between a menace and a sigh. As I sat opposite the Treasury Bench the Ministers reminded me of one of those marine landscapes not very unusual on the coasts of South America. You behold a range of exhausted volcanoes. Not a flame flickers on a single pallid crest. But the situation is still dangerous. There are occasional earthquakes, and ever and anon the dark rumbling of the sea."

Nevertheless Gladstone's first Government stands high in British history; but there were few fresh Liberal ideals to expound when Parliament was dissolved in 1874. He fought the election on a proposal to abolish the income-tax, which then stood at threepence in the pound, and to the end of his life he always regretted his failure to achieve this object. But the country was now against him and he lost. He went into semi-retirement, believing that the great reforming work of Liberalism had been completed. Most of his Whig friends agreed. The Radicals thought otherwise. All of them were wrong. "The Grand Old Man" was soon to return to politics, and return in a setting and amid a storm which would rend and disrupt the loyalties and traditions of English public life in a manner far more drastic than any of them yet conceived.

* * * * *

While his great adversary devoted his leisure to felling trees at Hawarden and writing articles about Homer Disraeli seized his chance. He had long waited for supreme power. For twenty-five years he had been the leader of the Conservative Party in the House of Commons, and now he was over seventy. His physique had never been robust, and his last years, made lonely by the death of his wife, were plagued by gout and other ailments. "Power—it has come to me too late. . . . There were days when, on waking, I felt I could move dynasties and Governments; but that has passed away." But at no time had his problems been simple. Apart from the interlude of the Peel Ministry of 1841–46, an interlude which had ended in party disaster, the Tories had been more or less in opposition for close on half a century. Labelled the party of reaction, its members mocked as the heirs of Eldon, Sidmouth, and other hard-shelled old Tories, it now had to face a democratic electorate. The fact that the extension of the franchise had been sponsored by the Tory leader made it no less "a leap in the dark" for them. But Disraeli had no doubts. He remained true to the spirit of the Young England movement, which he had founded a generation before, and he never believed that the working men of England were Radicals or would-be destroyers of the established order. He saw clearly that although many of the new electors were attracted by the ideas of tradition, continuity, and ordered social progress such feelings would never ripen into electoral advantage under the inert conservatism of his own back-benchers. He had not only to win over the electorate, but also to convert his own party.

Disraeli's campaign began long before Gladstone fell. He concentrated on social reform and on a new conception of the Empire, and both prongs of attack struck Gladstone at his weakest points. The Empire had never aroused his interest, and though passionate in defence of the political rights of the working class he cared little for their material claims. Disraeli, on the other hand, proclaimed that "the first consideration of a Minister should be the health of the people." Liberals tried to laugh this off as a "policy of sewage." In his first full session after reaching office Disraeli proceeded to redeem his pledge. He was fortunate in his colleagues, among whom the Home Secretary, Richard Cross, was outstanding in ability. A Trade Union Act gave the unions almost complete freedom of action, an Artisan's Dwelling Act was the first measure to tackle the housing problem, a Sale of Food and Drugs Act and a Public Health Act at last established sanitary law on a sound footing. Disraeli succeeded in persuading much of the Conservative Party not only that the real needs of the electorate included healthier conditions of life, better homes, and freedom to organise in the world of industry, but also that the Conservative Party was perfectly well fitted to provide them. Well might Alexander Macdonald, the miners' leader, declare that "The Conservative Party have done more for the working classes in five years than the Liberals have in fifty." Gladstone had provided the administrative basis for these great developments, but Disraeli took the first considerable steps in promoting social welfare.

The second part of the new Conservative programme, Imperialism, had also been launched before Disraeli came to power. Gladstone's passion for economy in all things military, his caution in Europe, and his indifference to the Empire jarred on a public which was growing ever more conscious of British Imperial glory. Disraeli's appeal was perfectly tuned to the new mood. "Self-government, in my opinion," he said of the colonies, "when it was conceded, ought to have been conceded as part of a great policy of Imperial consolidation. It ought to have been accompanied by an Imperial tariff, by securities for the people of England for the enjoyment of the unappropriated lands which belonged to the Sovereign as their trustee, and by a military code which should have precisely defined the means and the responsibilities by which the colonies should be defended, and by which, if necessary, this country should call for aid from the colonies themselves. It ought, further, to have been accompanied by the institution of some representative council in the Metropolis which would have brought the colonies into constant and continuous relations with the home Government. All this however was omitted because those who advised that policy—and I believe their convictions were sincere—looked upon the colonies of England, looked upon even our connection with India, as a burden upon this country; viewing everything in its financial aspect, and totally passing by those moral and political considerations which make nations great, and by the influence of which men alone are distinguished from the animals.

"Well, what has been the result of this attempt during the reign of Liberalism for the disintegration of the Empire? It has entirely failed. But how has it failed? Through the sympathy of the colonies for the Mother Country. They have decided that the Empire shall not be destroyed; and in my opinion no Minister in this country will do his duty who neglects any opportunity of reconstructing as much as possible our Colonial Empire, and of responding to those distant sympathies which may become the source of incalculable strength and happiness to this land."

At first Disraeli was brilliantly successful. The Suez Canal had been open for six years, and had transformed the strategic position of Great Britain. No longer was the Cape of Good Hope the key to the route to India and the Far East. The Foreign Office had been curiously slow to appreciate this obvious fact and had missed more than one opportunity to control the waterway. In 1875 Disraeli, on behalf of the British Government, bought, for four million pounds, the shares of the Egyptian Khedive Ismail in the Canal. This Turkish satrap was bankrupt and glad to sell; his holding amounted to nearly half the total issue. The route to India was safeguarded, a possible threat to British naval supremacy was removed, and—of fateful importance for the future—Britain was inexorably drawn into Egyptian politics. In the following year Queen Victoria, to her great pleasure, was proclaimed Empress of India. Such a stroke would never have occurred to Gladstone, or, indeed, to the next generation of Imperialists. But Disraeli's Oriental, almost mystical, approach to Empire, his emphasis on Imperial symbols, his belief in the importance of outward display, gave his policy an imaginative colour never achieved by his successors. His purpose was to make those colonies which he had once condemned as "millstones round our necks" sparkle like diamonds. New storms in Europe distracted attention from this glittering prospect.

*   *   *   *   *

In 1876 the Eastern Question erupted anew. The Crimean War had been mismanaged by the soldiers, and at the peace the diplomats had done no better. Most of the Balkans still remained under Turkish rule, and all attempts to improve the Ottoman administration of Christian provinces had foundered on the obstinacy of the Sultan and the magnitude of the task. Slavs, Rumanians, and Greeks were united in their detestation of the Turk. Revolt offered little hope of permanent success, and they had long looked to the Czar of Russia as their potential liberator. Here was a fine dilemma for the British Government. The possibility of creating independent Balkan states, in spite of Canning's example in the small Greek kingdom, was not yet seriously contemplated. The nice choice appeared to lie between bolstering Turkish power and allowing Russian influence to move through the Balkans and into the Mediterranean by way of Constantinople. The threat had long been present, and the insurrection which now occurred confronted Disraeli with the most difficult and dangerous situation for Great Britain since the Napoleonic wars.

Rebellion broke out in Bosnia and Herzegovina, where forty years later an assassin's bullet was to start the First World War. Germany, Austria, and Russia, united in the League of Three Emperors, proposed that Turkey should be coerced into making serious reforms. Disraeli and his Foreign Secretary, Lord Derby, resisted these plans, arguing that they "must end very soon in the disintegration of Turkey," and to emphasise British support of Turkey a fleet was dispatched to the Dardanelles. But these diplomatic manœuvres were soon overtaken by the news of terrible Turkish atrocities in Bulgaria. Disraeli, handicapped by faulty reports from his ambassador at Constantinople, who was an admirer of the Turks, failed to measure the deep stir in public opinion. In reply to a Parliamentary question in July he took leave to doubt whether "torture has been practised on a great scale among an Oriental people who seldom, I believe, resort to torture, but generally terminate their connection with culprits in a more expeditious manner." This tone of persiflage fanned into fierce and furious activity the profound moral feeling which was always simmering just below the surface of Gladstone's mind.

In a famous pamphlet, *The Bulgarian Horrors and the Question of the East,* Gladstone delivered his onslaught on the Turks and Disraeli's Government. "Let the Turks now carry away their abuses in the only possible manner, namely, by carrying off themselves. Their Zaptiehs and their Mudirs, their Bimbashis and their Yuzbachis, their Kaimakams and their Pashas, one and all, bag and baggage, shall, I hope, clear out from the provinces they have desolated and profaned. This thorough riddance, this most blessed deliverance, is the only reparation we can make to the memory of those heaps on heaps of dead; to the violated purity alike of matron, of maiden, and of child. . . . There is not a criminal in a European gaol, there is not a cannibal in the South Sea Islands, whose indignation would not arise and overboil at the recital of that which has been done, which has too late been examined, but which remains unavenged; which has left behind all the foul and all the fierce passions that produced it, and which may again spring up in another more murderous harvest, from the soil soaked and reeking with blood, and in the air tainted with every imaginable deed of crime and shame. . . . No Government ever has so sinned; none has proved itself so incorrigible in sin or—which is the same— so impotent for reformation." After this broadside relations between the two great men became so strained that Lord Beaconsfield (as Disraeli now was) publicly described Gladstone as worse than any Bulgarian horror.

At the end of the year a conference of the Great Powers was held in Constantinople at which Lord Salisbury, as the British representative, displayed for the first time his diplomatic talents. Salisbury was the direct descendant of Queen Elizabeth's great servant, William Cecil, and of James I's Minister, Robert Cecil, whose namesake he was. Over a period of twenty years, in both Houses of Parliament, he had been highly critical of his chief. He had joined Disraeli's Government only after much heart-searching. But in office gradually the two men grew togther. Salisbury's caustic, far-ranging common sense supplemented Disraeli's darting vision. As Secretary of State for India, and later at the Foreign Office, Salisbury established himself as the next predestined Tory leader. At Constantinople a programme of reform for Turkey was drawn up, but the Turks, sustained in part by a belief that Salisbury's zeal for reform did not entirely reflect the views of his Prime Minister and the British Cabinet, rejected it. The delegates returned to their capitals and Europe waited for war to break out between Russia and Turkey. When it came in the summer of 1877 the mood of the country quickly changed. Gladstone, whose onslaught on the Turks had at first carried all before it, was now castigated as a pro-Russian. Feeling rose as, month after month, in spite of heroic Turkish resistance, especially at Plevna in Bulgaria, the mass of Russian troops moved ponderously towards the Dardanelles. At last, in January 1878, they stood before the walls of Constantinople. Public opinion reached fever-point. The music-hall song of the hour was:

We don't want to fight, but by jingo if we do
We've got the ships, we've got the men, we've got the money too!
We've fought the Bear before, and while we're Britons true
The Russians shall not have Constantinople.

In February, after considerable prevarication, a fleet of British ironclads steamed into the Golden Horn. They lay in the Sea of Marmora, opposite the Russian army, for six uneasy months of truce; the whale, as Bismarck said, facing the elephant.

In March Turkey and Russia signed the Treaty of San Stefano. Andrassy, the Austrian Foreign Minister, in anger called it "an orthodox Slavic sermon." It gave Russia effective control of the Balkans, and was obviously unacceptable to the other Great Powers. War again seemed likely, and Lord Derby, who objected to any kind of military preparations, resigned. He was replaced at the Foreign Office by Lord Salisbury, who immediately set about summoning a conference of the Great Powers. They met at the Congress of Berlin in June and July. Business was dominated by Andrassy, Beaconsfield, Bismarck, and the Russian Minister Gortchakov, a quartet whose combined diplomatic talents would have been difficult to match. The result was that Russia gave up much of what she had momentarily gained at San Stefano. She kept Rumanian Bessarabia, which extended her territories to the mouths of the Danube, but the big Bulgaria which she had planned to dominate was split into three parts, only one of which was granted practical independence. The rest was returned to the Sultan. Austria-Hungary, as we must now call the Habsburg Empire, secured in compensation the right to occupy and administer Bosnia-Herzegovina. By a separate Anglo-Turkish convention Great Britain received Cyprus and guaranteed the territorial integrity of Turkey-in-Asia in return for yet another pledge by the Sultan to introduce proper reforms. Beaconsfield returned from Berlin claiming that he had brought "peace with honour." He had, indeed, averted war for the moment, Russia, blocked in the Balkans, turned her gaze away from Europe to the Far East. The arrangements at Berlin have been much criticised for laying the trail to the war of 1914, but the Eastern Question, as it was then posed before the nations, was virtually insoluble. No settlement could have been more than a temporary one, and the Congress of Berlin in fact ensured the peace of Europe for thirty-six years.

The following weeks saw the zenith of Beaconsfield's career. But fortune soon ceased to smile upon him. Thrusting policies in South Africa and Afghanistan led, in 1879, to the destruction of a British battalion by the Zulus at Isandhlwana and the massacre of the Legation staff at Kabul. Thse minor disasters, though promptly avenged, lent fresh point to Gladstone's vehement assault upon the Government, an assault which reached its climax in the autumn of 1879 with the Midlothian Campaign. Gladstone denounced a "vigorous, that is to say a narrow, restless, blustering, and self-assertive foreign policy, . . . appealing to the self-love and pride of the community." He argued that Britain should pursue the path of morality and justice, free from the taint of self-interest. Her aims should be self-government for subject peoples and the promotion of a true Concert of Europe. His constant theme was the need for the nation's policy to conform with the moral law. "Remember," he said at Dalkeith, "that the sanctity of life in the hill villages of Afghanistan among the

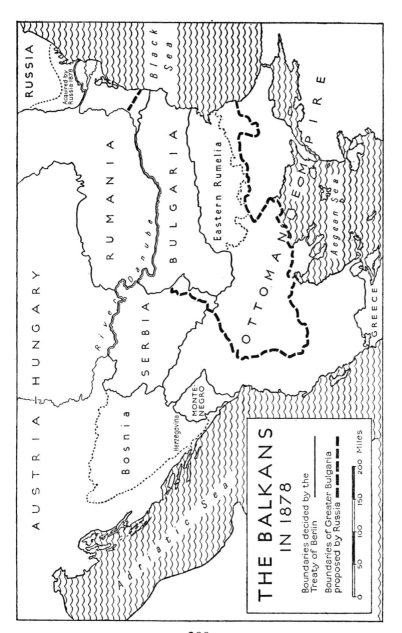

THE BALKANS
IN 1878

Boundaries decided by the
Treaty of Berlin ——————

Boundaries of Greater Bulgaria
proposed by Russia ▬ ▬ ▬ ▬

0   50   100   150   200 Miles

RUSSIA

Acquired by
Russia 1878

Black Sea

RUMANIA

River Danube

BULGARIA

Eastern Rumelia

OTTOMAN EMPIRE

Aegean Sea

GREECE

AUSTRIA-HUNGARY

SERBIA

Bosnia

Herzegovina

MONTE
NEGRO

Adriatic Sea

winter snows is as inviolable in the eyes of Almighty God as can be your own." This appeal to morality infuriated the Conservatives, who based their case on the importance of defending and forwarding British interests and responsibilities wherever they might lie. They maintained that Beaconsfield's policy had raised national power and prestige to new heights.

But the force of Gladstone's oratory was too much for the exhausted Ministry. Moreover, their last years in office coincided with the onset of an economic depression, serious enough for industry but ruinous for agriculture. When Beaconsfield dissolved in March 1880 the electoral result was decisive; the Queen was forced to accept as Prime Minister for a second time the man whom she described in a letter to her private secretary, Sir Henry Ponsonby, as "that *half-mad firebrand* who would soon ruin everything."

* * * * *

While the duel between Disraeli and Gladstone held the centre of the stage far-reaching movements were taking shape below the surface of Parliamentary politics. The Reform Act of 1867, in granting the vote to virtually every adult male resident in a borough, killed the modified eighteenth-century régime which had persisted since 1832. The emergence of a mass electorate called for a new kind of politics. Sheer numbers rendered the old techniques ineffective in the large cities. Two things were required: a party policy which would persuade the electors to vote, and an efficient organisation to make sure that they did so. Of the two leaders Gladstone was slow to see the implications of the new age. The great demagogue was bored by the ordinary everyday business of party. Disraeli, on the other hand, produced both a policy and an organisation. Twelve years earlier he had appointed John Gorst as party manager, under whose guidance the Conservative Party was completely overhauled. The Central

Office was established and a network of local associations was set up, combined in a National Union. The transition was remarkably smooth, and although there were to be storms in the early 1880's the system created by Disraeli still largely remains at the present time.

In the Liberal camp the situation was very different. Gladstone's coolness and Whig hostility prevented the building of a centralised party organisation. The impulse and impetus came not from the centre, but through the provinces. In 1873 Joseph Chamberlain had become Mayor of Birmingham. Aided by a most able political adviser, Schnadhorst, he built up a party machine which, although based on popular participation, his enemies quickly condemned as a "caucus." A policy of "Municipal Socialism" brought great benefits to Birmingham in the shape of public utilities, slum clearance, and other civic amenities. The movement spread to other towns and cities, and a National Liberal Federation was born. The aim of its promoters was to make the Federation the Parliament of the Liberal movement, which would work out a Radical programme and eventually replace the Whigs by a new set of leaders drawn from its own ranks. This was a novel phenomenon. Unlike Chartism and the anti-Corn Law League, movements for reform need no longer operate on the fringe of party. Radicalism was now powerful enough to make a bid for control. This change was greatly aided by the clustering of the parties round opposite social poles, a process well under way by 1880, and which Gladstone recognised in the course of his election campaign. "I am sorry," he declared, "to say we cannot reckon upon the aristocracy. We cannot reckon upon what is called the landed interest. We cannot reckon upon the clergy of the Established Church either in England or in Scotland. . . . We cannot reckon upon the wealth of the country nor upon the rank of the country. . . . In the main these powers are against us. . . . We must set them down among our most determined foes."

At the election Chamberlain and his followers put forward a programme of reform which was unacceptable to the Whigs, and indeed to Gladstone. Their success exposed and proclaimed the wide changes which the new franchise had wrought in the structure of the party system.

* * * * *

Gladstone and Disraeli had done much to bridge the gap between aristocratic rule and democracy. They both believed that Governments should be active, and the Statute Books for the years between 1868 and 1876 bulge with reforming measures. Elections gradually became a judgment on what the Government of the day had accomplished and an assessment of the promises for the future made by the two parties. By 1880 they were being fought with techniques which differ very little from those used to-day. Gladstone's Midlothian Campaign, the first broad appeal to the people by a potential Prime Minister, underlined the change. It shocked the Queen that he should make a speech about foreign policy from a railway carriage window, but her protest echoed an age that had already passed. This was the way to become "the People's William."

Beaconsfield died a year later. His great task, taken on almost single-handed, had been to lead the Conservative Party out of the despair of the period after 1846, to persuade it to face the inevitability of democracy, and to endow it with the policies which would meet the new conditions. That he was successful is a remarkable indication of his skill in all matters related to party. He made the Conservatives a great force in democratic politics. The large-scale two-party system with its "swing of the pendulum" begins with him. Tory democracy—working men by hundreds of thousands who voted Conservative—became the dominant factor. The extension of the franchise which had hitherto threatened to engulf the past bore it proudly forward. Whereas the Whigs vanished from the scene, the Tories, though they were slow to realise it, sprang into renewed life and power with a fair future before them. Such was the work of Disraeli, for which his name will be duly honoured.

American
"Reconstruction"

ACROSS the Atlantic the victory of Northern arms had preserved American unity. But immense problems had now to be faced. The most urgent was that of restoring order and prosperity to the defeated Confederacy. Great areas in the South, along the line of Sherman's march, and in the valley of Virginia, had been devastated. Atlanta, Columbia, Charleston, Richmond and other cities had been grievously damaged by bombardment and fire. The life of the South had come to a standstill. Farming, denied a market by the Northern blockade, had fallen into stagnation, despite the heroic efforts of Southern women and the faithful slaves to keep the land in cultivation. The blockade had also caused severe shortages in many common goods, and the breakdown of transport within the Confederacy had brought all within the grip of famine. The entire and inflated Southern banking system had collapsed. Confederate paper money and securities were now worthless. The whole region was reduced to penury. As the ragged, hungry soldiers of the Confederacy made their way homeward after Appomattox they were everywhere confronted by scenes of desolation and ruin.

Reconstruction was the word. But a prime difficulty in reconstructing the South was the future of the Negro. In spite of Lincoln's Proclamation of 1863, which nominally freed the slaves in the rebellious states, millions of them had con-

tinued throughout the war to work loyally for their old own-
ers. At the end of the war many of them believed that Emancipation meant that they need no longer work. They made
off to the nearest town or army camp, depriving the plantations of their labour and presenting the Union authorities
with an alarming problem. There was another reason for
tackling the question of the Negro, for in some parts of the
Union he was legally still a slave. Lincoln's Proclamation had
abolished salvery only in those areas under Confederate control. It had not applied either to the parts of the Confederacy
occupied by the Union or to the four slave states which had
remained loyal. Only two of these states, Maryland and
Missouri, had outlawed slavery within their limits. Further
action was needed, especially since doubts were expressed in
many quarters about the constitutional rightness of Lincoln's
Proclamation and of the Act passed by Congress in 1862
abolishing slavery in the Territories. The Thirteenth Constitutional Amendment was therefore proposed, prohibiting
slavery in all areas within the jurisdiction of the United States.

But here was a complication. The American Constitution
provided that no amendment was valid until it had been ratified by three-quarters of the states. As the Union now consisted of thirty-six states, some at least of the eleven former
Confederate states would have to ratify if the Thirteenth
Amendment was to become effective. The position of the
states which had seceded from the Union had to be defined.
If they had in fact left the Union should they return as the
equals of their conquerors? If so, on what conditions?

While the war was still in progress Lincoln had dismissed
the question of the legal status of the Confederate states as a
"pernicious abstraction." He had been concerned only with
restoring them to their "proper practical relation with the
Union." In December 1863 he had set out a plan for their

readmission. Pardon was offered, with a few exceptions, to all adherents of the Confederacy who would take an oath of loyalty to the Union. When such oaths had been taken by 10 per cent of the electorate of any state it remained only for state Governments to be established which were prepared to abolish slavery. Then they would be readmitted. Lincoln's "10 per cent plan" was never carried out. Reconstructed Governments were set up in 1864 in three of the Confederate states which had fallen under the control of Union armies, but Congress refused to seat the Senators and Representatives whom they sent to Washington.

* * * * *

Congress believed that Reconstruction was its business, and not the President's. The Radical Republicans who dominated Congress did not wish to smooth the path of the South's return to her allegiance. They wanted a harsh and vengeful policy, and they especially desired the immediate enfranchisement of the Negro. Radical vindictiveness sprang from various causes. The most creditable was a humanitarian concern for the welfare of the Negro. These feelings were shared only by a minority. More ignoble motives were present in the breasts of such Radical leaders as Zachariah Chandler and Thaddeus Stevens. Loving the Negro less than they hated his master, these ill-principled men wanted to humiliate the proud Southern aristocracy, whom they had always disliked, and at whose door they laid the sole blame for the Civil War. There was another and nearer point. The Radicals saw that if the Negro was given the vote they could break the power of the Southern planter and preserve the ascendancy over the Federal Government that Northern business interests had won since 1861. To allow the Southern states, in alliance with Northern Democrats, to recover their former voice in national affairs would, the Radicals believed, be incongruous and absurd. It would also jeopardise the mass of legislation on tariffs, banking, and public land which Northern capitalists had secured for themselves during the war. To safeguard these laws the Radicals took up the cry of the Negro vote, meaning to use it to keep their own party in power.

Even if Lincoln had lived to complete his second term he would have met with heavy opposition from his own party. The magnanimous policy he had outlined in April 1865, in the classic address delivered from the White House, was shattered by the bullet that killed him a few days later. The new President, Andrew Johnson of Tennessee, though sharing Lincoln's views on Reconstruction, was markedly lacking in political gifts. Nevertheless, from Lincoln's death until the end of the year, while Congress was in recess, Johnson was able to put into effect a Reconstruction plan closely resembling Lincoln's. Each Southern state, in conventions chosen by loyal electors, could qualify for readmission to the Union by repealing the Ordinances of Secession, repudiating the Confederate war debt, and abolishing slavery. The South, anxious, in the words of General Grant, "to return to self-government within the Union as soon as possible," was quick to comply. Southerners then proceeded to elect state legislatures and officials, chose Senators and Representatives to go to Washington, and ratified the Thirteenth Amendment, which went into force in December 1865.

When Congress reconvened in that same month it declined to seat the elected Representatives of the South. Ignoring Johnson's work, Congress went on to put its own ideas into practice. Its first step was to set up a Joint Committee on Reconstruction, charged with the task of collecting information about Southern conditions. Early in the new year this body, under Radical control, reported that drastic measures were necessary to protect the emancipated Negro. Congress promptly took action. First came the Freedmen's Bureau Bill, which prolonged the life and greatly extended the powers of an agency set up earlier to assist Negroes to make the transition to freedom. This was followed by a Civil Rights Bill, conferring citizenship on the Negroes and granting them equality of treatment before the law. Both these measures were vetoed by Johnson as unconstitutional infringements of the rights of the states. The Civil Rights Bill was repassed over Johnson's veto and became law. The Radicals meanwhile aimed at making doubly sure of their purposes by incorporating its provisions in the Fourteenth Amendment.

The quarrel between Johnson and the Radicals was now open and bitter, and the Congressional elections of 1866 witnessed a fierce struggle between them. The Radicals were much the more astute in presenting their case to the electorate. They pointed to a serious race riot in New Orleans as proof of Southern maltreatment of the Negro, and to the recently enacted Black Codes as evidence of an intention to re-enslave him. Their leaders carried more conviction with the Northern electors than did Johnson, whose undignified outbursts during a speaking tour lost him much support. The result was a resounding victory for the Radicals, who obtained a two-thirds majority in both Houses of Congress. The way was now clear for them to carry out their own plan of Reconstruction, for they were strong enough to override the President's vetoes. A series of harsh and vengeful Reconstruction Acts was passed in 1867. The South was divided into five military districts, each under the command of a Federal Major-General. The former Confederacy was to be subjected to Army rule of the kind that Cromwell had once imposed on England. In order to be readmitted to the Union the Southern states were now required to ratify the Fourteenth Amendment and to frame state constitutions which provided for Negro suffrage—and this in spite of the fact that very few of the Northern states had as yet granted the Negro the vote.

Not content with these successes, the Radical leaders then tried to remove the President from office by impeachment. This would have suited them well, for as the law then stood Johnson would have been replaced by the President of the Senate, who was himself a leading Radical. According to the Constitution, the President could be thus dismissed on conviction for treason, bribery, or other high crimes and misdemeanours. Yet Johnson's opposition to Radical policies had never overstepped constitutional limits, and his enemies were put to some difficulty in framing charges against him. After vain endeavours to find any evidence of treason or corruptibility, the Radicals put forward as a pretext for his impeachment Johnson's effort, in August 1867, to rid himself of his Secretary of War, Edwin M. Stanton. This unscrupulous politician had long merited dismissal. He had been in the habit of passing on Cabinet secrets to the Radical leaders while professing the utmost loyalty to the President. But when Johnson demanded his resignation Stanton refused to comply. For some months he continued to conduct the business of the War Department, in which he finally barricaded himself. Stanton justified his conduct by reference to the Tenure of Office Act, a measure recently adopted over Johnson's veto as part of the Radical effort to diminish the powers of the Presidency. No Cabinet officers, the Act had declared, were to be dismissed without the consent of the Senate. Failure to obtain consent was punishable as a high crime.

Thus in March 1868 the Radical leaders were able to induce the House to adopt eleven articles impeaching Andrew Johnson at the bar of the Senate. The only concrete charge against him was his alleged violation of the Tenure of Office

Act. Yet this measure was constitutionally doubtful, and its violation became a crime only because the Radicals said so. In spite of the weakness of their case they came within an ace of success. In the event they failed by a single vote to obtain the two-thirds majority in the Senate which they needed to convict the President. Seven Republican Senators, withstanding immense and prolonged pressure, refused to allow the impeachment process to be debased for party ends. They voted for acquittal.

By the narrowest possible margin a cardinal principle of the American Constitution, that of the separation of powers, was thus preserved. Had the impeachment succeeded the whole course of American constitutional development would have been changed. Power would henceforth have become concentrated solely in the legislative branch of the Government, and no President could have been sure of retaining office in the face of an adverse Congressional majority. Nevertheless the Radicals were strong enough in Congress during the rest of Johnson's term to be able to ignore his wishes. A further Republican victory at the polls in 1868 brought General Ulysses S. Grant to the White House. The triumph of the Radicals was now complete, for the ineptitude in high office of the victorious Union commander made him their tool.

The political reconstruction of the South ground forward in strict accordance with the harsh legislation of 1867. Under the superintendence of Federal military commanders elections were held in which the Negro for the first time took part. Almost a million coloured men were enrolled on the voting lists. At the same time more than a hundred thousand Southern whites were disfranchised because they had been in rebellion. Negro voters were in a majority in five states. Yet the Negro was merely the dupe of his ill-principled white leaders. These consisted either of Northern adventurers, known as "carpet-baggers," whose main purposes in going South were to make fortunes for themselves and to muster the Negro vote for the Republican Party, or of Southern "scalawags," who were prepared, for the sake of office, to co-operate with a régime that most Southern whites detested. Between 1868 and 1871 "carpet-bag" and "scalawag" Governments, supported by the Negro vote and by Federal bayonets, were installed in all the Southern states. When these states were deemed to have complied with the Radical requirements they were allowed to return to the Union.

Fraud, extravagance, and a humiliating racial policy were imposed upon the South by Radical rule. It could be maintained only by the drastic use of Federal power. To bolster up the "carpet-bag" Governments Congress initiated the Fifteenth Amendment, which laid down that suffrage could not be denied to any citizen on grounds of "race, colour, or previous condition of servitude." A series of laws placed Congressional elections under Federal management, and authorised the use of military force to suppress violence in the Southern states. These measures were prompted by the vigorous efforts of white Southerners, both by legal methods and by threats to Negro voters from secret societies like the Ku Klux Klan, to overthrow the "carpet-bag" Governments and restore white supremacy. For a time repression achieved its purpose, but gradually state after state was recaptured by white voters. This success was partly due to the stubbornness of Southern resistance and partly to a change in Northern sentiment. By the early 1870's the ordinary Northerner had become fully alive to the political shortcomings of the Negro and was scandalised by the corruption of the "carpet-bag" Governments. The Northern business man wanted an end to unsettled conditions, which were bad for trade. Above all,

Northerners became weary of upholding corrupt minority Governments by force. They began to withdraw their support from the Radical programme.

By 1875 the Radical Republicans had so far lost control that only South Carolina, Florida, and Louisiana were still in the hands of the "carpet-baggers." In the following year a way was opened for these states to recover control of their own affairs. After the Presidential election of 1876 disputes arose in these three states over the validity of the election returns. The matter was extremely important, since the nineteen electoral votes at stake were sufficient to decide the Presidential contest. The Democratic candidate, Samuel J. Tilden, had obtained 184 electoral votes, or one short of a majority. The Republican, Rutherford B. Hayes, therefore needed all the disputed nineteen. When the controversy was referred to the House of Representatives it was obvious that the Republican majority in that Assembly would decide in favour of Hayes. So as a sop to Democratic opinion generally, and to the South in particular, Hayes's supporters promised that Federal troops would be withdrawn from the South as soon as Hayes took office. Mollified by this concession, the South abandoned its opposition to Hayes. In April 1877, a month after Hayes assumed the Presidency, and twelve years after Lee's surrender at Appomattox, the last Federal garrisons left the South. The remaining "carpet-bag" Governments promptly collapsed, white supremacy was everywhere restored, and the period of Radical Reconstruction was over.

It had not been altogether an evil, for the "carpet-bag" legislatures promoted a number of long-overdue reforms and accomplished some good work in building roads and bridges. But it was on the whole a shameful and discreditable episode. In the judgment of an American historian, the "negro and carpet-bagger Governments were among the worst that have ever been known in any English-speaking land." Reconstruction left in the South a legacy of bitterness and hatred greater by far than that produced by four years of war. Remembering the Republicans as the party of Negro rule, the white South for the next fifty years would vote almost to a man for the Democratic Party. The Negro himself gained little lasting benefit from Reconstruction. His advancement had been the plaything of self-seeking and cynical men, and was set back for an incalculable period.

*   *   *   *   *

From the end of Reconstruction until the closing decade of the century American politics lacked interest. Memories of the Civil War remained fresh, especially in the South, and the passions aroused by it could still be revived. Indeed, they often were, especially by the Republican Party, which made a practice at election times of "waving the bloody shirt" and denouncing their Democratic opponents as rebels and traitors. Yet the issues of the war itself were dead, and unreplaced. No major questions divided the parties, no new policies were initiated, and scarcely a measure deserving the attention of the historian was placed on the Statute Book. Nor were the political personalities of the time any more exciting than the events in which they took part. A succession of worthy, mediocre men filled the Presidency, the chief virtue of their administrations being the absence of the corruption which had disgraced the two terms of the unfortunate General Grant. With few exceptions Congress too was filled with what one historian has called "sad, solemn fellows."

Yet if the politics of the period were insignificant its economic developments were of the first importance. Throughout the generation that followed the Civil War the pace of economic change quickened and the main outlines of modern America emerged. Between 1860 and 1900 the population of the Union soared from thirty-one to seventy-six millions. This increase was due in part to the heavy influx of European immigrants, who within forty years totalled fifteen millions. Cities grew fast. Great mineral deposits were discovered and exploited, giving rise to vast new industries. "No other generation in American history," it has been remarked, "witnessed changes as swift or as revolutionary as those which transformed the rural republic of Lincoln and Lee into the urban industrial empire of McKinley and Roosevelt."

Economic change transformed not only the regions which became great industrial centres, but the country as a whole. Even in the South a revolution was afoot. In Southern agriculture change was inevitable because of the disorganisation wrought by the war and the ending of slavery. Nearly all the great planters, impoverished by the war and crushed by taxation during the Reconstruction, were compelled to split their plantations and sell, often at absurdly low prices. Thousands of small farmers were thus able to increase the size of their holdings. An even greater number of Southern whites for the first time became landowners. The old sprawling plantations disappeared, and were replaced by an infinitely greater number of small farms, engaged for the most part in growing the same crops as before the war. Negroes however continued as in the days of slavery to provide the bulk of the labour for cotton cultivation. Because they lacked capital few of the coloured freedmen were able to buy farms or to pay rent. A novel form of tenantry known as "share-cropping" therefore came into being. Furnished by the farmer with land and equipment, the Negro—and later the landless white—gave their labour in return for one-third of the crop they produced. By these means Southern agriculture slowly revived. But it was almost twenty years before the cotton crop of the former Confederate states reached the level of 1860.

From then on expansion was rapid, and by 1900 the pre-war figures had been more than doubled.

This period saw also the beginnings of large-scale industry in the South. The Southern textile industry, very small before 1860, managed in time to recover and then to expand. Towards the end of the century the South, with its raw material at hand and its supply of cheap labour, possessed almost two million spindles and was daring to challenge New England's position in the home market. At the same time the tobacco industry flourished in North Carolina and Virginia, and the discovery of coal and iron deposits in Tennessee and Alabama led to the rise of a Southern iron industry. Yet the South remained predominantly agricultural, and the growth of Southern industry was insignificant compared with that of the North.

The Civil War had given a great impetus to Northern output. The Federal armies had needed huge quantities of arms and equipment, clothing and footwear. Fortified by Government contracts, Northern manufacturers embarked on large-scale production. Furthermore, in the absence of Southern representatives Congress passed into law the protective measures demanded by Northern industrialists and financiers. But the assistance thus afforded did no more than speed the coming of the American Industrial Revolution. The United States were, and still are, extraordinarily rich in mineral wealth. They possessed about two-thirds of the known coal deposits of the world, immense quantities of high-grade iron ore, equally great resources in petroleum, and, in the West, huge treasuries of gold, silver, and copper. Through their inventive ability and their aptitude for improving the inventions of others Americans grasped the power to turn their raw materials into goods. To this they added a magnificent transport system of railroads and canals which fed the factories and distributed their products. Moreover, America could look to Europe for capital as well as labour. The bulk of her industrial capital came from British, Dutch, and German investors. Much of the brawn and not a little of the brain that went into her making were also supplied by the great immigration from Europe.

Thus favoured, American industry forged swiftly ahead. Each decade saw new levels of output in the iron and steel mills of the Pittsburgh area, the oil refineries of Ohio, Pennsylvania, and elsewhere, the flour mills of Minneapolis and St Paul, the meat-packing plants of Chicago and Cincinnati, the clothing and boot and shoe factories of New England, and the breweries of Milwaukee and St Louis, to mention only the biggest of American industrial enterprises. In each of these fields great captains of industry arose, the most powerful of whom were Rockefeller in oil and Carnegie in steel. With untiring energy and skill, and with ruthless disregard for competitors, these men built up economic empires which gave them great wealth and a formidable power over the life of the community. Carnegie and Rockefeller, indeed, together with Morgan in finance and Vanderbilt and Harriman in railroads, became the representative figures of the age, in striking contrast to the colourless actors upon the political scene. Though the morality of their business methods has often been questioned, these men made industrial order out of chaos. They brought the benefits of large-scale production to the humblest home. By 1900, owing to their vigorous efforts, American industry was concentrated in a number of giant corporations, each practically a monopoly in its chosen field. This was a state of affairs presently to be challenged by Federal authority. But meanwhile the United States had ceased to depend on European manufactures; they were even invading Europe with their own. Thus America passed through a gilded age of which the millionaire seemed, at least to European eyes, the typical representative. Yet it was at the same time an age of unrest, racked by severe growing pains. There was much poverty in the big cities, especially among recent immigrants. There were sharp, sudden financial panics, causing loss and ruin, and there were many strikes, which sometimes broke into violence. Labour began to organise itself in Trade Unions and to confront the industrialists with a stiff bargaining power. These developments were to lead to a period of protest and reform in the early twentieth century. The gains conferred by large-scale industry were great and lasting, but the wrongs that had accompanied their making were only gradually righted. All this made for a lively, thrusting, controversial future.

America as a World Power

WHILE the United States were growing into the world's leading industrial Power their people were busily completing the settlement of the continent. At the beginning of the Civil War, after two and a half centuries of westward advance from the Atlantic coast, the frontier of settlement had reached roughly the line of the 97th meridian, which runs through Nebraska, Kansas, Oklahoma, and Texas. Between this frontier and the towns and cities of the Pacific seaboard lay a thousand miles of wilderness. Here were the Great Plains, about a million square miles in extent, where roamed many Indian tribes, and little else except the immense herds of buffalo on which they lived. The sparse rainfall of the Great Plains and lack of timber had made them seem unsuitable for farming and unlikely ever to be peopled. Yet in less than a generation large parts of this huge area were settled by white men and the natural frontier disappeared. The population west of the Mississippi rose in thirty years from about five millions in 1860 to almost eighteen millions, while the number of states in the Union increased from thirty-three to forty-four. By 1890 only four more states remained to be carved out of the West. These were Utah, Oklahoma, New Mexico, and Arizona, all admitted to the Union by 1912, when the political shape of the country became complete.

White settlement of the Great Plains was first prompted by the discovery of precious metals. In 1859 gold was found at Pikes Peak, on the eastern slopes of the Rockies, and miners began to flock into Colorado. As fresh deposits of gold, silver, and copper came to light there was a rush to Nevada, Arizona, Idaho, and Montana, and finally to the Black Hills of South Dakota. These sudden migrations in search of wealth did not always create lasting settlements, for many of the booms were short-lived. When precious ores ran low the whole population of the mining camps moved on elsewhere, leaving ghost towns to mark the site of their "diggings." Yet by speeding the political organisation of the West and encouraging the building of railroads the discovery of gold and silver did much to open up the Great Plains.

It was the railway indeed, more than any other factor, which threw wide the Plains to settlers. This was the great age of American railroad construction. At the close of the Civil War the United States had possessed about 35,000 miles of tracks, but in less than ten years that figure had been doubled, and by 1890 doubled again. The most prodigious feat was the building of a number of transcontinental railways. The first to cross the continent was completed in May 1869, when a link was made in Utah between the lines of the Union Pacific, stretching westward from Iowa, and the Central Pacific, reaching out eastward from California. This project was financed by a grant from Congress to the two companies of millions of acres of public land, a method which was also used elsewhere. Towards the end of the century three more transcontinental routes had been added, and other great lines had opened up the country. Many of the railroad companies took a direct part in peopling the West, for they realised that their lines could hardly pay until the country on either side of the tracks was settled. An extensive campaign to popularise the West was undertaken both in the Eastern States and in Europe. Because transport was cheap and land could be acquired on credit thousands of settlers were induced to seek new homes in the Great Plains.

Emigrants to the West could also buy land very cheaply from the state Governments, each of which had received from the Federal authorities large areas of the public domain. They could even obtain it free by virtue of the Homestead Act, which granted a quarter-section (160 acres) of public land to all white adult males who undertook to settle there. Although a loophole in the Act allowed land speculators to profit by it, this measure enabled large numbers of settlers, estimated in 1890 at more than a million, to obtain free farms for themselves, mostly to the west of the Mississippi.

The settlement of the West could only take place if the Indian barrier were removed. Already the the time of the Civil War the Indian had been obliged to retreat across half the continent in the face of white advance. Now, as the Red man was harried out of his last refuge, a further tragic chapter was added to his story. The threat to their hunting grounds, and indeed to their whole existence, delivered by the onrush of civilisation impelled the nomadic tribes of the Great Plains to resist the invaders with determination and savagery. From the Sioux and the Crows of the North to the Comanche and Apache of the South, these warlike tribesmen were magnificent horsemen and intrepid fighters. Their bows and arrows were much more effective than the muzzle-loading rifles with which the Federal troops were at first equipped. Yet their final defeat was inevitable. The introduction of the Winchester repeating rifle and the Colt revolver gave armed supremacy to the whites, who were already superior in organisation, numbers, and strategy. But the fatal blow was the wholesale slaughter of the buffalo, chiefly by professional hunters employed by Eastern leather manufacturers. By the early 1870's between two and three million buffalo were being killed annually for their hides, and ten years later a museum expedition seeking specimens could find only two hundred in the whole of the West. On the buffalo the Indian of the Plains had relied not only for food, but for a great variety of other things, from clothing to fuel. When the buffalo was virtually exterminated nomadic life became impossible. The Indians had to comply with the Government's plans and be herded into reservations.

Means had still to be found in the semi-arid West for making agriculture pay. The miner was at first succeeded not by the farmer but by the rancher, who for twenty years after the Civil War used the Great Plains as pasture for his cattle on the long drive from Texas to the Middle West. Although the journey involved passing through territory inhabited by hostile Indians, who frequently stampeded the cattle vast herds were led each year from the ranches of the South-West to the cattle centres of Kansas and Nebraska. Then, after being fattened for market, the cattle were shipped to the stockyards and canneries of Kansas City or Chicago. But the farmer still hung back from the Great Plains. In this extensive grassland there were very few trees, and no lumber for building houses, barns, and fences. More serious still, the annual rainfall between the 98th meridian and the Rockies was usually below the 20-inch minimum needed for agriculture.

Science now stepped in. A technique known as dry farming was developed. Deep ploughing loosened the soil sufficiently to allow water to move upwards, and frequent harrowing prevented evaporation. New strains of wheat were introduced from Russia, which were resistant to drought and to the disease of wheat-rust, then common on the Plains. But it was large-scale industry that really made farming possible.

A wide range of mechanical farm implements, reapers, harvesters, threshers, and improved types of plough enabled the Western farmer to cultivate large enough tracts of land to offset the low yield per acre. Moreover, the invention of barbed wire, though it ended the great cattle drives, solved the problem of fencing.

During the last quarter of the century large numbers of emigrant farmers were flowing into the Great Plains. By 1890 "the frontier"—which officially meant a region inhabited by more than two but less than six persons per square mile— had disappeared. The formerly unsettled area, the superintendent of the census explained, had now "been so broken into by isolated bodies of settlement that there [could] hardly be said to be a frontier line." The colonisation begun at Jamestown, Virginia, almost three centuries before was now complete. Hitherto the frontier had been America's safety-valve. Through it had passed ardent ambitions and bold, restless spirits. Now the safety-valve was shut, and the problems and pressures of dynamic growth within the United States were greatly intensified.

* * * * *

After slumbering since the end of Reconstruction American politics suddenly awoke. The alarm-clock was Populism. Sprung from deep-rooted discontent among farmers, this new movement made rapid headway. A climax was reached in 1896, when the Populists, merged by then with the Democratic Party, made a supreme effort at the polls. The Presidential campaign of that year was one of the fiercest and most spectacular in American history. It was concentrated on a single issue, namely, whether there should be both a gold and a silver currency, or monometallism *versus* bimetallism. Known as the Battle of the Standards, this contest was a passionate attempt by the farming interests to wrest control of the Federal Government from the financiers and industrialists, who had enjoyed its favour since the Civil War.

Agriculture, like all other branches of American life, had grown immensely since the Civil War. Within forty years the number of farms and the acreage under cultivation about trebled. Production of wheat, corn, cotton, and other commodities rose in similar proportion. But life had also become more difficult for the farmer. As production rose farm prices steadily fell. At the same time farm costs were rising, and large numbers of farmers faced hardship. Many had to become tenants, and mortgages multiplied.

For this decline there were several reasons. In some areas, especially in the Old South and the Middle West, the soil was exhausted by wasteful methods of cultivation. Elsewhere, as on the Great Plains, the farmer faced peculiar natural hazards. Yet these were difficulties which he had always had to endure, and the real explanation of his plight lay in another quarter. In spite of the rise in population, the growth of the cities, and the enormous demand for food, he always produced too much. Canada, South America, and Australia, all of which were experiencing similar agricultural booms, freely competed with the American farmer in the world market. Yet at home he had to buy his equipment and every essential of life in a protected market. The tariff policy of the Federal Government and the power of monopolies and trusts, made the price of the manufactured goods he needed artificially high. He was exploited not only by the manufacturer but by the railroad companies. Dependent on a single line to carry his produce to market, the Western farmer was made to pay for the losses of the railroads in carrying industrial freight. The charges for farm products were so crushing that at one time it was cheaper to burn corn as fuel than to sell it. This and other railroad practices were strongly resented.

Finally—and this seemed the most crippling burden—the high cost of money pressed heavily on a class which consisted overwhelmingly of debtors. More and more produce was needed to repay the same amount of money. Banking facilities in the West were inadequate, and this forced the farmer to borrow from Eastern financiers, whose interest rates ranged from 8 to 20 per cent. His grievances were inflamed by the deflationary fiscal policy of the Federal Government. At a time of unparalleled economic expansion the Government, in response to business interests which wanted a sound money policy, decided to contract the currency by ceasing to coin silver and withdrawing some of the "greenback" paper money issued during the Civil War.

Such consistent neglect of the farmers and their dependents by the Federal Government is surprising, since they still accounted for almost half the nation's population. But they were politically disunited, and there remained a wide gulf between Westerners and Southerners because of the smouldering prejudices of the Civil War. The South was solidly Democratic, the West in general Republican. Until agrarian problems could be isolated from other political issues, there was little hope that the farmers could induce the Federal Government to pay any attention to their demands. Only if they formed their own organisations, as "big business" and the working man had already done, could they save themselves from exploitation by stronger economic groups.

Accordingly nation-wide farmers' organisations began to grow. The first of these, an order called the Patrons of Husbandry, or, more popularly, the Grange, was established in 1867. For some years membership was not large, but after the depression of 1873 the movement quickly gained ground. Two years later Granges had been established in almost every state and there were 20,000 lodges and 800,000 members.

By this time the movement had ceased to be purely social in character, as had first been the case. Many state Granges ran co-operative business enterprises for marketing their produce and purchasing manufactured goods. By means of co-operative creameries, grain elevators, warehouses, loan agencies, and even factories, it was hoped to cut out the middleman's profit. In many states the Grange developed political off-shoots, and Farmers' Parties under various names came into being in the Upper Mississippi valley. All this may seem far removed from the realms of high politics, but America was the first country openly to show in her home affairs that great national decisions must depend upon the matching and mating of small, local causes. When control of a number of state legislatures had been won laws were passed to check the malpractices of the railroads, but these so-called Granger laws were not very effective. It proved impossible to frame regulations that the railroads could not evade. Enforcement was difficult because the judiciary sympathised with the railroads, and in the 1880's a series of Supreme Court decisions severely limited the regulatory powers of the states.

The Grange went rapidly into decline during the improvement in farming conditions that came in the late 1870's. Thus the first attempt at united action by the farmers ended in failure. When bad times returned, as they soon did, new farm organisations, known as the Farmers' Alliances, began to appear in the North-West and in the South. The Alliances conducted much the same kind of social and economic activities as had the Grange, on which indeed they were largely modelled. But, unlike the Grange, the Alliances, almost from the outset, adopted a political programme which called for tariff reduction, currency inflation, and stricter regulation of railroads. As time went on the political emphasis of the movement grew sharper, until finally Populism was born.

The Populist outburst arose from the sharp agricultural depression that began in 1887 and steadily gained in intensity. Severe droughts caused widespread crop failures. There followed a wholesale foreclosing of mortgages and the bankruptcy of a large section of the farming community. Since it was now obvious to the farmers that they could hope for nothing from either of the two major parties, the Alliance movement spread far and wide and was itself transformed into Populism.

Though owing its origin, as well as the main body of its supporters, to farmers' discontent, the Populist Party came to include many other groups. The struggling trade union organisation known as the Knights of Labour, survivors of such short-lived political organisations as the Greenback and Union Labour Parties, and a host of fanatics ranging from suffragists to single-taxers, all joined in. Such groups brought to the movement a number of cranks, but the farmers themselves provided Populism with a full share of picturesque and eccentric figures. From "Pitchfork" Ben Tillman of South Carolina and Jerry Simpson of Kansas, who enjoyed the nickname of "Sockless Socrates," to the revivalist Mary Ellen Lease, who advised the Plains farmers to "raise less corn and more Hell," the leaders of the Populist revolt were of a kind that American politics had not experienced hitherto.

After sweeping triumphs in the state elections of 1890 the Populists had high hopes of success in the Presidential election two years later. Their candidate was James B. Weaver, a former leader of the now defunct Greenback Party. But, for all their hardships, many farmers were still unwilling to abandon their traditional party loyalties. Though Weaver polled a million votes the Democratic candidate, Grover Cleveland, was successful by a narrow majority over his Republican rival, Benjamin Harrison.

No sooner had Cleveland's second term begun—he had already been President from 1885 to 1889—than economic disaster befell. A financial panic led to countless failures in the business world and heavy unemployment in the great cities. There was an outbreak of violent strikes, and a further collapse of agricultural prices. Cleveland could find no means of ending the depression, and discontent spread among his supporters. Many of them disagreed with his tariff policy and with his use of Federal troops to break the great Pullman strike in Chicago in 1894, which had immobilised half the country's railroads. But it was his refusal to follow an inflationary policy that drove despairing Democrats into the ranks of the Populists. The President's offense in the eyes of the inflationists was his use of the patronage at his disposal to force the repeal of the Silver Purchase Act of 1890, a measure which by doubling the amount of silver to be coined had sought to increase the volume of currency in circulation and improve farm prices. Its failure to achieve either of these aims showed, according to the bimetallists, that the Act had not gone far enough and that the only remedy was the free and unlimited coinage of silver. Cleveland, on the other hand, believed that the Act had sparked the panic of 1893, and that accordingly the gold standard must be upheld.

The free-silver question had been debated for some years before this, but the repeal of the Silver Purchase Act brought it into new prominence. Between 1893 and 1896 it gradually came to dwarf all other issues. The farmers, as we have seen, had long favoured inflation as a cure for low farm prices. Some of them had flirted earlier with the Greenback Party, which had promised inflation by printing more paper money. Now the agrarians hoped to restore prosperity by remonetising silver and coining all of the metal that the mines could yield. To business interests this seemed a sure road to bankruptcy, for inflation, they pointed out, was easier to start than to check. To them the gold standard seemed indispensable to stability. The next Presidential election was thus fought on the question of cheap money.

Whether the Populists would nominate a candidate of their own or amalgamate with the Democrats was at first in doubt. But the decision was given when the Democratic Convention met at Chicago in July 1896. With cheap-money men in control of the party machinery the Convention adopted a free-silver platform, and nominated as their candidate William Jennings Bryan, of Nebraska. Bryan's "Cross of Gold" speech to the Convention, containing an impassioned attack on the supporters of the gold standard, was to become one of the most celebrated examples of American oratory. Content with such a candidate and such a platform, the Populists endorsed Bryan. Though they did not entirely abandon their plans for a separate campaign, they marched with the Democrats against the Republican candidate, William J. McKinley, who stood for the gold standard. Byran had formidable disadvantages to overcome. His own party was sharply split, and against him were ranged the Press and the business and financial elements. He embarked on a strenuous campaign, in which his great rhetorical powers were employed to the full. Yet all his efforts were unavailing. McKinley, who stayed at home throughout the campaign, won by more than half a million votes.

Having staked all on Bryan's election, the Populists found it difficult to re-establish themselves once he was defeated. Although the Populist movement did not formally disband until much later, its demise may be dated from this election. Most of the measures that its followers demanded were taken up by new reform movements in the twentieth century, and nearly all were passed into law. Free silver was never attained, but the farmers reached their objective by another road. Through the discovery of new deposits in the Klondike and South Africa the world's supply of gold rose sharply in the last years of the nineteenth century. The volume of money in circulation increased, and when in 1900 Congress passed a Currency Act to place the United States on the gold standard it met with hardly any opposition. The free-silver agitation was all but forgotten.

*　*　*　*　*

When Bryan again unsuccessfully opposed McKinley in the Presidential contest the passions aroused four years earlier were wholly absent. The depression was over and prosperity had returned. Home affairs were ignored and American eyes were fixed on larger horizons, for between the two elections the United States had begun to play in world affairs a part commensurate with their strength.

Since the fall of Napoleon the American people had been so engrossed in settling the continent and in exploiting its natural resources that foreign affairs had interested them little. Now, with the process of settlement complete, and the work of economic development well in hand, they sought fresh fields in which to labour. By the 1890's the idea of Empire had taken hold of all the great industrial Powers. Britain, France, and Germany were especially active in acquiring new colonies and new markets. This European example was not lost upon America. For these and other reasons a vigorous spirit of self-assertion developed, which first became manifest in the Venezuelan boundary dispute with Britain in 1895.

Ever since the end of the Civil War Anglo-American relations had been distinctly cool. In spite of the settlement of the *Alabama* claims by Gladstone's Government, Britain's sympathy for the South during the great conflict had left its mark upon the Union. Constant bickering agitated the two countries over such matters as seal-fishing in the Behring Sea, the rights of American fishermen in Canadian waters, and interpretations of the Clayton-Bulwer Treaty of 1850 about the proposed Panama Canal. But all these disputes paled before the question of the Venezuelan boundary. The frontier between this South American republic and British Guiana had long been unsettled, and although the United States had frequently offered mediation her advances had always been declined by Britain. In the summer of 1895 the American State Department made yet another move in a communication which President Cleveland described as "a twenty-inch gun note." Britain was accused of violating the Monroe Doctrine, and was required to give a definite answer as to whether she would accept arbitration. Lord Salisbury bided his time, waiting for passions to cool. He replied in December, rejecting arbitration and telling the American Government that its interpretation of the Monroe Doctrine was at fault. At this Cleveland sent Congress a message announcing that America would fix the boundary line independently and oblige the disputants to accept her decision.

For a few days war with Britain seemed possible, and even imminent.[1] But the first patriotic outburst in America soon gave way to more sober feelings. In Britain opinion had reacted less violently. At the height of the crisis news arrived of the Kaiser's telegram to President Kruger in South Africa, congratulating him on the repulse of the Jameson raid. These Imperial perplexities, which are recounted in a later chapter, distracted attention in London. British wrath turned against Germany rather than the United States. Too involved in Europe and South Africa to think of quarrelling with America,

[1] I was returning from a visit to Cuba via America at this time and remember vividly looking at ships off the English coast and wondering which one would be our transport to Canada. W. S. C.

the British Government agreed to arbitration. Their claims in Guiana were largely conceded by the tribunal. There followed a steady improvement in Anglo-American relations, chiefly because Britain was awakening to the dangers of her isolation. Her growing alarm at German naval expansion led her to make friendly overtures to which the United States were fully ready to respond.

The exuberant pride of Americans could not long be held in check. In the Cuban revolt against Spanish rule it found an outlet. Ever since this revolt began in 1895 American popular sentiment had sympathised with the rebel fight for independence. Tempers rose at tales of Spanish atrocities. General Weyler's policy of herding civilians into concentration camps, where thousands died of disease, was vehemently denounced. These atrocities, sensationally reported and embellished by two rival New York newspapers, led to demands for American intervention. In 1898 popular clamour for war with Spain reached its height. In February the American battleship *Maine*, sent to Cuba to protect American lives and property, was blown up by a mine in Havana harbour, with the loss of most of her crew. At this the Spanish Government hastily made concessions to the United States, which President McKinley was at first disposed to accept. But public indignation was too strong for him, and on April 11 war was declared.

The conflict lasted only ten weeks, and was marked by a succession of overwhelming American victories. In Cuba an American expeditionary force, despite complaints about the mismanagement of the War Department and incompetent leadership in the field, won a series of rapid battles which brought about the surrender of all the Spanish forces in the island. At sea Commodore Dewey immobilised the main Spanish fleet in an engagement in Manila Bay on May 1. The

Caribbean squadron of the Spanish Navy was sunk outside the Cuban port of Santiago. In August Spain sued for peace, and in December a treaty was signed at Paris whereby Cuba became independent. The United States acquired Puerto Rico, Guam, and the Philippines.

All this did much to heal the wounds remaining from the Civil War. In the wave of patriotism that swept the country Northerner and Southerner alike took pride in the achievements of their common country. Young men from both regions rushed to join the expeditionary force and fought side by side for San Juan Hill. The famous Condederate cavalry leader Joe Wheeler exclaimed that a single battle for the Union flag was worth fifteen years of life. The venture also showed that the American people were now fully aware of their own strength as a world-Power. Their new colonial rôle was further stressed by the acquisition between 1898 and 1900 not only of the territory wrested from Spain, but of Hawaii, part of Samoa, and the vacant island of Wake in the Pacific. The United States, though not yet abandoning isolation, henceforward became less preoccupied by home affairs. They began to play an important rôle in the international scene. The Spanish War helped to promote a new and warmer friendship with Britain, for Britain, alone of the European nations, sympathised with the United States in the conflict. This the Americans appreciated, and as the nineteenth century drew to its end the foundations were laid for a closer concert between the two peoples in facing the problems of the world. We must now return across the Atlantic from the dazzling prospects that lay before the United States to the English party scene at Westminster.

Home Rule for Ireland

W HEN Gladstone in 1880 became Prime Minister for
the second time his position was not the comfortable
one he had held twelve years before. Then, with a determined Cabinet and a united party, he had presided over
the enactment of a great series of reforms. Expectation now
stood just as high, for a triumphant election campaign had
given him a majority of 137 over his Conservative opponents.
But almost as soon as the House assembled the Speaker remarked that Gladstone had "a difficult team to drive." So it
was to prove. Few periods of office have begun with higher
hopes; none has been more disappointing in its outcome.

The main fault lay in the composition of the Liberal Party.
For long it had prided itself upon the strength afforded by
diversity, but it soon began to find that the divisions between
Whig and Radical, Right and Left, were unbridgeable. In
the first Gladstone Government there had been little discord.
But the old Whig faction thought that reform had gone far
enough, and Gladstone himself had some sympathy with
them. He disliked intensely the methods of the Radical caucus
and scorned their policies of social and economic reform.
"Their pet idea," he wrote, "is what they call construction
—that is to say, taking into the hands of the State the business of the individual man." Moreover he found the Whigs

much better company than Radical newcomers like Joseph Chamberlain. Men such as the Foreign Secretary, Lord Granville, had been his friends and colleagues for many years, and Gladstone never lost his conviction that the natural leaders of the Liberal cause were a small, leisured, cultured aristocracy.

When it came to forming his Cabinet he had to conciliate these same Whigs. The Marquess of Hartington, who had led the party in the Commons during his chief's retirement, had never been happy about Gladstone's onslaught on Disraeli's Eastern policy. He and his friends were fearful of the direction that the Prime Minister's mind and energy were next likely to take. In the upshot only one Radical, Chamberlain, was admitted to the Cabinet, and to him was assigned what was then a lowly office, the Presidency of the Board of Trade. This was Gladstone's first great error. Not only was a Whig Cabinet profoundly unsuited to a time when the Liberal Party was becoming more and more Radical, but its leader was to find himself in direct clash and conflict with his own colleagues on the main political, Imperial, and foreign issues of the day, and above all on Ireland. A Cabinet with such deep cleavages was unlikely to prove an effective instrument of government. John Morley, Gladstone's biographer, wrote that it was not only a coalition, but "a coalition of that vexatious kind where those who happened not to agree sometimes seemed to be almost as well pleased with contention as with harmony." Over this ruled the Grand Old Man, as he was already considered at the age of seventy-one, his force and energy undimmed, his passions and enthusiasms growing more intense with every year that passed. He towered above his colleagues. When he was away from Cabinet, wrote one of them, it was as though he had "left us mice without the cat."

his preface that it would be, and his appraisals are the more fascinating, because of the revelations he again and again makes about himself.

Although he can dispatch a character with fine brevity, as when he dismisses William IV as "the most eccentric and least obnoxious of the sons of George III," Sir Winston is no debunker. He is a romantic openly in love with the turmoil and strife, the sweep and pageantry of history, who happens to be amazingly clear-eyed.

Q UITE UNDERSTANDABLY, it is as an Englishman in love with Britain that he surveys the English-speaking peoples during the 19th century, that age of the Industrial Revolution, of strong optimism and enormous prosperity when the sun never set on an expanding British Empire. We have so long been taught history only as seen through American eyes that it is a jolting relief to see it from another point of view. Sir Winston touches on American history at greater length in this volume than he has hitherto, daring even to poach for many pages on that land of Catton, the Civil War.

He is particularly illuminating in his account of how, because of the fear of occupation by land-hungry Americans, Canada in the years immediately following Appomattox was given Dominion status. What is amazing is Sir Winston's own dominion over the manifold and intricate materials with which he deals and his genius in presenting them. Few men who spend their lives merely writing history have written it with the vigor and skill of this man who has also made it.

BOOK-OF-THE-MONTH CLUB, INC.
345 Hudson Street, New York 14, N. Y.

Printed in U.S.A.

...since he is a great man himself, there is no reason he should not believe in what his own life documents. This does not mean that, in spite of welcoming the heroic, he sees all men as heroes. He is deeply aware, as everyone must be who has been a world leader, of human frailty, of the weaknesses in the strongest which by betraying them can alter

DISRAELI "In all his attitudes there was a degree of cynicism; in his make-up there was not a trace of moral fervour."

GLADSTONE "... his dominant theme was that conscience and the moral law must govern political decisions."

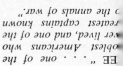

EE "... one of the ...oblest Americans who ...ver lived, and one of the ...reatest captains known ...o the annals of war."

history, and of the tragedies that occur when small men in high places must face up to big challenges.

A s a FORMER NAVAL PERSON, a former soldier and war correspondent too, he has a natural absorption in the clash of embattled forces, whether in the Crimea, our own Civil War, the Sudan or in South Africa, and his marching words as he refights these campaigns bring them and their leaders to life. In *The Great Democracies*, however, as in the three volumes which have preceded it, wars and rumors of war are by no means his only concern. He is as interested in those who govern (or misgovern) as in those who fight, and no less interested in the changing economic, social and international patterns of the century of reform and emerging democracies with which he deals. His subject is vast, world-spread and complex, and he approaches it not only as a portrait painter but as a panoramist. His touch remains the personal one he promised in

W
ITH THE GREAT DEMOCRACIES Winston Churchill brings to a triumphant close his History of the English-Speaking Peoples. One hates to have the series end. When the final sentence is read—a plea, by the way, for the ultimate union of Britain and this country—the cadences of Sir Winston's prose continue for some time to ring in the ears. Then there is a hush, a sudden and saddening hush, not as if a memorable concert had concluded but as if a great orchestra had disbanded.

Sir Winston has, of course, his own way of writing history no less than of making it. His is the grand style in print as well as in action. He moves into the past, near or distant, as if it were No. 10 Downing Street and takes possession of it with the same color and authority. And what a far-flung empire of history he has presided over as both a recorder and a shaper of events! His present series, which began in the dark remoteness of those days when a wide plain joined England and Holland, sweeps forward in this fourth volume to cover the decades from Waterloo to Victoria's death and those years at the dawning of the 20th century when Churchill himself was emerging as a public figure.

LINCOLN "... appeale... for strength in his inmos... thoughts to a power highe... than man's. Strength wa... certainly given him."

T
HOUGH THE GREAT DEMOCRACIES concludes his History of the English-Speaking Peoples, it does not conclude Churchill's chronicle of England. The narrative he leaves off here can be picked up in his monumental earlier works: The World Crisis (1911-1918), The Aftermath (1918-1928), and the six irreplaceable volumes of The Second World War which bring the story down to the Potsdam Conference and Churchill's defeat at the polls after having brought victory to Britain. Some insist that, by subscribing to the "great man" theory more fully than is now popular, Sir Winston is old-fashioned in his approach. But,

A HISTORY OF THE
ENGLISH-SPEAKING PEOPLES
VOLUME IV

The Great Democracies
by Winston S. Churchill

"Few men who spend their lives merely writing history have written it with the vigor and skill of this man who has also made it"

A Report by JOHN MASON BROWN
Reprinted from the Book-of-the-Month Club News

DEAR MEMBER

We are happy to tell you that after this book shipment you will receive a Book-Dividend with every second Book-of-the-Month Club selection or Alternate you purchase. Whenever you qualify for a Book-Dividend, the one then current will be shipped to you.

BOOK-OF-THE-MONTH CLUB, INC.

Meredith Wood PRESIDENT

But the Liberals, or rather the Whigs, were not alone in their troubles and anxieties. Shocked by the onset of democracy and its threat to old, established interests, the Tory leaders proceeded to forget the lessons which Disraeli had tried so long to teach them. Their leader in the Commons was Sir Stafford Northcote, who had once been Gladstone's private secretary and still stood in awe of the great man. His companions on the Front Bench, frightened by the prospect of universal suffrage, clung desperately to the faith, practice, and timidity of their youth. Into the breach stepped a small but extremely able group whose prowess at Parliamentary guerrilla fighting has rarely been equalled, the "Fourth Party" —Lord Randolph Churchill, A. J. Balfour, Sir Henry Drummond Wolff, and John Gorst. They teased and taunted Gladstone without mercy or respect. But Lord Randolph, who quickly rose to special prominence, reserved his fiercest criticism for the leaders of his own side. In a letter to *The Times* he charged them with "a series of neglected opportunities, pusillanimity, combativeness at wrong moments, vacillation, dread of responsibility, repression and discouragement of hard-working followers, collusions with the Government, hankerings after coalitions, jealousies, commonplaces, want of perception." His denunciations were not confined to Parliament. With the motto "Trust the People" and the slogan "Tory Democracy" he appealed to the rank and file over the heads of their nominal leaders. So dramatic was his success that his power soon became almost as strong as Salisbury's.

These were strange years for party warfare. The upsurge of the new forces, Radicalism and Tory Democracy, was playing havoc with the old Parliamentary system. Issues were confused and cut across party lines. Conflict was fierce, but often internecine. Chamberlain and Lord Randolph, though sometimes in bitter disagreement, had far more in common than they had with their own leaders. The confusion was not to be resolved until Gladstone, using Home Rule for Ireland like an axe, divided the political world by forcing men to make a clear and sharp decision about a single great proposal.

* * * * *

It was a constant complaint among Liberals that whenever they succeeded the Tories in office they fell heirs to a set of Imperial complications which involved them in enterprises hateful to their anti-Imperialist sentiments. So it was in 1880. One of their first troubles sprang from South Africa. There the Boer Republic of the Transvaal had long been in difficulties, threatened by bankruptcy and disorders within and by the Zulu warrior kingdom upon its eastern border. To save it from ruin and possible extinction Disraeli's Government had annexed it, an action which at first met with little protest. Disraeli looked forward to a union of all the white communities of South Africa in a self-governing Confederation on the Canadian model, but the times were not yet ripe. A fierce desire for renewed independence began to stir among the Transvaal Boers, and they looked for an opportunity to throw off British rule. As soon as British arms had finally quelled the Zulus in 1879 they felt safe enough to seize their chance. It was perhaps natural that they should expect their freedom from a Liberal Government. Gladstone had denounced the annexation of the Transvaal, but a powerful section of his party favoured the African natives more than the Boers. He himself was convinced that federation was the only solution for the South African puzzle, and he refused to make any immediate change. At the end of 1880 the Boers revolted and a small British force was cut to pieces at Majuba Hill. There was available in South Africa a force large enough to crush the Boers, but Gladstone declined to bow to the outcry for retaliation and continued with the negotiations that had already been under way at the time of Majuba. The outcome was the Pretoria Convention of 1881, which, modified in 1884, gave virtual independence to the Transvaal. This application of Liberal principles provided the foundation of Boer power in South Africa. All might have gone more smoothly in the future but for two developments. Immensely rich goldfields were discovered on the Rand and a large, bustling cosmopolitan mining community was suddenly planted in the midst of the Boer farmers' Republic. Meanwhile at Cape Town Cecil Rhodes had entered politics, resolved to create a vast, all-embracing South African dominion, and endowed by nature with the energy that often makes dreams come true. From these events sprang consequences which have yet to run their course.

*　　*　　*　　*　　*

As Gladstone had foreseen at the time, Disraeli's purchase of shares in the Suez Canal, brilliant stroke though it was, soon brought all the problems of Egypt in its wake. When he took office, Egypt, nominally ruled by the Khedive, was in effect under Anglo-French control. The Khedive had only temporarily been saved from bankruptcy by selling his Canal shares. Soon French and British Debt Commissioners were appointed to take charge of his finances, and of much else too. The British Commissioner was Evelyn Baring, later Lord Cromer, and one of the greatest of Imperial proconsuls. With a single break he was to preside over the destinies of Egypt for thirty years. At the end of 1881 however Anglo-French control was shattered by a nationalist revolt led by Colonel Arabi Pasha. It was backed by the Army and rapidly swept through the whole country. Gladstone tried in vain to apply the principles of the Concert of Europe. A sudden twist in the domestic politics of France forced her to stand aside, and the other European Powers remained aloof. On June 11, 1882, fifty Europeans were killed in riots in Alexandria. Arabi began to fortify the city in such a way as to threaten British ships in the harbour. Hence, exactly a month later, and after warning had been given, the forts were bombarded and the guns silenced. A few days later the Cabinet decided to dispatch an army under Sir Garnet Wolseley to Egypt. The decision was crowned by military success, and Arabi's army was decisively defeated at Tel-el-Kebir on September 13. Gladstone delighted in the victory, but was troubled in his conscience. The Liberal instinct was now to withdraw, but Egypt could not be left a vacuum. To annex her, though logical and expected by the other Powers of Europe, was too repugnant to the Liberal conscience. Gladstone therefore chose the worst of both worlds. The odium of occupation remained on the British, but much authority continued to be exercised by the Commissioners of the Debt, a state of affairs which allowed all the major European Powers to interfere. Nevertheless, after Baring became Consul-General in 1883, and in effect ruler of the country, a new era opened of much-needed reform.

Intervention in Egypt led to an even more perplexing entanglement in the Sudan. This huge territory, more than a thousand miles deep, stretched along the torrid banks of the Nile from the borders of Egypt down almost to the Equator. It formed a part of the Khedive's realm, and in spite of the efforts of British advisers it was woefully misgoverned by Pashas from Cairo. During the same year that the Egyptians revolted against France and Britain, the Sudanese rebelled against the Egyptians. They were led by the Mahdi, a Moslem fanatic who quickly destroyed an Egyptian army, and was soon in control of most of the Sudan. Gladstone spoke of the Sudanese as "a people rightly struggling to be free." This was a highly flattering way of describing the Mahdi's forces, whose blood-lust spread terror everywhere in their advance. Either the Sudan must be reconquered or it must be evacuated, and the Government in London chose evacuation. With this the Egyptians had to concur. At the end of 1883 the decision was made to withdraw their outlying garrisons scattered far to the South, for which Britain, as tutor to the Egyptian Army, had a general responsibility. To make the decision was easy; to carry it out more difficult. But on January 14, 1884, General Charles Gordon, who had achieved fame in Chinese wars, left London charged by the Cabinet with the task of evacuation.

Gordon had himself served in the Sudan, and had played a notable part in attempts to suppress the slave trade. He also had a conscience. It was to cost him his life. He arrived in Khartoum in February, and once there he judged that it would be wrong to withdraw the garrisons and abandon the country to the mercy of the Mahdi's Dervishes. He accordingly asked for reinforcements and put forward plans for counter-attack. In London the Government were taken aback by this change of front. They might have foreseen that a commander cast in heroic mould would not readily lend himself to withdrawal. Retreat was never to Gordon's liking. He was resolved to remain in Khartoum until his self-imposed mission was accomplished. His strength of will, often capricious in its expression, was pitted against Gladstone's determination not to be involved in fresh colonial adventures. Lord Randolph Churchill was the first to raise in the House of Commons the problem of Gordon's personal safety. In March he put a blunt question to the Government. "Are they going to remain indifferent," he asked, "to the fate of the one man on whom they have counted to extricate them from their dilemmas, to leave him to shift for himself, and not to make a single effort on his behalf?" Lord Randolph was met with evasive replies. Help for Gordon was to be long in coming, in spite of his urgent appeals, which were backed by dispatches from Baring in Cairo and by the advice of the foremost Imperial soldier of the age, Lord Wolseley. By May Gordon was cut off in Khartoum. Meanwhile the Cabinet, still insistent on the policy of "scuttling out," as Lord Salisbury called it, refused to dispatch a relieving army.

Throughout the spring and summer public opinion in England mounted, and large meetings were held demanding that Gordon must be saved. His stern religious faith, his Bible-reading, his assaults on slavery, his charitable work for the children of the poor, as well as his military prowess, had made him a popular figure, as gallant and noble as one of King Arthur's Knights. But Gladstone's mind was on other things. Reform of the franchise was one, and another was the case of the vehement atheist, Charles Bradlaugh, who had been elected to Parliament but refused his seat, and whose affairs perturbed the House of Commons and the Prime Minister's conscience for over six years. In May Lord Randolph said of Gladstone in the House of Commons: "I have compared his efforts in the cause of General Gordon with his efforts in the cause of Mr Bradlaugh. If a hundredth part of those invaluable moral qualities bestowed upon the cause of a seditious blasphemer had been given to the support of a Christian hero the success of Gordon's mission would have been assured."

Eventually, upon the insistence of Lord Hartington, then Secretary of State for War, who made it a matter of confidence in the Cabinet, the Government were induced to rescue Gordon. In September Wolseley hastened to Cairo, and in less than a month he had assembled a striking force of ten thousand men. He knew that a rapid foray against the massed spearmen of the Mahdi would accomplish nothing. Speed was essential, but disaster could not be risked. A campaign of six months, soundly based, was the fastest he could hope for. In October he set out from the borders of Egypt upon the eight-hundred-mile advance to Khartoum. Much of his way lay through uncharted reaches of the Nile; rapids and cataracts abounded, and the heat was heavy and wearisome. In the Northern Sudan the river Nile describes an immense bend to the east. Wolseley was aware that time was fatally short. He felt the eyes and anxieties of England focused upon Gordon and himself, and on the distance that lay between them. His main strength must proceed steadily up-river until, all cataracts surmounted, they would be poised for a swoop upon Khartoum. In the meantime he detached the Camel Corps under Sir Herbert Stewart to cut across a hundred and fifty miles of desert and rejoin the Nile to the north of Gordon's capital. Starting on December 30, Stewart acted with resolution. At Abu Klea, on January 17, a hundred and twenty miles short of his goal, Stewart was attacked by a Dervish host. His column of fewer than two thousand men confronted an enemy at least five times as numerous. Under a desperate onset the British square was broken by the Mahdi's fanatical hordes, but the battle was won. Two days later, amid constant harassments, Stewart's advanced troops reached the Nile, but he had been mortally wounded. His successor in command inherited a perilous situation. On January 21 steamers arrived from Khartoum, sent down-river by Gordon. There was a tragic but unavoidable delay while reconnaissances were made and the wounded tended. On the 24th a force of 26 British and 240 Sudanese sailed south on two of the steamers, assailed by Dervish musketry fire from the banks. On the 28th they reached Khartoum. It was too late. Gordon's flag no longer flew over the Residency. He was dead; the city had fallen two days before, after a prodigious display of valour by its defender. He had fallen alone, unsuccoured and unsupported by any of his own countrymen. In the eyes of perhaps half the nation Gladstone was a murderer. The Queen was so distressed that she made her own feelings clear to him in an open telegram. Gordon became a national martyr. It was true that he had disobeyed his orders, as indeed he admitted in his journal, but the fact remained that the Cabinet which had sent him out had then virtually abandoned him. The rescuing force, whose efforts had been so nearly crowned with success, retired to Egypt. Thirteen years went by before Gordon was avenged. As Gladstone later confessed, the Government had sent a "hero of heroes" to Khartoum with all the defects and virtues of his type and they had paid the penalty.

*   *   *   *   *

The position of the Liberal Party had been equally shaken by its activities at home. While the nation thought only of Gordon the Government was pressing ahead with its one considerable piece of legislation, a Reform Bill which completed the work of democratising the franchise in the counties. Almost every adult male was given a vote. Another Act abolished the remaining small boroughs and, with a few exceptions, divided the country into single-Member constituencies. All this was a logical extension of the Act of 1867, but it exasperated an already difficult situation. Single-Member constituencies stopped the old practice of running a Whig and a Radical in harness. The Liberals and Radicals were quick to press their advantage. Chamberlain had made onslaught after onslaught on the class who "toil not, neither do they spin," and with what is called his Unauthorised Programme, and its famous promise of "three acres and a cow," he now switched his main attack from town to country. The Whigs could not ignore the challenge; the division between them and the Radicals was too deep and fundamental for them ever to work together again, and by the autumn of 1885 Salisbury, the Tory leader in the House of Lords, and now Prime Minister, could assert, and with some truth, that Gladstone's "exhortation to unity was an exhortation to hypocrisy."

Further speculation about the future of English politics was abruptly cut short by the announcement of Gladstone's conversion to the policy of Home Rule. To comprehend the significance and impact of this event we must look back upon the melancholy story of Ireland. In the years since the Great Famine of the 1840's Ireland had continued in her misery. Her peasants, especially in the West, lived in a state of extreme poverty and degradation. General Gordon had thus described them some time before in a letter to *The Times:* "I must say, from all accounts and from my own observation, that the state of our fellow countrymen in the parts I have named is worse than that of any people in the world, let alone Europe." They were "living on the verge of starvation in places in which we would not keep our cattle." Ireland was, and is, a poor country, and in spite of famine and emigration she was still overpopulated. But these misfortunes were greatly aggravated by the policies of the English Government. The Irish peasant was crushed by a land system which he hated not only because it put almost absolute power into the hands of the landlord, but also because it rested on the expropriation of land which he considered, by right, to belong to him. His was a fierce, deep-rooted enmity. It was not just a matter of material poverty, of life passed in a one-roomed hut on a diet of potatoes. He felt he had been robbed of his heritage. For most of the nineteenth century the English answer was to ignore the hate and crush the crime which it produced. In the forty years before 1870 forty-two Coercion Acts were passed. During the same period there was not a single statute to protect the Irish peasant from eviction and rack-renting. This was deliberate; the aim was to make the Irish peasant a day-labourer after the English pattern. But Ireland was not England; the Irish peasant clung to his land; he used every means in his power to defeat the alien landlords.

It must not be supposed that the Irish picture can be seen from Britain entirely in black and white. The landlords were mostly colonists from England and of long standing; they believed themselves to be, and in many ways were, a civilising influence in a primitive country. They had often had to fight for their lives and their property. The deep hold of the Roman Catholic Church on a superstitious peasantry had tended on political as well as religious grounds to be hostile to England. Ireland more than once since the days of Queen Elizabeth had threatened to become a stepping-stone to the invasion of Britain from the Continent. Rick-burning, the assassination of landlords, and other acts of terrorism had contributed to a general acceptance in England of the landlord's case. It was hard to grasp that the vicious circle of unrest, heavy-handed repression, and rebellion could only be broken by remedying fundamental grievances.

From the moment when he first took office as Prime Minister Gladstone made Irish affairs his special concern, until at last they came to dominate his mind to the exclusion of almost everything else. His crusade for Ireland, for such it was, faced formidable opposition. English political society had little sympathy for Irish problems, and indeed many of its leading figures were members of the Irish aristocracy. In his first Ministry Gladstone had dealt successfully with the Irish dislike of an alien Church by disestablishing the Protestant

Church of Ireland. His second measure, a Land Act to prevent uncompensated eviction, had been passed in 1870, but proved a failure. Ten more years went by before he became convinced that the Irish peasant had to be given real security in the tenure of his land.

In 1873 Isaac Butt had founded the Home Rule League. It aimed to achieve Home Rule by peaceful, constitutional methods, and its leader, able, courteous, an admirable House of Commons man, put his faith in the persuasive processes of debate. But there was no response to his cause in England and no confidence in his methods in Ireland. Effective leadership of the movement soon passed into the hands of Charles Stewart Parnell. Parnell was a landlord, a Protestant, and a newcomer to Parliament. From his mother, the daughter of an American admiral who had won distinction fighting the British, he had acquired a hatred and contempt for English ways and institutions. A patrician in the Irish party, he was a born leader, with a power of discipline and a tactical skill that soon converted Home Rule from a debating topic into the supreme question of the hour. Ruthless in pressing his cause, and defiant of the traditions of the House of Commons, he swiftly gained such a position that an English politician said that "dealing with him was like dealing with a foreign Power."

The root of Parnell's success was the junction of the Home Rule cause with a fresh outburst of peasant agitation. A grave fall in world crop prices in the late seventies and a series of bad harvests accelerated the number of evictions as the impoverished peasants failed to pay their rents. This process was just beginning when, in 1877, Michael Davitt came out of prison after serving a seven-year sentence for treason. Davitt was a remarkable man who, in his love for Ireland and warm human sympathies, made a sharp contrast with Parnell. It was Davitt's belief that Home Rule and the land question could not be separated, and, in spite of opposition from the extreme Irish Nationalists, he successfully founded the Land League in 1879. Its objects were the reduction of rack-rents and the promotion of peasant ownership of the land. Davitt had previously assured himself of the material backing of the Irish in America. When Parnell declared his support for the League the land hunger of the peasant, the political demand for Home Rule, and the hatred of American emigrants for their unforgotten oppressors were at last brought together in a formidable alliance.

*   *   *   *   *

At the time none of this was immediately clear to Gladstone; his mind was occupied by the great foreign and Imperial issues that had provoked his return to power. His Government's first answer was to promote an interim Compensation for Disturbance Bill. When this was rejected by the House of Lords in July 1880 Ireland was quick to reply with Terror. In the last quarter of the year nearly two thousand outrages were committed. A new weapon appeared when Parnell advised his followers to make life unbearable for anyone who violated peasant law and custom "by isolating him from his kind as if he were a leper of old." One of the first victims was a land agent, Captain Boycott, whose name has passed into the English language. This was the period of the Land League's greatest success. Funds were pouring in from America and Australia, and, since the League effectively controlled more of Ireland than did the authorities in Dublin Castle, evictions almost ceased.

The Government then decided both to strike at terrorism and to reform the land laws. In March 1881 a sweeping Coercion Act gave to the Irish Viceroy the power, in Morley's phrase, "to lock up anybody he pleased and to detain him for as long as he pleased." It was during the debate on the

Coercion Bill that the climax came in Parnell's policy of obstruction. His aim in the House of Commons had been to bring government to a standstill by exploiting the fact that Parliamentary procedure rested on custom rather than rules. From January 31 until February 2 the House sat continuously for forty-one hours, and the end came only when the Speaker took the arbitrary step of "putting" the Question that the House should now "adjourn." Subsequently a resolution introducing the Closure was passed, thus making the first great breach in the traditional methods of carrying through Parliamentary business.

The Coercion Act was followed immediately by a Land Act which conceded almost everything that the Irish had demanded. The Act was based on the "three F's"—Fair Rents to be decided by a tribunal, Fixity of Tenure for all who paid their rents, and Free Sale by the tenant. This was far more generous than anything the Irish had expected, but Parnell, driven by Irish-American extremists and by his belief that even greater concessions could be extracted from Gladstone, set out to obstruct the working of the new land courts. The Government had no alternative, under the Coercion Act, but to arrest him. This it did in October. He was asked who would take his place. His reply was "Captain Moonlight." His prophesy was justified. Crime and murder multiplied, and by the spring of 1882 Gladstone was convinced that the policy of coercion had failed.

At the same time Parnell was anxious for release. As the extremists in Ireland were gaining ground it was vital for him to reassert his authority as leader. In April therefore what was called the "Kilmainham Treaty" was concluded, based on the understanding that Parnell would use his influence to end crime and terror in return for an Arrears Bill which would aid those tenants who, because they owed rent, had been unable to take advantage of the Land Act. W. E. Forster, Chief Secretary for Ireland and advocate of coercion, and the Viceroy, Lord Cowper, resigned. They were replaced by Lord Frederick Cavendish and Lord Spencer. Parnell and two of his henchmen were released on May 2, and it seemed that at last there was some likelihood of peace. But these bright prospects were destroyed by a terrible event. On May 6 Lord Frederick Cavendish landed in Dublin. A few hours after his arrival he was walking in Phoenix Park with his under-secretary, Burke, when both men were stabbed to death. The murderers were a group called the Invincibles. The object of their attack had been Burke. Lord Frederick, whom they did not know, was only killed because he had attempted to defend his companion. The English nation was shocked, the hand of the coercion party was strengthened, and all hope of any immediate conciliation was quenched. Gladstone did what he could to salvage a little from the wreck of his policy. He was now convinced that Parnell was a restraining influence in Ireland and that the only hope of any lasting success was to cooperate with him. This was not a view which commended itself to more than one or two members of his Cabinet. Parnell, for his part, was content to bide his time, and for three years Ireland was relatively quiet and peaceful.

* * * * *

Thus we return to the year 1885. On June 8 the Government was defeated on an amendment to the Budget, and Gladstone promptly resigned. Dissension and division in the Liberal Party had done their work, but a more direct cause was that the Irish Members voted with the Conservative Opposition. Lord Randolph Churchill had given Parnell to understand that a Conservative Government would discontinue coercion, and this was enough to swing Irish support. After some hesitation and difficulty Lord Salisbury formed a Government which was in a minority in the House of Commons. Lord Randolph took office as Secretary for India and his old enemy Northcote was elevated to the House of Lords, Sir Michael Hicks Beach becoming Chancellor of the Exchequer and Leader of the Commons. A most significant appointment was that of the Earl of Carnarvon as Viceroy of Ireland. It was well known that Carnarvon favoured a policy of Home Rule, and on August 1 he met Parnell in a house in Grosvenor Square. He left Parnell with the impression that the Government was contemplating a Home Rule measure. With an election approaching, Parnell had to make his choice. Through his mistress, Mrs O'Shea, who acted as intermediary, he made known to Gladstone the nature of the Conservative approach. Gladstone replied, "It is right I should say that into any counter-bidding of any sort against Lord R. Churchill I for one will not enter." The truth was that at this time Gladstone had already been converted to Home Rule, but was not prepared to bargain with Parnell, preferring to hold his hand and leave the next move to Salisbury.

When the election came in November Parnell, unable to extract a clear promise of support from Gladstone, ordered the Irish in Britain to vote Conservative. Ireland was not an important issue at these hustings. The election was mainly fought on the unhappy record of the late Government. Chamberlain's Unauthorised Radical Programme provided the only major diversion. The result could not have been more unfortunate. The Liberals lost a number of seats in the boroughs, but made some gains in the counties, where they attracted support from the recently enfranchised workers. In the new House of Commons the Liberal majority over the Conservatives was eighty-six. But Parnell had realised his dream. His followers, their ranks swollen by the operation of the Reform Act in the Irish counties, also numbered eighty-six. The position was exactly what Salisbury had described as "low-water mark—*i.e.* Tories + Parnellites = Liberals."

In these circumstances Gladstone continued to hope that the Parnellite-Conservative alliance would hold fast and that Home Rule would pass as an agreed measure without undue opposition from the House of Lords. Precedents like Catholic Emancipation, the Repeal of the Corn Laws, and the second Reform Act were much in his mind. To all Parnell's inquiries, put through Mrs O'Shea, he replied that it would be wrong for the Liberals to make any move until the Government had declared its policy. In December he saw A. J. Balfour, Salisbury's nephew, and on the 20th wrote to him, "I feel sure that this question can only be dealt with by a Government, and I desire specially on grounds of public policy that it should be dealt with by the present Government." The Conservatives treated this letter with contempt. A few days earlier the political situation had been transformed by the public disclosure of Gladstone's views on Home Rule by his son, Herbert. The "Hawarden Kite," as it came to be called, immediately brought to the surface all those forces which had been struggling, hidden from public view, in the political depths. The split in the Liberal Party which Gladstone had been so anxious to avoid became a reality. The Whigs, already alienated by the growing power of Radicalism, were solid against Home Rule. The attitude of the Conservatives hardened as they sensed the advantages they would gain from Gladstone's dramatic conversion. A possible alliance between them and the Whigs was already in the air. For Parnell the outcome was a disaster. His support had made the Conservatives a present of thirty seats. It proved to be a gift to the enemy.

It is doubtful whether there had ever been substance in Gladstone's hopes. Carnarvon represented himself and not his party or the Cabinet. His approach to Parnell had been tentative and the Government was uncommitted. Salisbury, for his part, was naturally content to have the Irish vote in a critical election, but his Protestantism, his belief in the Union, his loyalty to the landowners and to the Irish minority who had put their faith in the Conservative Party, were all far too strong for him ever to have seriously considered Home Rule. No leader has ever had less of the temperament of a Peel or a Gladstone. Enthusiasm of the kind that splits parties was quite outside Salisbury's nature.

By Christmas 1885 the die was cast. Carnarvon resigned in the New Year, and on January 26 Salisbury's Government announced that it would introduce a Coercion Bill of the most stringent kind. Without hesitation, almost without consultation with his colleagues, Gladstone brought about its defeat on an amendment to the Queen's Speech. There was no doubt that the new Government would be a Home Rule Government, and Hartington and the other leading Whigs refused to join. This was probably inevitable, but Gladstone destroyed any remaining hope of success by his treatment of Chamberlain. In the eyes of the country Chamberlain now stood next to his leader in the Liberal Party. But Gladstone gravely underrated his importance, had refused him the Colonial Office, and sent him to the Local Government Board. Chamberlain's views on Ireland had been changing rapidly during the previous year. His trust in Parnell had been shattered by what he considered the treacherous Irish switch to the Conservative side. The personal relations between the two men had also been poisoned by their intermediary, Captain O'Shea, the husband of Parnell's mistress. Chamberlain was opposed to any large scheme of self-government, and it would have needed all Gladstone's tact and persuasion to win him over. Gladstone made no attempt to do so. Chamberlain was not consulted in the preparation of the Home Rule Bill, and his own scheme for local government reform was ignored. He resigned on March 26, to become Gladstone's most formidable foe.

The Home Rule Bill was introduced into the Commons on April 8, 1886, by Gladstone in a speech which lasted for three and a half hours. He put the case for Home Rule as one of justice for Ireland and freedom for her people. It was an impressive performance, outstanding even in Gladstone's dazzling Parliamentary career. But his appeal to the Liberal principles of liberty and self-government struck against deep emotions. His sudden conversion to the new policy, his dependence upon the Irish vote for continuance in office, and the bitter memories of Irish crimes combined to deepen the fears and prejudices of his opponents. The emotions of race, religion, class, and economic interest all obscured the Liberal arguments which Gladstone used. Fire evoked fire. Gladstone's deep moral feeling found its answer on the other side, which believed him to be a hypocrite or worse. He had embarked on a sudden, destructive crusade. "And why?" asked Lord Randolph Churchill. "For this reason and no other: to gratify the ambition of an old man in a hurry."

The Bill was defeated on the second reading two months after its introduction. Ninety-three Liberals voted against the Government. Gladstone had a difficult decision to make. He could resign or dissolve. He chose the latter course and fought the election on the single issue of Home Rule. His zeal, enthusiasm, and energy were not enough to overcome the mighty forces arrayed against him. The new House contained 316 Conservatives and 78 Liberal Unionists, against 191 Gladstonians and 85 Parnellites. Gladstone resigned immediately, and Salisbury again took office.

Apart from one short spell the Conservatives were to remain in power for twenty years. The long period of Liberal-Whig predominance which had begun in 1830 was over. It

had been brought to an end by Whig distaste for social reform and by Gladstone's precipitate conversion to Home Rule.
The outlook for the Liberal Party was dark. In committing itself to a policy which was electorally unpopular in England
it had not only shed its Right Wing, but also the man who had
been by far the most outstanding of its young, reforming leaders. The turn of the wheel had brought fortune to the Conservatives, whose prospects had seemed so gloomy in 1880.
The opponents whom they had feared as the irresistible instruments of democracy had delivered themselves into their
hands.

Lord Salisbury's Governments

I T was not immediately perceived in the summer of 1886
that the controversy over Home Rule for Ireland had
wrought a deep change in the allegiance of English political
parties. Salisbury's Government depended upon the support of
the Liberal Unionists, led by Hartington, though their most
formidable figure, both in Parliament and in the country, was
Joseph Chamberlain. They protested that they were still Liberals, and for ten years they continued to sit on the Liberal
side of the House of Commons. This infuriated the followers
of Gladstone, many of whom bitterly and publicly likened
Chamberlain to Judas Iscariot. It was tacitly accepted, after
the failure of a Round Table Conference between the leaders
of the two sides, held at the beginning of 1887, that the gulf
was too wide to be bridged. This decisive split produced
strange bedfellows. Salisbury had to work with the man whom
he had denounced as a mob-leader and a "Jack Cade" only a
few months before. He had to accept part of Chamberlain's
programme as the price of his support. Chamberlain, now
tied to the Conservative chariot, was impelled for his part to
retract many of his former policies and opinions. On the Liberal side Gladstone, deprived of his Whig supporters, was
forced to make concessions to the Radical sections of his
party, whose views were far in advance of his own.

Salisbury's Government was not much different from that of the previous year, except that Hicks Beach insisted on standing down from the Leadership of the House of Commons. He argued that "the leader in fact should be leader in name." At the age of thirty-seven therefore Lord Randolph Churchill became Leader of the House and Chancellor of the Exchequer. His career had reached its pinnacle. In the course of six years his skill in debate and political tactics had carried him beyond all his rivals. His position in the Commons was unchallenged by any other member of his party, although many distrusted his methods and disliked his policies. Inside the Cabinet there was little harmony. Lord Randolph's ideas on Tory Democracy struck no spark in Salisbury's traditional Conservatism. The Prime Minister had no great faith in betterment by legislation. He believed that the primary business of government was to administer the existing order, and that the Conservatives owed their first duty to the classes who relied upon them to defend their interests. Lord Randolph wrote to him in November 1886, "I am afraid it is an idle schoolboy's dream to suppose that Tories can legislate—as I did—stupidly. They can govern and make wars and increase taxation and expenditure *à merveille,* but legislation is not their province in a democratic constitution." Salisbury replied, "We must work at less speed and at a lower temperature than our opponents. Our Bills must be tentative and cautious, not sweeping and dramatic." This clash was intensified by Lord Randolph's excursions into the field of foreign affairs. In October he had publicly attacked the reigning policy of friendship for Turkey and declared himself in favour of independence for the Balkan peoples. The differences between the two men, both in character and policy, were fundamental. The final collision occurred over a comparatively trivial point, Lord Randolph's demand for a reduction in the Army and

Navy Estimates. He resigned on the eve of Christmas 1886 at the wrong time, on the wrong issue, and he made no attempt to rally support. He lived for another nine years, enduring much ill-health, but already his career lay in ruins.

This dramatic fall came as the finale to a year of political sensations. It was the equivalent on the Conservative side to the Whig defection from Gladstone. Salisbury made George Goschen, a Liberal Unionist of impeccable Whig views, his Chancellor of the Exchequer, thus proclaiming that Tory Democracy was now deemed an unnecessary encumbrance. Thereafter his Government's record in law-making was meagre in the extreme. The main measure was the Local Government Act of 1888, which created county councils and laid the basis for further advance. Three years later school fees were abolished in elementary schools, and a Factory Act made some further attempt to regulate evils in the employment of women and children. It was not an impressive achievement. Even these minor measures were largely carried out as concessions to Chamberlain. From outside the Government he constantly preached the doctrine that the Unionist cause would be best served by a policy of active reform.

* * * * *

Salisbury's interest and that of a large section of public opinion lay in the world overseas, where the Imperialist movement was reaching its climax of exploration, conquest, and settlement. Livingstone, Stanley, Speke, and other travellers had opened up the interior of darkest Africa. Their feats of exploration paved the way for the acquisition of colonies by the European Powers. It was the most important achievement of the period that this partition of Africa was carried out peacefully. The credit is largely due to Salisbury, who in 1887 became Foreign Secretary as well as Prime Minister, and who never lost sight of the need to preserve peace while

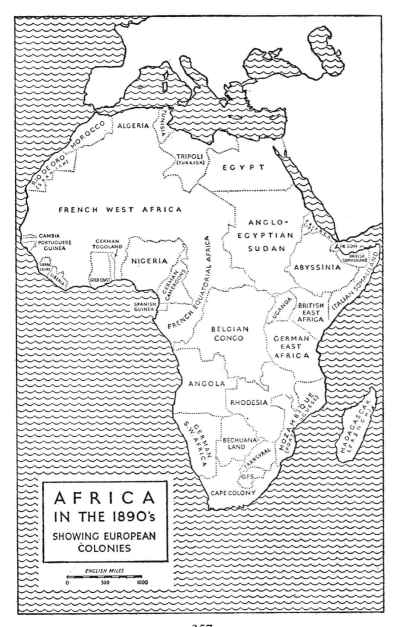

RIO DE ORO (SPANISH)

MOROCCO

ALGERIA

TUNISIA

TRIPOLI (TURKISH)

EGYPT

FRENCH WEST AFRICA

GAMBIA
PORTUGUESE GUINEA
SIERRA LEONE
LIBERIA

GERMAN TOGOLAND

GOLD COAST

NIGERIA

SPANISH GUINEA

GERMAN CAMEROONS

FRENCH EQUATORIAL AFRICA

ANGLO-EGYPTIAN SUDAN

ERITREA

FR. SOM.

BRITISH SOMALILAND

ABYSSINIA

UGANDA

BRITISH EAST AFRICA

ITALIAN SOMALILAND

BELGIAN CONGO

GERMAN EAST AFRICA

ANGOLA

RHODESIA

MOZAMBIQUE (PORTUGUESE)

MADAGASCAR (FRENCH)

GERMAN S.W. AFRICA

BECHUANA-LAND

TRANSVAAL

O.F.S.

CAPE COLONY

AFRICA
IN THE 1890's
SHOWING EUROPEAN
COLONIES

ENGLISH MILES
0   500   1000

the colonial map of Africa was being drawn. The French, seeking consolation for their defeat at the hands of the Prussians in 1870, had been first in the field, with the Germans, in the early eighties, not far behind. Gladstone and Disraeli, had they wished, with the naval and economic power at their disposal, could have annexed much of the continent which their countrymen had mapped and explored. But neither showed any enthusiasm for adventures in tropical Africa. The task of forwarding British interests was largely carried out by men like Cecil Rhodes, Sir William Mackinnon, and Sir George Goldie, who, in spite of the indifference of the Government at home, carved out a great new empire.

When Salisbury took office he himself promoted no great schemes of Imperial expansion, but he was prepared to back up the men on the spot. The work of consolidation and political control was entrusted, after the Elizabethan model, to three chartered companies. The Royal Niger Company operated in Nigeria, the British East Africa Company controlled what is now Kenya and Uganda, and the British South Africa Company acquired the territory of the Rhodesias. All were launched between 1886 and 1889. Rhodesia is the only self-governing member of the British Commonwealth which bears the name of the man who founded it, and foresaw its future. Its capital, Salisbury, commemorates the Prime Minister. Many border disputes with the other colonising Powers arose, but Salisbury pursued a steady policy of settlement by negotiation. It culminated in the signing of agreements with Germany, France, and Portugal in 1890. The German agreement, which was the most important of the three, defined the boundaries of the two countries' possessions in Central and South Africa. As part of the bargain Heligoland was ceded to Germany in compensation for the recognition of the British protectorate of Zanzibar. A future German naval base was traded for a spice island. By 1892 Salisbury had largely succeeded in his aims. The assertion of British control over the Nile Valley and the settlement of the boundaries of the West African colonies were the only outstanding problems.

Salisbury's foreign policy was largely swayed by these colonial affairs. Attached in principle to the idea of the Concert of Europe, he was inevitably drawn closer to Bismarck's Triple Alliance of Germany, Austria-Hungary, and Italy. Britain was in more or less constant conflict with France in West Africa and with Russia in the Near and Far East. The key to Salisbury's success lay in his skilful handling of the innumerable complications that arose between the Powers in an age of intense national rivalries. He once said that "British policy is to drift lazily downstream, occasionally putting out a boat-hook to avoid a collision." No British Foreign Secretary has wielded his diplomatic boat-hook with greater dexterity.

*   *   *   *   *

The relentless question of a sullen and embittered Ireland overshadowed domestic politics. "What Ireland wants," Salisbury had asserted during the election campaign, "is government—government that does not flinch, that does not vary," and in his nephew, A. J. Balfour, who became Irish Secretary in 1887, he found a man capable of putting into practice the notion that all could be solved by "twenty years of resolute government." The situation that Balfour faced was very difficult. Agricultural prices were steadily falling, but the Government had rejected Parnell's argument that the only way to prevent mass evictions was to reassess rents. The Irish peasants, organised by William O'Brien and John Dillon, had taken matters into their own hands by launching the "Plan of Campaign." The basis of the Plan was that tenants in a body should ask for a reduction of rent. If the landlord refused rents were to be withheld and the money paid into a campaign fund. The Plan was enforced with the terrorist methods which had now become an implacable feature of Irish land disputes. The Government's answer was to make a few concessions, and pass a Crimes Act which gave to the executive arbitrary powers of the most sweeping kind. Balfour stretched his authority to the limit and acted with a determination that fully matched the ruthlessness of his Irish opponents. In defending his actions in the House of Commons he displayed such skill and resource that he rose rapidly to the front rank of Parliamentarians.

Parnell stood aloof from these tumults. He now perceived that Home Rule could only be won by conciliating a broad section of English opinion. But his adherence to cautious and constitutional action was stricken by the publication in *The Times* on April 18, 1887, of a facsimile letter, purporting to bear his signature, in which he was made to condone the Phoenix Park murders. Parnell, while denouncing the letter as a forgery, refused to bring an action in an English court. Such forbearance, and the public acceptance by men as eminent as Salisbury that this and other letters were authentic, convinced most Englishmen of his guilt. But in the following year the Government set up a commission of three judges to investigate the whole field of Irish crime. They had been sitting for six months when, in February 1889, they at last began to probe the letters. They discovered that they had been forged by a decrepit Irish journalist named Richard Piggott. Piggott was betrayed by a fatal inability to spell correctly and crushed by the brilliant cross-examination of Sir Charles Russell. He broke down in the witness-box, and later confessed. A few weeks afterwards he blew out his brains in a hotel in Madrid. The effect on the public was most dramatic. For a few months Parnell rode the crest of the wave. Long execration turned into sudden, strange, and short-lived popularity. A General Election was approaching, the Government was out of favour, and nothing, it seemed, could prevent a victory for Gladstone and Home Rule.

But the case was altered. On November 13, 1890, the suit of O'Shea *v.* O'Shea and Parnell opened in the Divorce Court. A decree *nisi* was granted to Captain O'Shea. Parnell, as co-respondent, offered no defence. He had been living with Mrs O'Shea for ten years. Posterity was to learn that the circumstances were not so dishonourable to Parnell as they then appeared, but public opinion at the time was severe in condemnation. The Nonconformist conscience, powerful in the Liberal Party, reared its head. Gladstone, single-minded for Home Rule, refused to join in the moral censure, but he was convinced that the only way to stop the Conservatives from exploiting Parnell's adultery was for the Irish leader to retire, at any rate for a while. "It'll no' dae," was his constant reply to the suggestion that Parnell should remain. Tremendous pressure was put on the Irish leader. His friend and admirer Cecil Rhodes telegraphed, "Resign—marry—return." It was wise advice. But Parnell was not to be moved; the passion which had burned for so long beneath his cold exterior burst into flame. His pride revolted. He refused to bow to "English hypocrisy," whatever the cost to his country or his cause.

As a last measure Gladstone wrote to Parnell that he would cease to lead the Liberal Party unless the Irishman retired. Before the letter could be delivered the Irish Party confirmed Parnell in his leadership. Gladstone, in despair, sent his letter to the Press. It was an irretrievable step, a public ultimatum. Next morning Gladstone wrote, "For every day, I may say, of those five years we have been engaged in laboriously rolling uphill the stone of Sisyphus. Mr Parnell's decision . . .

means that the stone is to break away from us and roll down again to the bottom of the hill. I cannot recall the years that have elapsed." The rest of the story is anti-climax. After Parnell had made a bitter attack upon Gladstone the Catholic Church declared against him, and he was disavowed by most of his party. In vain he made a series of wild and desperate efforts to regain power. Within a year he died.

Liberal prospects, which had been so bright in 1889, were now badly clouded. They were not improved by the adoption of the comprehensive "Newcastle Programme" of 1891. In trying to meet the demands of every section of the party this programme gave far more offence than satisfaction. When the election came in the summer of the following year the result was a Home Rule majority of only forty, dependent on the Irish Members. In the House there were 275 Liberals and 82 Irish Nationalists, as against 269 Conservatives and 46 Liberal Unionists. The majority was too thin for Gladstone's purposes, but he formed a Cabinet which included men as gifted as Harcourt, Rosebery, Morley, and Campbell-Bannerman. The brightest star of them all was H. H. Asquith, the most able Home Secretary of the century.

Gladstone was resolute. Work began immediately on a second Home Rule Bill, and in February 1893 he introduced it himself. At the age of eighty-four he piloted the Bill through eighty-five sittings against an Opposition led by debaters as formidable as Chamberlain and Balfour. There have been few more remarkable achievements in the whole history of Parliament. It was all in vain. Passing through the Commons by small majorities, the Bill was rejected on the second reading in the Lords by 419 votes to 41. Thus perished all hope of a united, self-governing Ireland, loyal to the British Crown. A generation later civil war, partition, and the separation of the South from the main stream of world events were to be

Ireland's lot. The immediate reaction in England was one of indifference. Encouraged by their victory, the Lords hampered the Government incessantly. Only one major issue was successful, a new Local Government Act, which established urban, rural district, and parish councils. After the defeat of the Home Rule Bill Gladstone fell increasingly out of sympathy with his colleagues. They refused to support his scheme for a dissolution and an attack on the Lords. He, for his part, hated their plans for heavier taxation and increased expenditure on armaments. "The plan is mad," he said of one proposal. "And who are they who propose it? Men who were not born when I had been in public life for years." He resigned on March 3, 1894, fifty-two and a half years after his swearing in as a Privy Counsellor. His parting with his Ministers was affecting. Harcourt made a tearful speech of farewell, and there was much emotion. Gladstone, who remained unmoved, afterwards referred to this meeting as "that blubbering Cabinet." He died in 1898. His career had been the most noteworthy of the century, leaving behind innumerable marks on the pages of history. He was the greatest popular leader of his age, and he has hardly been equalled in his power to move the people on great moral issues. He stands, too, in the very front rank of House of Commons figures. Few of his conceptions were unworthy. Gladstone's achievements, like his failures, were on the grand scale.

* * * * *

In January 1893 the Independent Labour Party had been founded at a conference at Bradford, with J. Keir Hardie, the Scottish miners' leader, as its chairman. The aims of the I.L.P., as it was called, were the popularisation of Socialist doctrine and the promotion of independent working-class candidates at Parliamentary elections. Here was a sign, not much noticed in the great world of politics, of new forces which were coming to the surface in the industrial areas of Britain. The lull which followed the collapse of the Chartist movement had already been broken some years before by an outburst of Socialist propaganda and a wave of Trade Union activity. The first manifestation was the founding in 1881 of the Democratic Federation, which was converted to Marxism by the energy and money of a wealthy exponent of the principles of class-warfare and revolution, H. M. Hyndman. But the working class found Marxism unattractive even when expounded by a rich man, and the movement had little success.

Of far greater importance in England was the emergence about the same time of the Fabian Society, run by a group of young and obscure but highly gifted men, Sidney Webb and George Bernard Shaw among them. They damned all revolutionary theory and set about the propagation of a practical Socialist doctrine. They were not interested in the organisation of a new political party. Socialist aims could be achieved by "permeating" the existing political parties, and, largely through the agency of Sidney and Beatrice Webb, they attained some measure of success. The stream of publications which flowed from the Fabian pens, especially the *Fabian Essays* of 1889, did much to shape the course of Labour politics. The outlook, in the main, was practical and empirical, owing little to dogmatic theory and nothing to Marx. Great stress was placed on the slow and intricate nature of the change to Socialism—the "inevitability of gradualness."

Most working men knew little of these higher intellectual activities. They were absorbed in efforts to raise their standards of living. During the mid-Victorian years Trade Union organisation had been largely confined to the skilled and relatively prosperous members of the working class. But in 1889 the dockers of London, a miserably underpaid group, struck for a wage of sixpence an hour. John Burns, one of the organisers of the strike, reminded the dockers of the relief of Lucknow. "This, lads," he said, "is the Lucknow of Labour, and I myself, looking to the horizon, can see a silver gleam —not of bayonets to be imbrued in a brother's blood, but the gleam of the full round orb of the dockers' tanner." It was indeed the Lucknow of Labour. The dockers' victory, made possible by much public sympathy and support, was followed by a rapid expansion of Trade Union organisation among the unskilled workers.

Throughout the country small groups of Socialists began to form, but they were politically very weak. Their sole electoral success had been the return for West Ham in 1892 of Keir Hardie, who created a sensation by going to the House for his first time accompanied by a brass band and wearing a cloth cap. The greatest difficulty for these Socialist groups was that their fervent beliefs evoked no response either among the mass of working men or among Trade Union leaders, most of whom continued to put their trust in the Liberals and Radicals. But Keir Hardie patiently toiled to woo the Unions away from the Liberal connection. He had some success with the new Unions which had expanded after the dock strike and were willing to support political action. He was greatly aided in his task by the reluctance of the Liberal Party to sponsor working-class candidates for Parliament, apart from a handful, known as "Lib-Labs," most of whom were miners.

The outcome was a meeting sponsored by the Socialist societies and a number of Trade Unions which was held in the Memorial Hall, Farringdon Street, London, on February 27, 1900. It was there decided to set up a Labour Representation Committee, with Ramsay MacDonald as its secretary. The aim of the committee was defined as the establishment of "a distinct Labour group in Parliament who shall have their own Whips and agree upon policy." The Labour Party had been founded. MacDonald in the twentieth century was to become the first Labour Prime Minister. He was to split his party at a moment of national crisis, and die amid the execrations of the Socialists whose political fortunes he had done so much to build.

*　*　*　*　*

Gladstone had been succeeded as Prime Minister by Lord Rosebery. Rosebery had the good luck to win the Derby twice during his sixteen months of office. Not much other fortune befell him. Rosebery had a far-ranging mind, above the shifts and compromises indispensable in political life. He had been most at ease as Foreign Secretary, contemplating the larger issues of the world and delicately considering British action. He was the Queen's own choice as Prime Minister, and his Imperialist views made him unpopular with his own party. The Lords continued to obstruct him. At this moment the Chancellor of the Exchequer, Sir William Harcourt, included in his Budget proposals a scheme for the payment of substantial death duties. This caused violent feeling throughout the capitalist class affected. The Cabinet was rent by clashes of personality and the quarrels of Imperialists and "Little Englanders." As Rosebery later said, "I never did have power." His was a bleak, precarious, wasting inheritance. When the Government was defeated on a snap vote in June 1895 it took the opportunity to resign. The quarrels of the Liberal leaders were now no longer confined by the secrecy of the Cabinet, and the years that followed were dark ones for the Liberal Party. At the General Election the Conservative–Liberal Unionist alliance won a decisive victory. Its majority over the Opposition, including the Irish Nationalists, was 152.

Lord Salisbury thereupon formed a powerful administration. He once again combined the offices of Prime Minister and Foreign Secretary, and his position in his own party and in the country was unrivalled. His methods of dispatching business were by now unorthodox. It is said that he sometimes failed to recognise members of his Cabinet when he met them on rare social occasions. He loved to retire to the great Cecil house at Hatfield, whence he discharged his vast responsibilities by a stream of letters written in his own hand. His leisure was spent in making scientific experiments in his private laboratory; he also enjoyed riding a stately tricycle around his park. His authority and prestige derived in part from the air of patrician assurance which marked his public speech and action. In character he presented the aristocratic tradition in politics at its best. He cared little for popular acclaim, and such disinterestedness in a democratic age was accepted and even approved. His deputy and closest adviser was his nephew, Arthur Balfour, who became First Lord of the Treasury. But the man who in the public eye dominated the Government was the Liberal Unionist leader, Joseph Chamberlain, now at the height of his powers and anxious for the office which had been denied to him for so long by the events of 1886. By his own choice Chamberlain became Colonial Secretary. His instinct was a sure one. Interest in home affairs had languished. In its five years of office the Government passed only one substantial reforming measure, the Workmen's Compensation Act of 1897. The excitement of politics lay in the clash of Imperial forces in the continents of Africa and Asia, and it was there that Chamberlain resolved to make his mark.

Chamberlain approached his task with the reforming enthusiasm of his Radical days. A great change had taken place in him. The Municipal Socialist and Republican of his Birmingham years was now the architect of Empire. "It is not enough," he declared, "to occupy certain great spaces of the world's surface unless you can make the best of them—

unless you are willing to develop them. We are landlords of a great estate; it is the duty of a landlord to develop his estate." Chamberlain could not fulfil this promise in the way he would have wished, although some advances were made, especially in West Africa. From the moment he took office projects of reform were pushed into the background by the constant eruption of questions inseparable from a policy of expansion. The first was a small one, that of the Ashanti, who continued to terrorise much of the Gold Coast by their slave-raiding. An expedition was sent against them under Wolseley, and by January 1896 the Ashanti kingdom had been crushed. The situation in Nigeria was much more difficult, since another Great Power was involved. The French, by moving overland to the south of the Sahara Desert, were attempting to confine the British to the coastal areas by using their superior military strength. Chamberlain, who, as Salisbury said, hated to give anything away, retaliated by organising the West African Frontier Force, under Sir Henry Lugard. His measures were completely successful; skilful diplomacy backed resolute action, and the Anglo-French Convention of June 1898 drew boundary lines in West Africa which were entirely satisfactory to the British.

A few months later a far more dangerous dispute broke out between Britain and France over the control of the Upper Nile. Since the death of Gordon the Dervishes had held unquestioned sway in the Sudan. Their prophet, the Mahdi, was dead, but his successor, the Khalifa as he was called, kept their loose military empire in his grip. He also cherished ambitions for enlarging his domains at the expense of Egypt and Abyssinia. Meanwhile the Egyptian Army, reorganised and reformed by British officers, successfully defended the Lower Nile and the Red Sea coast from Dervish incursions. In 1896 the time had come for the British Command in Egypt to strike back at the restless fanatics to their south. French moves towards the sources of the Nile were already taking place, and must be forestalled; the Italian settlements on the Red Sea needed support; the slave-trade, which the Dervishes had revived, called for suppression; and at home Lord Salisbury's Government was not averse to an Imperial advance. In March Sir Herbert Kitchener, Sirdar of the Egyptian Army, launched his campaign for the avenging of Gordon and the reconquest of the Sudan. This vast tract of African territory could no longer be left a prey to barbarous rule, or remain a magnet for European rivalries.

The desert and the harsh tropical climate presented a formidable challenge to Kitchener's expedition, and he left nothing to chance. His great capacity, now to be displayed, was his foresight in organisation. The River War on the banks of the Nile was a painstaking operation, well planned and well directed. A single reverse would have aroused an outcry of criticism in Britain, and only carefully calculated risks could be taken. Supply was the chief problem, and to meet the needs of Kitchener's columns far in the interior of the African continent over five hundred miles of railway were built through arid and unsurveyed regions. It was largely an engineers' war, enlivened by many short, fierce, gallant actions. Kitchener started the campaign with 15,000 men, and at the end commanded 25,000, of whom 8,000 were British. The Khalifa's forces were at least three times as numerous, devoted to their cause, ferociously brave, and wily in the ways of the desert. After two and a half years the Dervish Army was finally confronted and destroyed outside Khartoum at the Battle of Omdurman on September 2, 1898. This, as described at the time by a young Hussar who took part in the battle, was "the most signal triumph ever gained by the arms of science over barbarians." The Khalifa and his surviving lieutenants were gradually hunted down, and the Sudan then entered upon a period of constructive rule.

Five days after the Battle of Omdurman news reached Khartoum that there were Europeans at Fashoda, a post high upon the White Nile. They were Major Marchand and his officers, with a platoon of West African soldiers, who had marched for two years from the Atlantic coast across 2,500 miles of jungle in the hope of establishing France astride the sources of the Nile between the Congo and Abyssinia. Kitchener himself sailed up-river to meet Marchand in person. Courtesies were exchanged between the two soldiers, but it was evident who held the ground in greater force. For a time the French flag flew alongside the British and the Egyptian at Fashoda fort while matters were referred to London and Paris. In both capitals there was a flurry of talk about war. But French claims to the provinces of the Southern Sudan could not be sustained in the light of the British victory in the River War. The French gave way, and by the Convention of March 1899 the watershed of the Congo and the Nile was fixed as the boundary separating British and French interests. This was virtually the last of the colonial disputes which for some decades had poisoned relations between Britain and France. Henceforward, under the growing menace of Germany, the two countries found themselves in constantly increasing harmony.

These were not the only external preoccupations of the Government. At the end of 1895 a crisis occurred with the United States, when, as has been related, President Cleveland claimed the American right to make an arbitrary settlement of the boundary between British Guiana and Venezuela. Throughout these years Germany was hard at work promoting her plans for the penetration of Asia Minor, and there was much talk of a Berlin-Baghdad railway. To this Salisbury raised no objection. He preferred to see the Germans rather than the Russians busy in Turkey. In the Far East the Russian threat to China, made possible by the building of the trans-Siberian railway, perpetually agitated the Foreign Office. The province of Manchuria, with the naval base of Port Arthur, was falling into the grasp of the Russians. Few foresaw at that time the startling defeats which Japanese arms would shortly inflict upon the Czar. Chamberlain, who had a large say in foreign affairs, was provoked into making an ill-considered bid for an alliance with Germany. Salisbury held aloof, and restrained his ardent colleague, perceiving more perils in a European alliance than in a policy of isolation. His confidence in Britain's power to stand alone was now to be tested. For the great events on the world stage, and the diplomatic manœuvres that attended them, were for the Island eclipsed by the struggle in South Africa.

The South African War

BRITAIN entered the twentieth century in the grip of war. She placed nearly half a million men in the field, the biggest force she had hitherto sent overseas throughout her history. The conflict in South Africa, which began as a small colonial campaign, soon called for a large-scale national effort. Its course was followed in Britain with intense interest and lively emotion. Scarcely a generation had gone by since the Franchise Acts had granted a say in the affairs of State to every adult male. The power to follow events and to pass judgment upon them had recently come within the reach of all through free education. Popular journals had started to circulate among the masses, swiftly bringing news, good, bad, and sometimes misleading, into millions of homes. Yet the result of this rapid diffusion of knowledge and responsibility was not, as some had prophesied, social unrest and revolutionary agitation. On the contrary, the years of the Boer War saw a surge of patriotism among the vast majority of the British people, and a widespread enthusiasm for the cause of Empire.

Of course there were vehement critics and dissentients, the pro-Boers, as they were derisively called. They included some influential Liberal leaders, and in their train a rising young Welsh lawyer named Lloyd George, who now first

made himself known to the nation by the vigour of his attacks upon the war and the Government. Nevertheless the general feeling in the country was staunchly Imperialist. There
was pride in the broad crimson stretches on the map of
the globe which marked the span of the British Empire, and
confidence in the Royal Navy's command of the Seven Seas.
Europe was envious. Most of the Powers made plain their
sympathy for the Boers, and there were hints of an allied
combination against the Island kingdom. She might not have
been allowed to escape from her colonial war with an easy
victory, but her dominion of the seas caused second thoughts.
On the outbreak of war a flying squadron of the Royal Navy
was mobilised at Portsmouth, and this upon consideration
from many angles proved effective in overawing Europe. The
lesson was not lost upon the German Kaiser. The spectacle
of British sea-power exercising unchallengeable authority
made him redouble his efforts to create a mighty ocean-going
German battle fleet. Dire consequences were to flow from his
spirit of emulation.

*   *   *   *   *

The South African War had its roots deep in the past. Two
landlocked Boer Republics, owing a vague suzerainty to Britain, were surrounded on all sides, except for a short frontier
with Portuguese Mozambique, by British colonies, protectorates, and territories. Yet conflict was not at first inevitable.
The large Dutch population in Cape Colony appeared reconciled to British rule and supported Cecil Rhodes as their
Premier. The Orange Free State was friendly, and even in the
Transvaal, home of the dourest frontier farmers, a considerable Boer party favoured co-operation with Britain. Hopes of
an Anglo-Boer federation in South Africa were by no means
dead. But all this abruptly changed during the last five years
of the nineteenth century.

When Joseph Chamberlain became Colonial Secretary in 1895 he was confronted by a situation of great complexity. The Transvaal had been transformed by the exploitation of the extremely rich goldfields on the Witwatersrand. This was the work of foreign capital and labour, most of it British. Within a few years Johannesburg had developed into a great city. The Uitlanders—or Outlanders, as foreigners were called —equalled the native Boers in number, but the Transvaal Government refused to grant them political rights, even though they contributed all but one-twentieth of the country's taxation. Paul Kruger, the President of the Republic, who had taken part in the Great Trek and was now past his seventieth year, determined to preserve the character and independence of his country. He headed the recalcitrant Dutch, unwilling to make common cause with the British, and opposed to the advance of industry, though ready to feed on its profits. The threat of a cosmopolitan goldfield to a close community of Bible-reading farmers was obvious to him. But his fears were intensified by the encircling motions of Rhodes' British South Africa Company, which already controlled the territories to the north that were to become the Rhodesias, and was now trying to acquire Bechuanaland to the west. Rhodes, who had large financial interests on the Rand, dreamt of a United South Africa and a Cape-to-Cairo railway running through British territory all the way.

The political and economic grievances of the Uitlanders made an explosion inevitable, and Chamberlain by the end of 1895 was ready to meet it. Unknown to him however Rhodes had worked out a scheme for an uprising of the British in Johannesburg to be reinforced by the invasion of the Transvaal by a Company force. This was to be led by the Administrator of Rhodesia, Dr Leander Starr Jameson. At the last moment the rising in Johannesburg failed to take place, but

Jameson, not having counter-instructions from Rhodes, invaded the Transvaal with five hundred men on December 29. It was, in Chamberlain's words, "a disgraceful exhibition of filibustering," and it ended in the failure which it deserved. On January 2 Jameson and his force surrendered to the Boers at Doornkop. The raid was a turning-point; the entire course of South African history was henceforth violently diverted from peaceful channels. The atmosphere of the country was poisoned by national and racial prejudice; the Dutch at the Cape, in natural sympathy with the Transvaal Boers, began to growl at the British. Rhodes was forced to resign his Premiership; but his great popularity in England served only to sharpen Boer suspicion of a deep-laid plot against the life of their republics. The Orange Free State threw in its lot with Kruger. In the Transvaal his purpose was strengthened; the party of reaction gained the upper hand and armaments were purchased on a large scale for the conflict that loomed ahead.

The next three years were occupied by long-drawn-out and arduous negotiations, Chamberlain's determination being more than matched by Kruger's tortuous obstinacy. In March 1897 Sir Alfred Milner, an outstanding public servant, became High Commissioner in South Africa. He was an administrator of great talents, but he lacked the gift of diplomacy. Within a few months he had made up his mind; he wrote to Chamberlain, "There is no ultimate way out of the political troubles of South Africa except reform in the Transvaal or war. And at present the chances of reform in the Transvaal are worse than ever." But Chamberlain was anxious to avoid war, except as a last resort, and even then he hoped that the responsibility for its outbreak could be fixed on the Boers. He believed, as did Rhodes, that Kruger, under pressure, would yield. They underestimated the pioneers of the veldt.

The climax was reached in April 1899, when a petition, signed by more than 20,000 Uitlanders, arrived in Downing Street. It was followed in May by a dispatch from Milner which stated that "The spectacle of thousands of British subjects kept permanently in the position of helots . . . does steadily undermine the influence and reputation of Great Britain and the respect for the British Government within the Queen's Dominions." A period of negotiation followed, with the British Government demanding a vote for every citizen after five years' residence in the Transvaal and putting forward the old claim to "suzerainty." A conference at Bloemfontein in June between Kruger and Milner settled nothing. Milner was convinced that the Boers, now armed to the teeth, were aiming at the establishment of a Dutch United States of South Africa. Kruger was equally convinced that the British intended to rob the Boers of their freedom and independence. "It is our country you want," he said, as tears ran down his face. Chamberlain made several more attempts to come to an agreement, but by this time both sides were pressing ahead with military preparations. On October 9 the Boers delivered an ultimatum while the British forces in South Africa were still weak. Three days later their troops moved over the border.

* * * * *

At the outbreak of the war the Boers put 35,000 men, or twice the British number, in the field, and a much superior artillery derived from German sources. They crossed the frontiers in several directions. Their army was almost entirely mounted. They were armed with Männlicher and Mauser rifles, with which they were expert shots. Within a few weeks they had invested Ladysmith to the east, and Mafeking and Kimberley to the west. At Ladysmith, on the Natal border, 10,000 men, under Sir George White, were surrounded and

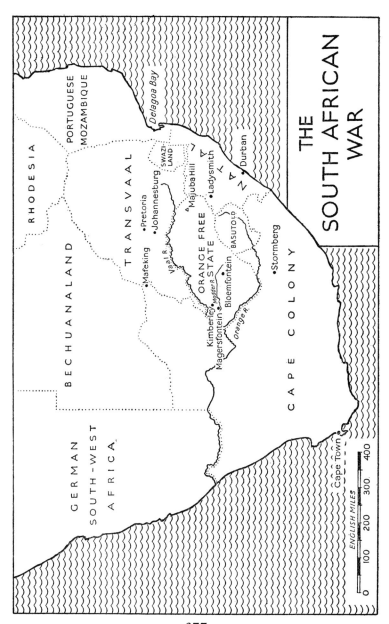

THE
SOUTH AFRICAN
WAR

RHODESIA

PORTUGUESE
MOZAMBIQUE

Delagoa Bay

BECHUANALAND

TRANSVAAL

SWAZI-
LAND

•Pretoria
•Johannesburg

▲Majuba Hill

N A T A L

•Ladysmith

•Durban

GERMAN

SOUTH-WEST

AFRICA.

•Mafeking

Vaal R.

ORANGE FREE
STATE

BASUTOLD

•Stormberg

Kimberley•
Magersfontein•

Modder R.
•Bloemfontein

Orange R.

CAPE COLONY

•Cape Town

ENGLISH MILES

0   100   200   300   400

· 377 ·

besieged after two British battalions had been trapped and forced to surrender with their guns at Nicholson's Nek. At Mafeking a small force commanded by Colonel Baden-Powell was encircled by many times its number under Pete Cronje. At Kimberley Cecil Rhodes himself and a large civilian population were beset. After the seasonal rains there was fresh grazing on the veldt, which had been deliberately stimulated by Boer burnings at the end of the summer. The countryside was friendly to the Boer cause. World opinion was uniformly hostile to the British. Meanwhile a British army corps of three divisions was on the way as reinforcement, under the command of Sir Redvers Buller, and volunteer contingents from the Dominions were offered or forthcoming. The phrase "unmounted men preferred" used in official correspondence was typical of the want of knowledge prevailing at the War Office. The troops were good, but the enemy weapons and conditions were entirely misunderstood.

Kruger had long wanted a salt-water port under his independent control. Beyond the mountain passes of Natal lay Durban harbour, which could be captured if only he could reach it. Durban was linked with the Transvaal by a railway which, by comparison with the long line to Cape Town, was short, manageable, and on his doorstep. Here would be the end of many disputes about customs dues, freight charges, and much else besides, and it was in this region that the main effort of both sides was at first concentrated.

The British army corps, as it arrived, was distributed by Buller in order to show a front everywhere. One division was sent to defend Natal, another to the relief of Kimberley, and a third to the north-eastern district of Cape Colony. Within a single December week each of them advanced against the rifle and artillery fire of the Boers, and was decisively defeated with, for those days, severe losses in men and guns. At

Colenso, in Natal, where Buller himself commanded, at the Modder River on the road to Kimberley, and at Stormberg in the east of Cape Colony the Boers held their front and invaded the country before them. Although the losses of under a thousand men in each case may seem small nowadays, they came as a startling and heavy shock to the public in Britain and throughout the Empire, and indeed to the troops on the spot. But Queen Victoria braced the nation in words which have become justly famous. "Please understand," she replied to Balfour when he tried to discuss "Black Week," as it was called, "that there is no one depressed in *this* house. We are not interested in the possibilities of defeat. They do not exist." Lord Roberts of Kandahar, who had won fame in the Afghan Wars, was made the new Commander-in-Chief, Lord Kitchener of Khartoum was appointed his Chief of Staff, and in a few months the two already illustrious generals with an ever-increasing army transformed the scene. Buller meanwhile persevered in Natal.

The new British command saw clearly that forces must be used on a large scale and in combination, and the Boer capitals, Bloemfontein and then Pretoria, became their sure objective. Cronje at Mafeking was deceived into thinking that the main blow would fall on Kimberley, and he shifted the larger portion of his troops to Magersfontein, a few miles south of the diamond centre. Here he entrenched himself and awaited the attack. Kimberley indeed was one of Roberts' objectives, but he gained it by sending General French on a long encirclement, and French's cavalry relieved it on February 15. The threat from the rear now compelled Cronje to quit his earthworks and fall back to the north-east. Twelve days later, after fierce frontal assaults by Kitchener, he surrendered with four thousand men. Thereafter all went with a rush. On the following day Buller relieved Ladysmith; on

March 13 Roberts reached Bloemfontein, on May 31 Johannesburg, and on June 5 Pretoria fell. Mafeking was liberated after a siege which had lasted for two hundred and seventeen days, and its relief provoked unseemly celebrations in London. Kruger fled. The Orange Free State and the Transvaal were annexed, and in the autumn of 1900 Roberts went home to England. After almost exactly a year of lively fighting, and with both the rebel capitals occupied, it seemed to the British people that the Boer War was finished, and won. At this Lord Salisbury, on Chamberlain's advice, fought a General Election and gained another spell of power with a large majority.

*   *   *   *   *

On January 22, 1901, Queen Victoria died. She lay at Osborne, the country home in the Isle of Wight which she and Prince Albert had designed and furnished fifty-five years before. Nothing in its household arrangements had been changed during the Queen's long widowhood. She had determined to conduct her life according to the pattern set by the Prince; nor did she waver from her resolution. Nevertheless a great change had gradually overtaken the monarchy. The Sovereign had become the symbol of Empire. At the Queen's Jubilees in 1887 and 1897 India and the colonies had been vividly represented in the State celebrations. The Crown was providing the link between the growing family of nations and races which the former Prime Minister, Lord Rosebery, had with foresight christened the Commonwealth. Disraeli's vision and Chamberlain's enthusiasm had both contributed to this broadening Imperial theme. The Queen herself was seized with the greatness of her rôle. She sent her sons and grandsons on official tours of her ever-increasing dominions, where they were heartily welcomed. Homage from a stream of colonial dignitaries was received by her in England. She appointed Indian servants to her household, and from them learnt Hindustani. Thus she sought by every means within her power to bind her diverse peoples together in loyalty to the British Crown, and her endeavours chimed with the Imperial spirit of the age. One of her last public acts, when she was over eighty years of age, was to visit Ireland. She had never believed in Irish Home Rule, which seemed to her a danger to the unity of the Empire. Prompted by a desire to recognise the gallantry of her Irish soldiers in South Africa, she travelled to Dublin in April 1900, wearing the shamrock on her bonnet and jacket. Her Irish subjects, even the Nationalists among them, gave her a rousing reception. In Ireland a fund of goodwill still flowed for the Throne, on which English Governments sadly failed to draw.

In England during the Queen's years of withdrawal from the outward shows of public life there had once been restiveness against the Crown, and professed republicans had raised their voices. By the end of the century all this had died away. High devotion to her royal task, domestic virtues, evident sincerity of nature, a piercing and sometimes disconcerting truthfulness—all these qualities of the Queen's had long impressed themselves upon the minds of her subjects. In the mass they could have no knowledge of how shrewd she was in political matters, nor of the wisdom she had accumulated in the course of her dealings with many Ministers and innumerable crises. But they justly caught a sense of a great presiding personage. Even Ministers who in private often found her views impulsive and partisan came to respect the watchful sense of duty that always moved her. She represented staunchness and continuity in British traditions, and as she grew in years veneration clustered round her. When she died she had reigned for nearly sixty-four years. Few of her subjects could remember a time when she had not been their Sovereign. But all reflecting men and women could appreciate the advance of British power and the progress of the British peoples that had taken place during the age to which she gave her name. The Victorian Age closed in 1901, but the sense of purpose and confidence which had inspired it lived on through the ordeals to come.

* * * * *

The war in South Africa meanwhile continued. In the past the Boers had never shown themselves docile or obedient to political authority, even when exercised by their own leaders, and British occupation of their principal townships and British seizure of the railways seemed an insufficient reason for abandoning the struggle. The veldt was wide, and from its scattered farmhouses a man could get news, food, shelter, forage, a fresh horse, and even ammunition. Roberts and Buller had hardly left the shores of South Africa when the war flamed into swift-moving, hard-hitting guerrilla. Botha, Kritzinger, Hertzog, De Wet, De la Rey, to name only five of the more famous commando leaders, soon faced Kitchener with innumerable local battles and reverses which were not to end for another seventeen months. The Boers were only to be subdued by extraordinary British exertions. In February 1901 Botha struck at Natal, and was thrown back by General French after laying waste large areas of the country. The other leaders invaded Cape Colony, hoping to rally its Dutch inhabitants. Very few responded, but they were enough to destroy all hopes of a speedy peace. After the raiders were expelled Kitchener and Botha met at the end of the month to arrange terms. Each of these leaders wanted an amnesty for the Cape rebels; but Milner, the High Commissioner, was adverse, and the Cabinet in London supported him. Thus frustrated, and much against his judgment and personal inclination, Kitchener was driven to what would nowadays be called a "scorched earth" policy. Blockhouses were built along the railway lines; fences were driven across the countryside; then more blockhouses were built along the fences. Movement within the enclosures thus created became impossible for even the most heroic commandos. Then, area by area, every man, woman, and child was swept into concentration camps. Such methods could only be justified by the fact that most of the commandos fought in plain clothes, and could only be subdued by wholesale imprisonment, together with the families who gave them succour. Nothing, not even the incapacity of the military authorities when charged with the novel and distasteful task of herding large bodies of civilians into captivity, could justify the conditions in the camps themselves. By February 1902 more than twenty thousand of the prisoners, or nearly one in every six, had died, mostly of disease. At first the authorities denied that anything was wrong, or that any alleviation was possible, but at length an Englishwoman, Miss Emily Hobhouse, exposed and proclaimed the terrible facts. Campbell-Bannerman, soon to be Prime Minister, but at this time in Opposition, denounced the camps as "methods of barbarism." Chamberlain removed them from military control; conditions thereupon speedily improved, and at last, on March 23, 1902, the Boers sued for peace.

Three days later Cecil Rhodes died of heart disease. In one of his final speeches he thus addressed the Loyalists of Cape Town: "You think you have beaten the Dutch. It is not so. The Dutch are not beaten. What is beaten is Krugerism, a corrupt and evil Government, no more Dutch in essence than English. No! The Dutch are as vigorous and unconquered today as they have ever been; the country is still as much theirs as yours, and you will have to live and work with them hereafter as in the past." Certainly the peace which was signed at Vereeniging on May 31 tried to embody this spirit, and its provisions may be judged magnanimous in the extreme. Thirty-two commandos remained unbeaten in the field. Two delegates from each met the British envoys, and after much discussion they agreed to lay down their arms and ammunition. None should be punished except for certain specified breaches of the usages of war; self-government would be accorded as soon as possible, and Britain would pay three million pounds in compensation. Such, in brief, were the principal terms, of which the last may be reckoned as generous, and was at any rate unprecedented in the history of modern war. Upon the conclusion of peace Lord Salisbury resigned. The last Prime Minister to sit in the House of Lords, he had presided over an unparalleled expansion of the British Empire. He died in the following year, and with him a certain aloofness of spirit, now considered old-fashioned, passed from British politics. All the peace terms were kept, and Milner did much to reconstruct South Africa. Nearly half a million British and Dominion troops had been employed, of whom one in ten became casualties. The total cost in money to the United Kingdom has been reckoned at over two hundred and twenty million pounds.

* * * * *

We have now reached in this account the end of the nineteenth century, and the modern world might reasonably have looked forward to a long period of peace and prosperity. The prospects seemed bright, and no one dreamed that we had entered a period of strife in which command and ascendancy by a single world-Power would be the supreme incentive. Two fearful wars, each of about five years' duration, were to illustrate the magnitude which developments had reached during the climax of the Victorian era. The rise of Germany to world-Power had long been accompanied by national assertiveness and the continuous building up of armaments. No one could attempt to measure the character and consequences of the impending struggles. To fight on till victory was won became the sole objective, and in this the power of the nations engaged was to prove astounding. It seemed so easy in the course of the closing years of the passing century to take as a matter of course the almost universal system of national armies created by general conscription and fed by the measureless resources of industrial progress. Order and organisation were the salient features of modern life, and when Germany threw all her qualities into the task the steps became obvious, and even inevitable. Nay, it could be argued, and perhaps even proved, that the wise and normal method of modern progress, which all the Continent of Europe adopted in one form or another, was the principle of rearmament on the highest scale. Such was the vitality of the human race that it nevertheless flourished undeterred.

Alone of the Great Powers of Europe, which ordained that every man should be trained as a soldier and serve for two or even three years, Great Britain availed herself of her island position and naval mastery to stand outside the universal habit—for such it had become. And yet this abstention was by no means to allay the growth of the danger. On the contrary, in South Africa Britain took, unconsciously no doubt, a leading part in bringing about the crisis. She exhibited herself to all the nations as supreme. For three long years the process of conquering the Boers continued, leaving the rest of Europe and America the facts of Empire and much else to meditate upon. All the Powers began to think of navies in a different mood. Germany saw that her world preponderance would not be achieved without warships of the greatest strength and quality, and France and other nations followed her example. It was indeed a new outlet for national pride and energy, of which Japan, at the opposite side of the globe, took eager advantage. To the vast military staffs were added naval formations which pointed out the logic and importance of all their doings. The conquest of the air was also on the way. Britain would have been content to rule alone in moderation.

Nearly a hundred years of peace and progress had carried Britain to the leadership of the world. She had striven repeatedly for the maintenance of peace, at any rate for herself, and progress and prosperity had been continuous in all classes. The franchise had been extended almost to the actuarial limit, and yet quiet and order reigned. Conservative forces had shown that they could ride the storm, and indeed that there was no great storm between the domestic parties. The great mass of the country could get on with their daily tasks and leave politics to those who were interested as partisans without fear. The national horse had shown that the reins could be thrown on his neck without leading to a furious gallop in this direction or that. No one felt himself left out of the Constitution. An excess of self-assertion would be injurious. Certainly the dawn of the twentieth century seemed bright and calm for those who lived within the unequalled bounds of the British Empire, or sought shelter within its folds. There was endless work to be done. It did not matter which party ruled: they found fault with one another, as they had a perfect right to do. None of the ancient inhibitions obstructed the adventurous. If mistakes were made they had been made before, and Britons could repair them without serious consequences. Active and vigorous politics should be sustained. To go forward gradually but boldly seemed to be fully justified.

The United States remained, save in naval matters, largely aloof from these manifestations. Her thoughts were turned inwards on her unlimited natural resources, as yet barely explored and still less exploited. Her population still owed much of its amazing increase to immigrants from Europe, and these, out of temper with the continent of their origins and perhaps misfortunes, had no wish to see their new home entangled in the struggles of the old. The vast potentialities of America lay as a portent across the globe, as yet dimly recognised, save by the imaginative. But in the contracting world of better communications to remain detached from the preoccupations of others was rapidly becoming impossible. The status of world-Power is inseparable from its responsibilities. The convulsive climax of the first Great War was finally and inseparably to link America with the fortunes of the Old World and of Britain.

*   *   *   *   *

Here is set out a long story of the English-speaking peoples. They are now to become Allies in terrible but victorious wars. And that is not the end. Another phase looms before us, in which alliance will once more be tested and in which its formidable virtues may be to preserve Peace and Freedom. The future is unknowable, but the past should give us hope. Nor should we now seek to define precisely the exact terms of ultimate union.

INDEX

INDEX

INDEX

INDEX

291–2; Imperial policy of, 291–4; and Eastern Question, 294–8; party organisation of, 300–1; death of, 302; annexes Transvaal, 336; mentioned, 88
Dissenters, 91
"Doctrine of lapse" (India), 83
Doornkop, 375
Douglas, Stephen A., and transcontinental railway, 158; Presidential candidate, 161, 163, 164; supports Lincoln, 168
Draft riots, 231
Drummond Wolff, Sir Henry, 335
Durban, 378
D'Urban, Sir Benjamin, 110
Durham, John Lambton, first Earl of, 53, 102, 123
Dutch settlers in South Africa, 106–10; discovery of Australia, 114. *See also* Boers
Dutch East India Company, 106–8

Early, General Jubal A., 225, 227, 260
East India Company, India under, 80–3; Bengal Army of, 83–6; loyal armies of, 85; abolition of rule of, 88
East Point, Georgia, 256
Eastern Question, 294–8; origin of, 32; Russia and, 69–71, 79
Education Act, Forster's, 287, 289
Egypt, purchase of Suez Canal shares from, 293; revolt of Arabi Pasha in, 337; British intervention in, 337–8; Sudan revolts against, 338; Army of, 368
Eldon, John Scott, first Earl of, Lord Chancellor, 5, 17; on state of monarchy, 22; mentioned, 33
Elgin, James Bruce, eighth Earl of, 103
Emancipation Edict, 215–7
England, disaffection in, 44–6; in 1848, 66; politics in mid-Victorian, 90; religious preoccupations in, 91; slave trade of, 150–1. *See also* Britain
Enlistment Act, 288
Erie Canal, 136
Erie, Lake, 133
Eupatoria, 74
Evolution, theory of, 92
Ewell, Richard S., 233–8

Fabian Society, 364
Factory Acts, 53, 356
Fair Oaks, Battle of, 194
Farmers' Alliances (United States), 325
Farragut, Admiral David G., 242, 257
Fashoda incident, 370
Federal Army, 169; changes in generalship of, 176, 180, 218–20, 234, 248; invasion routes for, 176–7; routed at Bull Run, 178–80; rifled guns of, 183, 196, 239; of Mississippi, 183–4, 242–3; coastal successes of, 190; and McClellan, 210, 217–8; desertion and absenteeism in, 223, 231; conscription to, 231; unity of command in, 251; occupation of Southern states by, 308, 310–2. *See also* Potomac, Army of
Federal Bank, 131, 142
Federal Government, slave-owning states remaining to, 173–5; unified control of, 176; Joint Committee of, 186–8; relations between McClellan and, 209–11,

216–7; crisis between British Government and, 231–2; tariff policy of, 323; neglect of the farmer by, 323–4
Federal Navy, 173; arrests Confederate agents on *Trent*, 181–2; at Yorktown, 192; in conflict with the *Merrimac*, 200–2; in Mississippi, 222, 242; and *Alabama*, 231–2
Ferdinand VII, King of Spain, 27
Fish River, 107, 109
Fitzgerald, Vesey, 36
Fitzherbert, Maria, 16, 40
Five Forks, Battle of, 261
Florida, purchased from Spain, 132; secession of, 164; "carpet-bagger" Government of, 312
Floyd, John Buchanan, 166, 185
Force Act, 141
Forrest, General Nathan B., 258
Forster, W. E., 348; Education Act of, 287
Fort Donelson, Tennessee, 184, 185
Fort Henry, Tennessee, 184, 185
Fort Sumter, South Carolina, 166, 168, 259
Fortress Monroe, Virginia, 200, 251; landings at, 187, 191; embarkation of McClellan's army at, 205
Fourteenth Amendment, 308
Fourth Party, 335
Fox, Charles James, 14, 16
France, peace with, 6–8; army of occupation in, 6, 8; intervenes in Spain, 27, 132; agrees not to intervene in South America, 28; intervenes in Greece, 32; July Revolution, in 42, 43; danger of intervention of, in Belgium, 44, 46; 1848 Revolution in, 64; foreign trade of, 68; in Crimean War, 72, 73, 78; Nice and Savoy ceded to, 92; commercial treaty with, 96; and New Zealand, 124; slave trade of, 150–1; and war for Schleswig-Holstein, 270; German threat to, 274; and Spanish succession, 275; at war with Prussia, 277–9; harsh terms for, 279, 281; British colonial quarrels with, 282, 359, 368–70; and Egypt, 3*d*7; African interests of, 358–9; improved relations with Britain, 370; Navy of, 385
Franchise, extension of, 95; and increase in education, 287, 372. *See also* Reform Bill
Franchise Acts, 372; Disraeli's, 95–7, 291, 300; Gladstone's, 97, 342
Francis Joseph, Emperor of Austria-Hungary, 65
Franco-Prussian War, 268
Frankfort, 1849 Parliament at, 65; Bismarck the Prussian representative at, 267–9
Franklin, Kentucky, 259
Frayser's Farm, Battle of, 198
Frederick, Maryland, 210, 234
Frederick William IV, King of Prussia, 65
Fredericksburg, 194; Battle of, 220–1; Sedgwick at, 234–8
Free trade, Pitt's policy of, 24; Peel and, 58–62; Gladstone and, 95–6
Freedman's Bureau Bill, 308
Frémont, General John C., 186, 194
French, General Sir John, 379
Friendly Islands, 114
"Frontier, the," 322

INDEX

Fugitive Slave Law, 157; Northern defiance of, 159, 162, 163

Gaines's Mill, Battle of, 197
Gambetta, Leon, 279
Garibaldi, Giuseppi, 93, 272
Garrison, William Lloyd, 144, 153
Geneva Convention (1864), 79
George III, King of Great Britain, madness of, 14; sons of, 17; death of, 18
George IV, King, as Regent, 15; marriages of, 16; his hatred for Princess Caroline, 17–20; coronation of, 21; opposes recognition of South American republics, 30; chooses successor to Lord Liverpool, 33; opposed to Catholic Emancipation, 38–9; death of, 40
George, David Lloyd, 372
Georgia, secession of, 164; fighting in, 247, 254; Confederates driven back into, 249; Sherman devastates, 258–9
German Confederation, and Schleswig-Holstein, 269; eliminating Austria from, 272, 273
Germany, revolts in, 44, 65; attempt to unite, 65; foreign trade of, 68; unification of, 267–9, 280; menace of powerful, 281, 370; and Jameson raid, 330; African interests of, 358–9; Heligoland ceded to, 358; in Triple Alliance, 359; penetration of Asia Minor by, 370; Chamberlain bids for alliance with, 371; creation of Navy of, 373, 385; rise of, to world-power, 385
Gettysburg, Battle of, 235–41
Gladstone, Herbert, 350
Gladstone, W. E., 95–7; Disraeli seeks co-operation of, 90; Prime Minister, 97, 283, 286–90, 300, 333–5, 351, 361; Confederate sympathies of, 181, 217; versus Disraeli, 283–4, 295; moral fervour of, 284, 298, 300, 352; converted to Home Rule, 284, 336, 343, 349, 362; relations with Queen Victoria, 285–6; in semi-retirement, 290; no social reformer, 291; and Empire, 291–2, 358; on Bulgarian horrors, 295–6; Midlothian Campaign of, 298, 300, 302; on social differences of parties, 301; Whig sympathies of, 333–4; South African policy of, 336–7; Egyptian policy of, 337–8; and Gordon, 339–42; his crusade for Ireland, 343–5, 348, 351–2; and Parnell, 347–9, 360–2; resigns, 348, 363; incurs enmity of Chamberlain, 351; Home Rule Bills of, 352, 362–3; makes concessions to Radicals, 354; popularity of, 363
Glendale, Battle of, 198
Glenelg, Lord, 110
Goderich, first Viscount, 35
Gold, in Australia, 99, 119–21; in Canada, 99, 104; in United States, 119, 146, 319; in New Zealand, 126; in Transvaal, 329, 337, 374; in Klondike, 329
Gold Coast, slave-raids into, 368
Gold standard, in Britain, 12; in the United States, 328–9
Goldie, Sir George, 358
Gordon, General Charles, 339–43; on Ireland, 343; avenging of, 369

Gordon Riots, 15
Gordonsville, Virginia, 204, 218
Gorst, John, 300, 335
Gortchakov, Prince, 297
Goschen, George, 356
Grand Gulf, Mississippi, 243–4
Grange, the, 324–5
Granger laws, 325
Grant, General Ulysses S., in Mexican War, 145–6; seizes Fort Henry and Fort Donelson, 185; at Shiloh, 190; attacks Vicksburg, 221–2, 232, 243–4; given command in West, 248; given complete command, 251; plan of, 251; campaign of, against Lee, 251–4; ruthlessness of, 253; takes Richmond, 261–2; Lee surrenders to, 261; Presidency of, 310, 313
Granville, second Earl, 334
Gravelotte, Battle of, 278
Great Exhibition, 67–8
Great Lakes, disarmament on, 131
Great Plains, cultivation of, 157; free soil and slavery in, 158–61; white settlement of, 318–22
Great Trek, 110–11
Greece, War of Independence of, 31, 70; intervention in, 32, 35; and Turkey, 294
Greeley, Horace, 216, 258
Greenback Party, 326, 327
Greville, Charles, 41, 48
Grey, second Earl, and Princess Caroline, 21; and franchise reform, 45; Prime Minister, 46, 153; demands creation of new peers, 50; retires, 51
Grey, third Earl, 118
Guam, 332
Gurkhas, 85

Hagerstown, Maryland, 233
Halleck, General Henry W., caution of, 184, 191; military adviser to Lincoln, 187; in command in West, 190; General-in-Chief, 199; and McClellan, 209; refuses to withdraw garrisons, 210; and Hooker, 234; and Rosecrans, 248
Hamilton, Alexander, 131, 155
Hampton Roads, peace talks in, 260
Hanover, at war with Denmark, 269; absorbed by Prussia, 273
Harcourt, Sir William, at Gladstone's retirement, 363; Chancellor of the Exchequer, 366; mentioned, 284, 362
Hargraves, Edward, 119
Harpers Ferry, 187; Brown liberates slaves at, 162; Confederates hold, 177–8; recovered by Federal Army, 178; Jackson captures, 210–12
Harriman, E. H., 316
Harrisburg, Pennsylvania, 233
Harrison, Benjamin, 326
Harrison's Landing, 197
Hartington, Marquess of (later eighth Duke of Devonshire), distrusts Gladstone, 334, 351; and rescue of Gordon, 340; leads Liberal Unionists, 354
Hatteras Inlet, 190
Hauhans, cult of, 125
Havana, 331
Havelock, General Sir Henry, 87
Hawaii, 114, 332
"Hawarden Kite," 350

INDEX

Hayes, Rutherford B., Presidency of, 312
Hazel Grove, 228, 229
Heligoland, 358
Henry Hill, the, 179
Herbert, Sidney, 77, 79; on Whigs, 94
Hereros, 108
Hertzog, General J. B. M., 382
Herzegovina, 294, 298
Hesse, 273
Hicks Beach, Sir Michael, 349, 355
Hill, General Ambrose P., at Antietam, 213; at Chancellorsville, 229; in invasion of Pennsylvania, 233; at Gettysburg, 235–8; mentioned, 155
Hill, Sir Rowland, 59
History of England, by Macaulay, 66
Hobart, 117
Hobhouse, Emily, 383
Hobson, Captain William, 124
Hohenzollern-Sigmaringen, Prince Leopold of, 275–6
Holmes, General Theophilus H., 221
Holstein, 268, 269
Holy Alliance, 7; and Spanish rising, 27, 132; split by Greek revolt, 32
Home Rule, Gladstone converted to, 284, 336, 343, 349, 362; League, 345; Conservatives and, 348–50; Liberal Party splits on, 350–3; Bill of 1886, 352; Bill, second, 362
Homestead Act, 320
Hood, General John B., 197; in command in West, 254, 256–9
Hooker, General Joseph, given command, 220, 223; plan of campaign of, 225–6; at Chancellorsville, 226–9, 241; crosses the Potomac, 234; resigns, 234
Hospitals, and Florence Nightingale, 79
Houston, General Sam, 144
Hudson's Bay Company, 104
Hungary, risings in, 65; Bismarck's agents in, 273
Hunt, Leigh, 20
Huskisson, William, advocates Free Trade, 24; at Board of Trade, 25; mentioned, 32, 36
Hyndman, H. M., 364

Idaho, 319
Illinois, high road to, 136; threatens to acknowledge Confederacy, 231; mentioned, 161
Income tax, of Pitt, 12–3; of Peel, 58; Gladstone proposes abolition of, 290
Independent Labour Party, 363
India, Russian threat to, 70, 81; under East India Company, 80; missionaries in, 80; British expansion in, 82; causes for disaffection in, 83–5; loyalty in, during Mutiny, 85, 88; rule of East India Company ends in, 88; shortened route to, 293; Empress of, 293, 380–1
Indian Mutiny, 80, 85–8; conditions leading to, 82–3; conditions after, 88, 90
Indiana, threatens to acknowledge Confederacy, 231
Industrial Revolution, problems posed by, 8, 23, 52; unrest and rioting due to, 9; in United States, 313–7
Inkerman, Battle of, 76
Iowa, 319

Ireland, Castlereagh in, 4; Protestant ascendancy in, 5, 36; Peel in, 24–5; British failure in, 36, 343; and Catholic Emancipation, 37; potato famine in, 60, 99, 343; Home Rule for, 284, 345; scheme to make Prince of Wales Viceroy of, 285; attempts to pacify, 287; miserable conditions in, 343; terrorism in, 344, 346–7, 360; Gladstone's crusade for, 344–5, 351, 361–2; Parnell's work for, 345–7, 360–2; policy of coercion in, 346–7, 351, 359–60; Phoenix Park murders in, 348; rejection of Home Rule for, 362; Queen Victoria visits, 381
Ironclad ships, 200–3, 232
Isandhlwana, 298
Islands, Bay of, 123
Ismail, Khedive, 293, 337
Italy, Queen Caroline in, 18–21; 1848 revolt in, 64; unification of, 92, 272; ally of Prussia against Austria, 273, 274; no ally for France, 275; in Triple Alliance, 359

Jackson, Andrew, in Florida, 132; Presidency of, 138–9, 142; problems before, 139, 142; refuses to renew Bank charter, 142
Jackson, Mississippi, 243
Jackson, General Thomas ("Stonewall"), 170; at Harpers Ferry, 178, 210–11; at Bull Run, 179–80; Shenandoah campaign of, 194–5; fails to reach Lee in time, 196–7; at Glendale, 198; at Cedar Mountain, 204; destroys Pope's supplies, 206; at Antietam, 212–3; in withdrawal, 218; at Fredericksburg, 220; at Chancellorsville, 225–30; death of, 229–30; mentioned, 187
James River, McClellan retreats to, 197–8; blockade of mouth of, 200; *Merrimac* in, 203; Federal forces at mouth of, 224; Grant crosses, 253, 259; mentioned, 177, 187, 224
Jameson, Dr Leander Starr, 374–5
Jameson Raid, 375; Kaiser's telegram on, 330
Japan, 371, 386
Java, 114
Jefferson, Thomas, 28, 131, 133, 138; idea of sovereign state rights of, 155
Jefferson City, Missouri, 174
Jersey, Countess of, 17
Jerusalem, dispute over shrines in, 71
Johannesburg, 324; capture of, 380
Johnson, President Andrew, reconstruction plan of, 307; struggle between Congress and, 308–9; impeachment of, 309
Johnston, General Albert Sidney, defeated on Mississippi, 183–5; in supreme command in West, 190; death of, 190
Johnston, General Joseph E., at Harpers Ferry, 177–8; at Bull Run, 179; plan for attack on, 186; threatens Washington, 187; retires behind Rapidan, 191; wounded at Seven Pines, 195; in command in West, 221; needs reinforcement, 232; fails before Vicksburg, 244; plan for campaign of, 250–1; campaign against, 251, 254; dismissal of, 254; re-

· 395 ·

INDEX

Lookout Mountain, 248, 249
Lords, House of, and trial of Queen Caroline, 19–20; opposes Reform Bills, 49; creation of new peers in, 50; defeats Home Rule Bill, 362
Lorraine, ceded to Germany, 279
Louis Napoleon, Prince—*see* Napoleon III
Louis Philippe, King of the French, 43, 64
Louisa Court House, 226
Louisiana, secession of, 164; "carpetbagger" Government of, 312
Louisiana Purchase, 137, 156
Louisville, Kentucky, 184, 232; Railway, 250
Lowe, Robert, 287
Lucknow, 86, 87
Luddite riots, 9
Lugard, Sir Henry, 368
Lyon, General Nathaniel, 174

MacArthur, John, 116
Macaulay, Lord, 66–7, 81
McClellan, General George B., in Mexican War, 145; in command of Federal Army, 180; plans of campaign of, 180, 186, 192, 199; relieved of general direction of armies, 188; crippling of operations of, 188, 192, 194; advance of, towards Richmond, 192–3, 194; retreats to James River, 197–8; at Battle of Seven Days, 199; ordered to hand over troops, 199, 209; embarkation of army of, 205; relations between politicians and, 209–10, 217–8; army returned to, 210; Maryland campaign of, 211–4; against Emancipation Edict, 216–8; pursues Lee, 218; relieved of command, 219; Grant follows plan of, 253; stands for Presidency, 256–7
Macdonald, Alexander, 292
MacDonald, Ramsay, 365
McDowell, General Irvin, at Bull Run, 178–80; Rappahannock command of, 188; McClellan needs corps of, 194–5
McKinley, William J., Presidency of, 328–9, 331
Mackinnon, Sir William, 358
McLaws, General Lafayette, 211
MacLean, Sir Donald, 125
MacMahon, Marshal, 278, 280
Macquarie Harbour, 117
Madison, James, 28, 133
Mafeking, 376, 379
Magersfontein, 379
Magruder, General J. B., at Yorktown, 186, 192; defends Richmond, 196; attacks at Savage Station, 198
Mahdi, the, 338, 341, 368
Mahomet Ali, Pasha of Egypt, 32
Maine, admitted to Union, 137
Maine, U.S.S., 331
Majuba Hill, Battle of, 336
Malvern Hill, Battle of, 198
Manassas, first Battle of, 178; Junction, 191; burning of stores at, 206; second Battle of, 208
Manchester, demonstrators from, 12; Anti-Corn Law League in, 59
Manchuria, 371
"Manifest Destiny," 144–6
Manila Bay, Battle of, 331

Manitoba, 104, 105
Maori wars, 125–6
Maoris, 122–4
Marchand, Major J. B., 370
Maritime Provinces, 100, 105
Marsden, Reverend Samuel, 123
Martinsburg, West Virginia, 210, 233
Marx, Karl, 280, 364
Marxism, 364
Maryland, and secession, 167, 175; Lee invades, 210–3; abolishes slavery, 305
Mason and Slidell, arrest of, 181
Matabele, 110
Meade, General George G., given command, 234; at Gettysburg, 236–40; slow pursuit of, 240–1; ordered to follow Lee, 251
Mechanicsville, Virginia, 196
Meerut, mutiny at, 85
Melbourne, Victoria, 118, 120
Melbourne, second Viscount, transportation of farm workers by, 46; Prime Minister, 51, 56; and Queen Victoria, 57; mentioned, 102
Memphis, Tennessee, 185, 242
Mendaña, Alvaro de, 114
Menschikoff, Prince A. S., 71
Merrimac, the, 200–3
Metternich, Prince K. W. von, 7, 26–7, 65
Metz, 277–8
Mexican War, 143–6; territory acquired by U. S. in, 156
Mexico, Gulf of, trade in, 136; Confederate Navy in, 231
Mexico City, capture of, 145
Mfecane, 111
Middle classes, enfranchisement of, 11; fear revolution, 12; acquire political power, 286
Middle West, anti-slavery feeling in, 154
Midlothian Campaign, 298, 302
Mill, James, 47, 286
Milner, Sir Alfred (later Viscount), 375–6, 382, 384
Milroy, General Robert H., 194
Milwaukee, 316
Minneapolis, 316
Minnesota, the, 201
Missionary Ridge, 248, 249
Mississippi River, steamboats on, 136; as route for invasion, 176, 183–4; Island No. 10 in, 184, 191; in Federal hands, 242–4; increase in population west of, 318
Mississippi State, secession of, 164; Grant invades, 221–2; Lee's help sought for, 232
Mississippi valley, states of, 133–4; cotton cultivation in, 135; Confederate defeats in, 183–5; recovered for Union, 249; farmers' parties in Upper, 325
Missouri, admission of, to Union, 137; Compromise, 156, 158, 160; slavery in, 160; and secession, 167, 173, 174; abolishes slavery, 305
Mobile, Alabama attack on, 251, 257
Modder River, Battle of, 379
Mohawk Indians, 101
Moldavia, 72
Moltke, Count Helmuth von, 267, 273, 276
Monitor, the, 202

INDEX

Monometallism *versus* bimetallism, 322, 327–9
Monroe Doctrine, 29–30, 132; and Venezuelan boundary question, 330
Montana, 319
Montgomery, Alabama, 173
Morgan, John Pierpont, 316
Morley, John, first Viscount, 362; on Coercion Bill, 346
Mormon settlement, 147–8
"Municipal Socialism," 301
Murfreesboro, Tennessee, 221; Battle of, 222

Nana Sahib, 86–7
Napier, General Sir Charles, 82
Naples, Kingdom of, 27, 93
Napoleon III, Emperor of the French, President of France, 64; opposes Russia over Jerusalem, 71; and Crimean War, 72, 78; and Italian unity, 93; Confederate sympathies of, 181; double diplomacy of, 270; tricked by Bismarck, 272, 274–5; mobilisation scheme of, 277; defeated in battle, 278; surrender of, 278; mentioned, 267
Napoleonic wars, Tories and, 3; peace after, 5–8; ruin to Dutch trade in, 108
Nashville, Tennessee, 190, 222, 232; Battle of, 259
Natal, founding of, 111; in Boer War, 378, 382
National Liberal Federation, 301
National Republicans, 138, 142
Navarino, Battle of Bay of, 35
Nebraska, 158, 318, 321
Negro, slavery of, in U. S., 137, 142, 149–62, 163; emancipation of, 216–7, 304–5; problems of free, 304; enfranchisement of, 306, 308, 310; Radical measures to protect, 308, 313; political shortcomings of, 311; part of, in Southern farming, 314
Netherlands, Kingdom of the, 43, 44
Nevada, 319
New Bern, North Carolina, 190, 224
New Brunswick, 104
New Caledonia, 114
New England, prosperity in, 131; colonisation of, 134; loyalty to Union in, 140; anti-slavery feeling in, 154; industries of, 315
New Hebrides, 114
New Mexico, 146, 157; admitted to Union, 318
New Orleans, railway route through, 158; fall of, 242; race riot in, 308
New South Wales, transportation of Tolpuddle "Martyrs" to, 53–4; convict settlement in, 115; "offspring" of, 117–8; gold in, 119–21
New York, anti-slavery campaign in, 153; draft riots in, 231
New York State, 136
New Zealand, Cook discovers, 114, 123; affected by Australian gold rush, 120, 126; Maoris of, 122–5; first British settlements on, 123–6; Maori wars in, 125–6; farming industry in, 126; political development of, 126–7
New Zealand Association, 123

"Newcastle Programme," 362
Newman, Cardinal John Henry, 92
Nguni, 108
Niagara Falls, peace parleys at, 258
Nicaragua, 162
Nice, 92
Nicholas I, Czar of Russia, suppresses nationalist risings, 65; and Turkey, 70–3; and Crimean War, 73
Nicholson, John, 82, 86
Nicholson's Nek, Battle of, 378
Niel, Marshal Adolphe, 274
Nigeria, 358, 368
Nightingale, Florence, 79
Nile River, Wolseley's expedition up, 340–1; British control over valley of, 359, 368–9; French expedition to, 370
Nonconformists, emancipation of, 36; prevalence of, 91
Norfolk, Virginia, naval base at, 177; *Merrimac* at, 200; evacuation of, 202
North Anna River, 220
North Carolina and secession, 167, 173; Federal successes on coast of, 190; tobacco industry in, 315
North German Federation, 267
Northcote, Sir Stafford (later Lord Iddesleigh), 335, 349
Northern states, anti-slavery feeling in, 153–4, 158–62; Federal conceptions of, 155; and transcontinental railway, 158; not prepared for coercion, 166–9; called to arms, 169, 178; task before, 172; strength of, 183; discouraged by losses, 215; peace terms of, 260; attempt to retain ascendancy of business interest of, 306; turn against Radicals, 312; Industrial Revolution in, 315. *See also* Federal Government
Northern Virginia, Army of, 195; 1862 campaign of, 204–14; faces Hooker's army (1863), 223–6; reorganised for invasion of Pennsylvania, 233; decisive defeat of, 238–42; Grant's campaign against, 251–4; terms for surrender of, 261
Nova Scotia, 104

O'Brien, William, 359
O'Connell, Daniel, 36, 38; Irish votes of, 48, 52
Ohio River, Cumberland high-road across, 136; as route for invasion of South, 176, 184
Ohio State, helps West Virginia, 175; oil refineries of, 316
Oklahoma, 318
Omdurman, Battle of, 370
Ontario, 100, 104
Orange Free State, origin of, 112; friendly to British, 373; joins Kruger, 375; annexation of, 380
Orange River, 107, 111
Oregon, 143, 145; Treaty, 103, 147
Origin of Species, The (Darwin), 92
O'Shea, Captain W. H., 351, 361
O'Shea, Mrs, 349–50, 361
Otago, 126
Oudh, 83, 87
Outram, General Sir James, 87
Oxford Movement, the, 91

INDEX

INDEX

DESIGN BY AVERY FISHER

IT IS FITTING THAT BOTH THE DISPLAY
AND TEXT TYPE FACES USED IN THIS BOOK
ARE OF ENGLISH ORIGIN. THE BINDING,
TITLE PAGE AND IMPORTANT HEADINGS
ARE SET IN PERPETUA, THE CREATION OF
ERIC GILL. THE ORIGINAL FORMS FROM
WHICH THE TYPE WAS CUT BY THE MONO-
TYPE CORPORATION WERE SIMPLY LET-
TERS DRAWN WITH BRUSH AND INK.

THE TEXT HAS THROUGHOUT BEEN SET
IN TIMES ROMAN, INITIALLY DESIGNED
BY STANLEY MORISON FOR USE IN THE
LONDON TIMES. ITS EXTREME LEGIBIL-
ITY AND ATTRACTIVE 'COLOR' IN MASS
ARE ITS MOST DISTINCTIVE CHARACTER-
ISTICS.

MAPS BY JAMES MACDONALD

COMPOSITION, PRESSWORK AND BINDING
BY KINGSPORT PRESS, INC.